QUALITATIVE RESEARCH USII
SOCIAL MEDIA

Do you want to study influencers? Opinions and comments on a set of posts? Look at collections of photos or videos on Instagram? *Qualitative Research Using Social Media* guides the reader in what different kinds of qualitative research can be applied to social media data. It introduces students, as well as those who are new to the field, to developing and carrying out concrete research projects. The book takes the reader through the stages of choosing data, formulating a research question, and choosing and applying method(s).

Written in a clear and accessible manner with current social media examples throughout, the book provides a step-by-step overview of a range of qualitative methods. These are presented in clear ways to show how to analyze many different types of social media content, including language and visual content such as memes, gifs, photographs, and film clips. Methods examined include critical discourse analysis, content analysis, multimodal analysis, ethnography, and focus groups. Most importantly, the chapters and examples show how to ask the kinds of questions that are relevant for us at this present point in our societies, where social media is highly integrated into how we live. Social media is used for political communication, social activism, as well as commercial activities and mundane everyday things, and it can transform how all these are accomplished and even what they mean.

Drawing on examples from Twitter, Instagram, YouTube, TikTok, Facebook, Snapchat, Reddit, Weibo, and others, this book will be suitable for undergraduate students studying social media research courses in media and communications, as well as other humanities such as linguistics and social science–based degrees.

Gwen Bouvier is a professor at the Institute of Corpus Linguistics and Applications, Shanghai International Studies University, China. Professor Bouvier's publications have drawn on critical discourse analysis, multimodality based on social semiotics, and online ethnography. She is the Associate Editor for the journal *Social Semiotics*.

Joel Rasmussen is a senior lecturer in the School of Humanities, Education and Social Sciences at Örebro University, Sweden. His research focuses on how communication processes shape responsibilities and measures regarding risk and health in organizations and society. He is interested in how public-sector institutions are refashioning identity through social media. His work is published in international journals such as *Human Relations*, *Discourse & Communication*, *Safety Science*, *PLoS ONE*, and others.

"An indispensable guide for those who want to learn about, and practically undertake, qualitative social media research of popular platforms."

—**Professor Per Ledin**, *Södertörn University and author of* Doing Visual Analysis, From Theory to Practice

"Bouvier and Rasmussen provide an informative, clearly written and indispensable guide for readers investigating social media data or contemplating doing so. A welcome handbook for all research methods courses that seek to remain informed and up to date."

—**Paul Cobley**, *Professor in Language and Media, Middlesex University*

QUALITATIVE RESEARCH USING SOCIAL MEDIA

GWEN BOUVIER AND JOEL RASMUSSEN

Routledge
Taylor & Francis Group

LONDON AND NEW YORK

Cover image: Vladimir Vladimirov

First published 2022
by Routledge
4 Park Square, Milton Park, Abingdon, Oxon OX14 4RN

and by Routledge
605 Third Avenue, New York, NY 10158

Routledge is an imprint of the Taylor & Francis Group, an informa business

© 2022 Gwen Bouvier and Joel Rasmussen

The right of Gwen Bouvier and Joel Rasmussen to be identified as authors of this work has been asserted in accordance with sections 77 and 78 of the Copyright, Designs and Patents Act 1988.

All rights reserved. No part of this book may be reprinted or reproduced or utilised in any form or by any electronic, mechanical, or other means, now known or hereafter invented, including photocopying and recording, or in any information storage or retrieval system, without permission in writing from the publishers.

Trademark notice: Product or corporate names may be trademarks or registered trademarks, and are used only for identification and explanation without intent to infringe.

British Library Cataloguing-in-Publication Data
A catalogue record for this book is available from the British Library

Library of Congress Cataloging-in-Publication Data
Names: Bouvier, Gwen, author. | Rasmussen, Joel (Sociologist), author.
Title: Qualitative research using social media / Gwen Bouvier and Joel Rasmussen.
Description: 1 Edition. | New York, NY : Routledge, 2022. | Includes bibliographical references and index. |
   Identifiers: LCCN 2021048281 (print) | LCCN 2021048282 (ebook) | ISBN 9780367333508 (hardback) |
   ISBN 9780367333478 (paperback) | ISBN 9780429319334 (ebook)
Subjects: LCSH: Qualitative research. | Online social networks—Research. | Social sciences—Research—
   Methodology.
Classification: LCC H62.B6188 2022 (print) | LCC H62 (ebook) | DDC 300.72—dc23/eng/20211004
LC record available at https://lccn.loc.gov/2021048281
LC ebook record available at https://lccn.loc.gov/2021048282

ISBN: 978-0-367-33350-8 (hbk)
ISBN: 978-0-367-33347-8 (pbk)
ISBN: 978-0-429-31933-4 (ebk)

DOI: 10.4324/9780429319334

Typeset in Times New Roman
by Apex CoVantage, LLC

CONTENTS

Acknowledgments		ix
1	Introduction	1
	Asking questions about social media	1
	Social media and voices from below	2
	Nodes and echo chambers	6
	The power of algorithms	7
	Affective communities	10
	Influencers	13
	The ephemeral nature of social media use	14
	Social media and news	17
	The ethics of researching social media	20
	Consent and information	21
	Confidentiality and anonymity	22
	Opportunities and limitations for social research	23
	So what do we use?	23
2	Qualitative content analysis: text and speech-based material	25
	Introduction	25
	Qualitative content analysis: meaning making and text	26
	Fitting QCA into the research process	28
	The research design phase	29
	Organizing and analysis of data	32
	Presentation of results	37
3	Qualitative visual content analysis	39
	Introduction	39
	History and current research	40
	Defining and working with key theoretical concepts	43
	Research design and preparation	45
	Questions of data collection and generalization	47
	Coding frame and examples of analytical tools	49
	Presentation of results	56
4	Analyzing social media language with critical discourse analysis	58
	Introduction	58
	What is CDA?	59
	Why word choice is political	61

How words suggest models of how the world works	63
How to do CDA	63
Revealing the scripts or 'doings' of discourse	64
Summary	67
Participants	67
Actions	67
Doing a project with CDA: fitness influencers on Chinese Weibo	67
Research question	68
Literature review	68
Choosing and gathering data	69
The analysis	70
Being independent	70
Choice	70
Self-management	74
Striving	75
Consuming Western products	77
Drawing conclusions	78

5   Multimodal critical discourse analysis   79

Introduction	79
What is MCDA?	84
Visual communication involves choices	85
The choices we make are political	85
How choices tell bigger stories about the world	86
Codification and classification	87
How to do MCDA	88
Revealing the scripts or 'doings' of discourse	88
Analyzing participants	88
Analyzing actions	90
Shaping viewer engagement	92
Personal address	92
Perspective	93
Distance	94
Settings in images	94
Images in compositions	94
Images can create hierarchies	95
Images can be coordinated	95
Doing a project with MCDA: fitness influencers on Chinese Weibo	95
Research question	96
Literature review	97
Choosing and gathering data	98
The analysis	98
A decontextualized world	99
Coordinated life domains	99
The people and actions in the images	102
Drawing conclusions	102

6 Multimodal narrative analysis of video clips — 103

Introduction — 103
Telling stories about the world — 103
Film clips and models of the world — 104
Identifying the discursive scripts in film clips — 105
    Participants — 106
    Social action and social interactions — 106
    Settings — 107
    Language, narration, and captions — 107
The stages in film clips — 107
The problem-solution structure — 108
Recounting events — 113
Projection narratives: possible worlds — 119
Projection sequence in the fitness influencer clip — 128
Doing a research project using film clips as data — 130
Creating a literature review — 130
Gathering and managing the data — 132
Carrying out the analysis — 133
Presenting the findings — 133
Drawing conclusions — 134

7 Online ethnography — 135

Introduction — 135
A brief history of online ethnography — 136
Current research areas and case studies — 139
Planning an online ethnography — 141
Combining research materials and methods — 143
    Archival, elicited, and field note data — 144
    Different degrees of researcher participation — 144
Writing up and presenting ethnographic findings — 145

8 Focus group interviews — 150

Introduction — 150
History and current research — 151
The purpose of focus group research — 153
Developing themes and research questions — 155
Selecting and reaching informants — 157
Creating an interview guide — 161
    Different types of interview questions — 162
Online spaces for conducting interviews — 164
    Asynchronous online focus groups — 165
    Synchronous online focus groups — 166
Transcription — 167
Analyzing focus groups — 169
Presenting results — 170

9 Conclusion 172
   Situating the book: social media data in media and communication studies 172
   Qualitative methodology in an evolving world 173
   The book in relation to big data and quantification 173
   The value of case study research 174
   Coda 175

Bibliography **176**

Index **200**

ACKNOWLEDGMENTS

This project would not have been possible without the support of my esteemed research assistant Wenting Zhao. Thank you for your intelligence, patience, and thoroughness. I'd also like to thank my dear husband, David Machin. I am immensely grateful for you always being kind and supportive. My heartfelt thanks to you both.

—Gwen

Many thanks to Gwen for inviting me to this project. Warmest thanks also to my family, Sara, Nicole, and Noelle for always being there, adding so many colors to our lives together and putting things in perspective that it's a little easier to sometimes do one thing a whole lot, like co-writing this book. You are the best.

—Joel

INTRODUCTION

Chapter 1

Asking questions about social media

Social media are embedded in and shape all parts of life. At the turn of this century, Howard (2000) noted that people were becoming increasingly reliant on the Internet to accomplish basic daily tasks, to do shopping, find a playground for the children, learn how to play the piano, or check out a diagnosis for that rash on a child's foot. This marked a huge shift in society in many ways. Perhaps the first significant change was that information became so much more easily accessible. Formerly, it may have taken a trip to a library, or even ordering a specialist book. Optimists at the time saw the potential for all human knowledge to be immediately available to anyone with a few clicks on their keyboard. There was much excitement that anyone with a computer and Internet connection could upload content. Formerly, knowledge had always come top down, from publishers, media companies, and other institutions. This sounded incredibly democratizing.

Since Howard wrote this, a huge part of being online can involve, or is integrated with, social media. This means that these same tasks of gaining information, acquiring knowledge, and developing skills may be accomplished on different social media platforms. We may rely on social media to engage with and understand major events happening in society and politics, to go about our daily working activities, or to communicate with our dentist. More specialist sites and feeds will address and cater for specific interests and communities. They allow us to build remote international communities. In fact, one of the earlier slogans of Facebook was the idea of connecting all of humanity. Some put it that social media are not so much simply embedded in our everyday lives, but rather our lives are embedded in social media (Thurlow et al., 2004: 75).

Researchers are still working out the consequences all this has. Many things are now done so differently than before and are in transition as the former ways change or exist in parallel. In this chapter, we look at some of the key areas in this body of research. We cannot cover all research done on social media in a single chapter, but as researchers seeking to start projects in social media communication, there are a set of themes that provide the basis for grasping how and why we might want to ask questions about it. As the Internet matured, it soon became clear that the knowledge people want, have the capacity for, or will even tolerate, may be selective. Not everyone seems to want to be connected to certain other kinds of people. It also became clear that there were great profits to be made by those who provided the technical infrastructures through which people were steered through all these sites and information. And, as with older forms of media and communication, those who best understand it and know how to use it may come to have more influence.

In this chapter, the themes we look at all relate to these basic issues. Researchers show how they raise issues about political participation and social justice, but also call us, most importantly, to understand more about the actual nature of social media communication per se. All these issues can feed into any social media communications

DOI: 10.4324/9780429319334-1

research project, and this chapter is also intended as a resource to foster research ideas and to provide a springboard for journeys into more specific areas of interest.

We certainly may not want, or need to cite, much of this research, but as researchers we need to know what kinds of issues and questions are being raised by communications scholars as being important in regard to social media. Many of the issues we will want to investigate in our own projects are likely to touch on some of these questions in different ways. Research is all about contributing to knowledge, and the assembled body of knowledge should act as a resource of guiding principles and ideas to help you better formulate your own ideas.

Social media and voices from below

One area of research on social media has related to its potential to allow voices formerly lacking a platform to now speak, be heard, come together, share ideas and interests, and mobilize (Castells, 2015). The impact of hashtags such as #MeToo and #BlackLivesMatter are typically listed as examples of how this process can bring injustices into wider public view, creating pressure to make perpetrators accountable, and even lead to challenges of power relations (Bouvier and Cheng, 2019). Researchers provide compelling examples from a range of international contexts (Florini, 2014; Tufekci, 2017; Jackson et al., 2020).

Following is a post using the #MeToo hashtag:

> Change is coming to the U.S. House today: Lawmakers voting to add House Rule to explicitly prohibit lawmakers from having sexual relationships with staffers. Makes it an Ethics violation to do so. Part of broader effort to change culture of Capitol Hill following #metoo movement

Here we see that the hashtag presents a voice that formerly had no clear outlet. Mainstream media may have a number of reasons for not wanting to address accusations of sexual misconduct. This could be through fears of legal reprisals, or simply that media organizations are often run by men. This hashtag allowed many women to recount experiences where formerly they had felt alone. Since this time, many have questioned the nature and success of #MeToo, for instance, that while its basic driving message may have been important, it became too broad, unfocused, and was elitist (Zarkov, 2018). Yet ultimately, we could argue that issues of sexual conduct by men towards women and women's rights take a higher profile now, at least in some societies.

Other research shows how social media have been used by activists in democratic movements around the world. In particular, Twitter has been used as a tool to help disseminate information and to organize in protests in the Middle East (Bruns et al., 2013; Jansen, 2010), and to negotiate state control of media and censorship (Penney and Dadas, 2013; Poell and Van Dijck, 2015), such as in Turkey (Tufekci, 2017) and in China (Yang, 2014).

Other scholars have focused more specifically on political participation in the form of protests. Valenzuela et al. (2012), for example, looked at protest behavior among young people, noting that social media facilitates access to contacts, which makes it possible for movements to get off the ground and come into the public eye. Simply, social media platforms can provide information in a single central place as a sort of rallying point, which can inspire a sense of focus. These platforms can facilitate the formation of collective identities, which, the authors argue, is an important feature of protest behavior (2012: 303).

How does this translate to actually getting people to participate in protests? Bosch (2017: 224) noted that social media have enabled protest participation by increasing users' possibilities to engage in collective action, such as organizing protests, creating petitions, strategizing to put together writing campaigns that put pressure on companies, etc. One important feature allowing this, Penney and Dadas (2013) argue, is Twitter's horizontally structured organization that is non-hierarchical and has peer-to-peer communication, which is particularly useful for the coordination of users and events of social movements.

One simple example of a petition-like use of social media is the #StopFundingHate hashtag. This hashtag was created to address the notion that the British press was anti-immigration. Its purpose was to raise awareness about companies that advertised with these titles. Here we see a tweet by the toy company Lego that aligns with the hashtag:

> Replying to @StopFundingHate we have finished the agreement with The Daily Mail and are not planning any future promotional activity with the newspaper

Others used the hashtag to bring attention to wider forms of racism in the media. Here we see how Facebook (posted on Twitter) carries racist posts about the Roma (Figure 1.1). The idea is that the hashtag becomes a way to call attention to how media organizations can be part of sustaining racist attitudes.

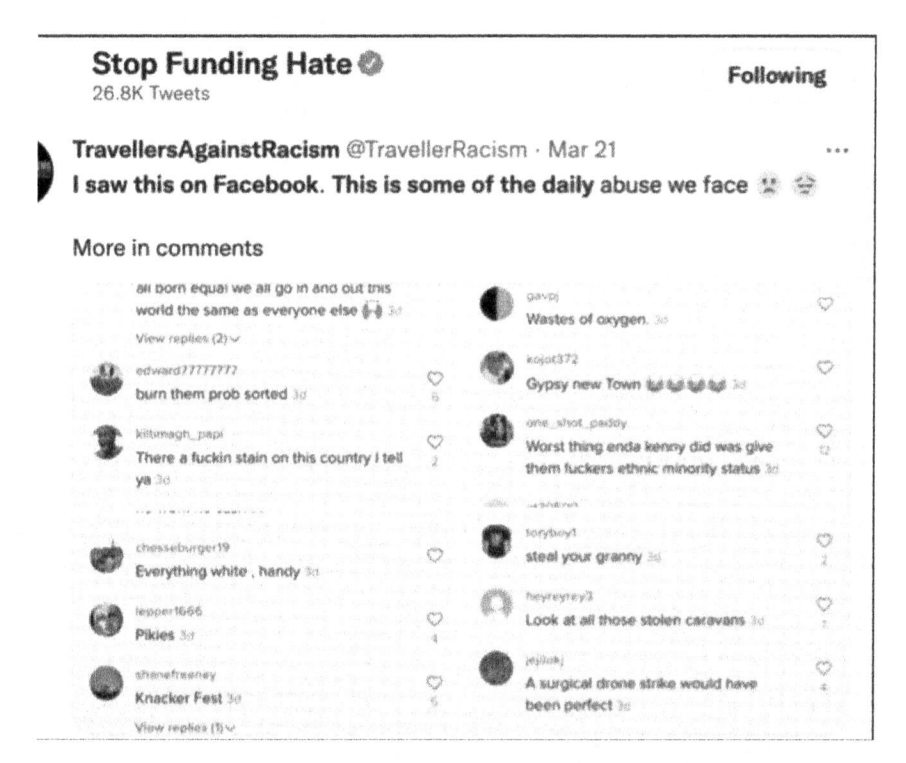

Figure 1.1 Tweet aligning with the hashtag #StopFundingHate

Figure 1.2 Tweet aligning with the hashtag #BringBackOurGirls

At the time of this writing, the hashtag #BringBackOurGirls was also receiving much international attention. This hashtag was set up when 276 Nigerian schoolgirls were kidnapped by Boko Haram in 2019. At the top right (Figure 1.2), we see Michelle Obama showing her allegiance.

Such hashtags can all be thought of in terms of voices from below, calls for action and justice, or raising awareness of cruelty, abuse, and inequalities in a manner facilitated by social media.

The possibility to carry a range of media formats, including images and film clips, on social media such as Twitter has also been pointed to as being hugely helpful in increasing the scope and potential impact of its messages. In the case of #BringBackOurGirls, it was possible to spend hours looking at different kinds of content. Users can then share fragments of film clips, news footage, and images as part of creating mobilization (Gleason, 2013). Such hashtags can interlink with others carrying related concerns, which together can bring more users into participation around a core principle. For example, there was cross-posting on #BringBackOurGirls from a range of other hashtags related to sex trafficking of young women, such as #RealMenDontBuyGirls (Figure 1.3).

#BringBackOurGirls brought about major international attention and intervention from America. Yet this campaign ultimately did not bring back the girls. While we might argue that these hashtags raise awareness and can play a role in shifting attitudes, others, in this instance, suggest that hashtags can be a kind of 'clicktivism' (Dean, 2010). The situation in Nigeria is complex, often grossly simplified by Western media as being about religion and terrorism, and these kidnappings have been and are still ongoing (Shearlaw, 2015). In fact, as we look at the research areas in this chapter, we learn more regarding how to think about and approach these kinds of issues of engagement and impact, but what is also clear is that we need more research about individual cases and different contexts. Nevertheless, scholars have reminded

Figure 1.3 Tweet aligning with the hashtag #RealMenDontBuyGirls

us that social media technology with its possibilities for creating these dynamic, interlinking communities must not be confused with having a set of users who are well informed and civically aware, nor that people have the motivation and commitment to go beyond the act of posting their outrage on social media (Bakardjieva, 2009, 2010).

Researchers have also shown that social media can equally be used to share ideas and mobilize people around ideas that are much less related to social justice and democratic ideals (Creemers, 2017). This can be where authoritarian regimes use platforms to steer discussions and embed information (MacKinnon, 2011). Social media has also been an important tool for organizations promoting extremist ideas and violence, or looking to radicalize potential recruits (Gentleman, 2011; Huey, 2015). More right-wing groups are also using social media to promote their ideas and attack ethnic minorities (Heikkilä, 2017). Matamoros-Fernández (2017) has, in particular, looked at the relatively unregulated way that racism takes place across many social media platforms. We have already seen one example of this on the #StopFundingHate hashtag, where Facebook users come together to share racist comments about Roma travelers. This may not necessarily be in more overt forms that are so easily picked up as hate speech. Breazu and Machin (2021), carrying out research into racism against the Roma across social media platforms, show how much of this takes place in ways that are less easy to control. Here is an example from their data, where users post under a news clip reporting on a Roma village being quarantined during the Covid pandemic:

> I would put everyone in construction and agriculture . . . Including those from gangs . . . Why put them in jail so that we pay for everything . . . Isolation at Home . . . and work for the benefit of the state . . . Foot chains . . . with GPS . . . and you'll see how good they turn to be after 3 years of hard work.

Running through these comments, the authors show, is a clear sense that users feel the Roma are a social problem, they are lazy, and they need to be controlled – here by forced labor and foot chains. While YouTube can be quite strict with overt forms of racism in posted videos, users are free to leave these kinds of comments.

For media and communications researchers, this idea that we can now have voices from below, whether more democratic or more intolerant, brings a new set of possibilities (KhosraviNik, 2017). Formerly, knowledge and what we can call dominant ideologies were disseminated top-down by mainstream news media. In other words, the model of the world found in the news, on television, and in movies tended to carry representations of events, persons, and processes that were less critical of the status quo. This model is linked to being owned by corporations, and therefore needing to align with the interests of advertisers, or being operated by the state. For example, the news media have been observed to be generally xenophobic (Van Dijk, 1998), supportive of Western governments in military conflicts (Bouvier, 2014), and simply take business and global capitalism for granted (Hertz, 2002). A former task for critical discourse analysis and other media and communications scholars has been to reveal how these ideologies are buried in media texts. With social media comes the opportunity to consider how these ideologies are taken on by ordinary people, how they are challenged or negotiated, and how these ideologies exist across platforms (KhosraviNik, 2017). However, as Bouvier and Way (2021) argue, the question should rather be to ask what ideologies are embedded in any instance of communication. Even where we appear to deal with a 'voice from below' (e.g., a social justice movement that appears to offer a challenge to a form of social inequality), to what extent do these communications carry, at their roots, forms of ideas and thinking that reflect the logics of the dominant ideology?

In terms of research, we are clearly still finding out how ideas and the mobilization of communities take place on and through social media. What kinds of communities come together, for what reasons, and how? The research that follows in this book also gives us clues about other things we need to bear in mind as we do so. These call us to question what we mean by communities and to think more carefully about the extent to which they are coherent and what participation in them looks like. We also need to think about what kinds of community voices come to the surface, and why.

Nodes and echo chambers

Social media platforms can facilitate the formation of communities or networks of connections. As we saw earlier, this can mean that we can link up with others who share our interests and concerns. This affordance, to link people, even those scattered around the planet, has been explored by researchers. This can be how local communities come together around a specific issue (Medina and Diaz, 2016). It can relate to how refugees maintain contact while in different transit camps (Charmarkeh, 2013), or how a global diaspora creates community (Conversi, 2012). Such research often ties into the more optimistic view of social media and its possibilities for bringing people together. While some pointed to the limitations of the #MeToo or #BringBackOurGirls hashtags, these can bring people together in new ways and yield new opportunities. Although, of course, we might also find communities that have extremist or violent views may come together.

One observation about such communities or networks of connections is that they can tend to be rather 'nodal' and insular (KhosraviNik, 2017). In other words, on social media we tend to be attracted to, or at least channeled towards, those who share similar outlooks and ideas (Matamoros-Fernández, 2017). And in one sense, it has been suggested, social media is a kind of consumer-centric medium since we shop around, finding the things and opinions that best please us (Khamis et al., 2016: 4).

Such nodes have also been talked about in terms of 'echo chambers' (Hall Jamieson and Capella, 2010). Here, users tend to come across views that confirm their existing ideas and values. We may even find that their views become reinforced and hardened as they tend not to come across alternative ideas (Baumgaertner et al., 2016). Social media feeds or hashtags can therefore be occupied by niche opinion and interest groups.

Scholars have looked at how this situation can restrict opportunities for users to be exposed to alternative perspectives and ideas (Sunstein, 2001; Shirky, 2001, 2003; Adamic and Glance, 2005). In more extreme cases, this limitation can be dangerous, where groups can become radicalized and xenophobic (Conversi, 2012), or where people find themselves in networks where racist views become naturalized (Matamoros-Fernández, 2017). This is one concern of Breazu and Machin (2021) in their account of where users post on YouTube about the Roma, as we saw earlier. Scholars have also shown that social media feeds related to what appear to be clear matters of social justice can, on closer inspection, have a nodal and echo chamber quality, where there is no room for viewpoints that may even complicate the 'shared' stance, even where this may carry some important oversights and simplifications (Bouvier, 2020a, 2020b). In all cases of how we seek out and experience knowledge and understandings of events in the world, online and through social media platforms, we may ignore that which does not suit our preferences and needs, and seek comfort in having our views confirmed and supported (Stroud, 2010: 556). This may all have huge implications for how people come to think about knowledge and information, and about others who are not part of their node of mutual reinforcers.

When users look for information or search on social media, there is also the issue that search engine algorithms will offer a set of options based on the tracking of their preferences (Brossard and Scheufele, 2013; Jacobson et al., 2016). As such, it has been argued that we can all become stuck in a 'filter bubble', created by our user history (Pariser, 2011). Algorithms, which seek to keep us on site for longer and align us with suitable advertising, track our choices and customize our online experience so we are surrounded with information that fits our political views.

The power of algorithms

Social media is driven by the need to produce profits. As we use various social media, they study our preferences. They also use algorithms to continually compute who our family, friends, and former school friends are likely to be. All of this – the knowledge about who we are, our opinions and interests – can be tied to our consumer patterns and preferences (Fuchs, 2011). While social media present in terms of connectivity, which is always presumed to be a good thing, many platforms are in competition and lock each other out (van Dijck, 2013). Bigger platforms may include the buttons of other bigger platforms, but the aim is ultimately to lock users into their own chain of platforms (Van

Dijck, 2003: 156). This is important to channel users from networking into consumer activity. Google aims to lock users into their own algorithmic flow of buttons.

We are continually being told what is already the most successful comment, idea, picture, or story, and in this context 'what you might also like', whether a product, a news story, or a social media influencer. In this way, algorithms signal up what your network community values, and cement what kinds of ideas and attitudes are common across the section of connectivity (Rambukkana, 2015). Things that get liked more get higher rankings and then will get more interest. They can then become high profile, attracting further discussions and bringing into focus other, similar content. Poor-quality content may come to the surface simply because of how it gets signaled and then attracts clicks. This can relate to which hashtags and issues gain traction and which do not. The #MeToo hashtag was around for some time before it began trending, as celebrities began to participate. Bouvier (2019) shows how one hashtag among many, offering competing perspectives, became dominant once a TV presenter used it in a tweet. What is 'trending' and what goes beneath the radar is clearly a complex thing, and not simply related to what is most naturally salient as a civic issue, nor the most useful interpretation of it (Enli and Simonsen, 2017).

The naming of social media feeds and hashtags has in itself received critical attention. Hashtags raise a particular issue of interest, at least at first, within a network of users. This invites us to connect about a set of concerns (Rosenbaum, 2018). We can also use hashtags to find feeds or posts that we may want to challenge (Conover et al., 2011: 94), but hashtags can also have a shaping and defining role. Those who create them seek to shape events with associations and meanings that support their own interests (Rambukkana, 2015). There can be a kind of race to create a defining hashtag that gets to dominate how something is shaped – a kind of "framing contest" (Enli and Simonsen, 2017: 1085).

Hashtags can even misrepresent the nature of processes, events, and things, for example, where they suggest some kind of people's uprising, which it may not be (Papacharissi, 2016), or a challenge to racism (Bouvier, 2020). Yet, particularly where they provide a good news hook, these hashtags may become widely accepted as a coherent and faithful stance. For example, Bouvier (2019) shows how one hashtag, relating to the debate about abortion in Ireland, became reported in the news as the singular stance against the control over abortion. In fact, there were a range of stances, and this particular one was felt by some to be damaging to the actual cause of getting the law changed in a country where the Catholic Church still holds much power. Here, the hashtag presented the journey of a woman, accompanied by her friend, to have an abortion in England. The headline from the British BBC news site was as follows:

#TwoWomenTravel – Live-tweeting the journey for an abortion (BBC Trending)

Yet as Bouvier's analysis shows, and as other commentators at the time noted, it was not clear that such a journey had actually taken place. The hashtag was compellingly composed at its start, where the tweets did not mention procedures, or even the actual political issue and what was at stake. Rather, they posted bleak images of the journey, showing grey skies and streets through a taxi window, and slightly depressing waiting rooms, and were commenting on 'feeling cold' or, as we see in Figure 1.4, being 'away from home'.

Figure 1.4 A @TwoWomenTravel post showing a bleak, generic setting: Pretty ordinary sights, in a place away from home. Can't say it's comforting, though @Enda KennyTD #twowomentravel

Other hashtags being used to campaign for a change in law, using different strategies, were ignored by the news media. The hook of the images, the emotion, and the symbolism of the hashtag #TwoWomenTravel became presented as the case against abortion per se. Those tweeting on the hashtag did not question how real it was, nor show awareness of the complexity of those seeking to bring about a change in the law.

> What these women have done today is beyond important and brave @TwoWomenTravel #repealthe8th #twowomentravel
>
> @TwoWomenTravel What a brave woman u are, I am so sorry this already horrible experience has been made worse #twowomentravel #repealthe8th

The process of getting hashtags to the surface can mean competition among activists, as well as advertising companies, mainstream media, or even politicians who seek to manipulate the hashtag's meaning to their own benefit (Rambukkana, 2015). We should remember that while anyone can create a hashtag, not all will attract interest, either by algorithms or users. Trending hashtags are rarely 'bottom-up', but are generated by elite users, journalists, influencers, and celebrities (e.g., Bruns et al., 2013; Enli and Simonsen, 2017). In the #TwoWomenTravel case, it was only when the comedian James Cordon tweeted using the hashtag that it began to have any traction. In the case of this particular hashtag, the creator was also clearly well-skilled in using the medium.

Research shows that in the cases of trending hashtags, we often find that the same elite users are those getting retweeted, often by each other, who understand the processes that drive trending (Hermida et al., 2014; Page, 2012; Papacharissi and de Fatima Oliveira, 2012; Siapera et al., 2015).

Coming back to the idea of nodes, we could think about issues being represented by communities of mutual reinforcers where hashtags frame things, persons, and events in accordance with their more or less mutually shared and establish narratives, buzzwords, and symbolism. Again, there is much more work to be done in different specific cases to help us to understand how hashtags compete, come to the surface and shape, or even recontextualize how events, processes, and persons appear.

Affective communities

We now move on to consider observations made by researchers that allow us to think about the nature of communication on social media. This relates to how people contribute to feeds. Such observations encourage us to look more closely at exactly what is going on when people post to a feed about an issue of social justice, or even one that may be more xenophobic and racist. They also allow us to think more about what is going on in nodes.

Scholars have drawn attention to how social media feeds appear to be not so much characterized by coherent rational discussion, but more by floods of emotion or what is called 'affect' (Papacharissi, 2016). On such feeds, there may be an overall sense of an issue, for example, such as #MeToo or #TwoWomenTravel, but when we look closer, actual issues or aims may not be so obvious (Bouvier, 2020). What might be clear is a shared feeling of outrage and a powerful sense of shared agreement and mobilization around a simple narrative formed by buzzwords and symbolism. This can be the case both for ideas that we may consider as being democratic and about justice, as well as those against them. As scholars have shown, such feeds that have this emotionally charged sense of purpose will also be able to carry a great variety of contradictory and unconnected ideas, so long as these align with the broader affectivity and mutual agreement (Bouvier, 2019). In the work of one of the authors, a closer look is taken at a Twitter hashtag where users criticized a person captured on film making a xenophobic outburst. Bouvier found there was huge incoherence in what users posted. Some see the person as 'white trash', as poorly educated, as a white supremacist, as indicative of people from a particular region, or as an exceptional type of arrogant person found in all countries. The overall issue of racism or how to understand a xenophobic outburst becomes rather fuzzy. Yet those postings appear united by a sense of shared outrage and affect.

Following are three tweets from the #MeToo hashtag. These appeared quite close together in time, and they give us some insight into how affect can unite users:

> 3x as many male managers are now uncomfortable mentoring women in the wake of #MeToo. This is a huge step in the wrong direction. We need more men to #MentorHer.

> How about vegans stop complaining about feminists supporting rape by eating dairy and instead work to rid rape + rape culture within the animal rights movement! Maybe then, feminist would take vegans more seriously and be more willing to join the animal rights movement. #MeToo

> To the guy who wouldn't stop touching my butt on the tube, thanks for the reminder that although it was important to mark #Suffrage100, we're still a long way from achieving equality. Gonna do my bit to smash the patriarchy today in your honour #metoo

We can see that all of these tweets are emotionally engaged with issues of male-female relationships and abuse of power. The last one seems more directly the case, where a woman reports being assaulted on the Tube (i.e., London Underground public transit), but the first is more a related issue as to whether this will mean that male managers will become more reluctant to mentor female colleagues. This is clearly important, but when we come to the second tweet, which introduces the issue of veganism, we begin to see that this is less about a single, clearly demarcated issue where there are easy-to-identify problems, causes, and solutions. Rather, a range of things become loaded onto the hashtag, but they are united by the outrage, and where men and sexual abuse lie at the core. In the last of the three tweets, the female user comments: 'Gonna do my bit to smash the patriarchy today in your honour', referring to the man on the tube. Here, 'smash the patriarchy today' is more of a symbolic statement than a concrete and specific act.

The following meme (Figure 1.5) was also posted on the hashtag around the same time as these other posts. Here, humor is used to express that when women have had enough, they fight back. Some scholars ask us to consider what it means when we do social and political debate on social media, not by clear and transparent argument, but by symbolism and buzzwords (Krzyzanowski and Ledin, 2017). This does not mean that such hashtags cannot bring about change or mobilize people against a form of injustice in society, but just as hashtags can define how an event, process, or issue

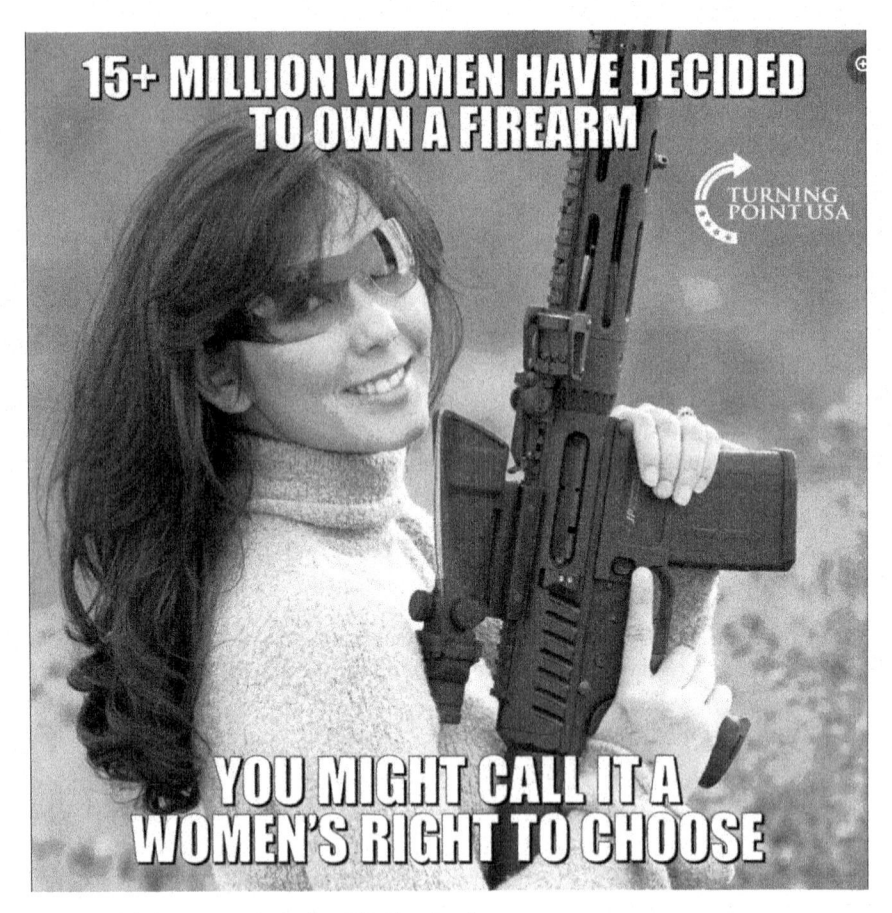

Figure 1.5 Meme posted on the #MeToo feed

might become framed, we might also look carefully at what kind of framing takes place on the social media feeds. In fact, in an analysis of anti-racism hashtags, one of the authors shows how racism becomes somehow easier to dismiss when we can account for it as the actions of 'white trash' or neo-Nazis. It means we may not ask why someone who may otherwise be a decent person, a hard and conscientious worker, produces xenophobic or racist sentiments when drunk. We look more at this issue in the research examples in the following chapters.

Papacharissi (2016) suggested that we might best think of the kinds of collective alignment found on such feeds as 'affective communities'. This means those posting engage around a kind of emotionally driven issue. When someone posts about veganism, or jokes about gun sales, we tend not to find other users saying that this is not what they are really dealing with on the hashtag, or that jokes about gun sales have no place there. There is rather a sense that they all align in this affective connectivity.

For Papacharissi (2016), the affective nature of social media communities does not mean that they cannot bring about some kind of social change; however, this may be more to do with raising awareness and introducing issues into the public space, rather than being able to bring about real change in terms of laws or the allocation of government spending. Other authors have also asked questions about the actual levels of commitment to issues on social media, where, as we see, the binding ties are not always so clear (De Zuniga and Valenzuela, 2010). In addition, actions carried out over social media do not require much effort at all, which could mean that we end up with passive activism or 'slacktivism' (Davies, 2013). Much of the activity found on the hashtags we have looked at so far in this chapter involved retweets and posting material found on other platforms, where users demonstrate their approval. This means supporting issues by 'likes', shares, subscribing, or clicking on a petition (Housley et al., 2018: 2). Of course, this is not always the case, where scholars have shown, for example, that social media have been used to draw people to protests and demonstrations (Tufekci and Wilson, 2012). Again, more research is needed to look at specific cases across a range of issues and user groups.

Influencers

To this we must add the key force driving many social media feeds, which is the desire of users to create engaging posts that will garner likes, shares, and subscribers (Rambukkana, 2015). This means that the tenor of tweets may in part be driven by the need to capture attention, which can create a push for those that provoke high emotion, polarity, sarcasm, and humor (Breazu and Machin, 2019). This combines with self-promotionalism (Page, 2012), where posts can be about impression management and self-branding (Enli, 2015; Kreiss, 2016; Page, 2012). Some scholars argue that issues that may have high social and political relevance are now carried out through combinations of all these things (Udupa, 2017).

Although many users may strive for likes, researchers point to the role played by influencers who use social media as a kind of self-branding, to increase personal capital and to sell products (Burke et al., 2011, 2010; Ellison et al., 2007; Valenzuela et al., 2009). These kinds of users can use morally charged feeds such as #MeToo or #BlackLivesMatter in order to gain such moral capital, also linking to their own blog or company profile (Bouvier, 2020). Such users, where successful, will tend to understand how to strategically use the medium. These influencers are those who understand the processes of self-promotion and 'pseudo-events' that can drive trending (Page, 2012). These users, therefore, know how to address, engage, and steer opinion nodes (Singh and Jain, 2010). Here is a tweet taken from the #MeToo hashtag, posted around the time of those shown earlier:

> Here's an unpopular opinion: I'm actually not at all concerned about innocent men losing their jobs over false sexual assault/harassment allegations.

This particularly provocative comment carries links to the user's own blog, where we find out she is a columnist. As Udupa (2017) notes, social media feeds tend to reward those who produce either more extreme, sarcastic, or memorable posts. Breazu and Machin (2019), analyzing racism against the Roma on Facebook, show how users seem to compete to provide the most outrageous comment, with each user getting carried along with the fun. In this case, the tweet seeks to attract attention to drive traffic to a blog.

Influencers may have a range of motivations, including to drive users to their websites, to promote their business, or to foster a political ideology. Researchers point, in particular, to how influencers have transformed how marketing and branding take place (Ferrari, 2015; Riboni, 2017). Some influencers take on the status of what have been called 'micro-celebrities' (Riboni, 2017: 190). These have an advantage over mainstream celebrities in that they can appear less corporate and more everyday, or a layperson (Cheung and Lee, 2012). They can claim a different level of trustworthiness and authenticity (Kádeková and Holienčinova, 2018), and they can also more naturally align with the local culture and fashion of a particular node of users (Pereira et al., 2018: 108). Authenticity here appears to become a key factor for followers. This may be carefully staged and managed (Gaden and Dumitrica, 2014), but will be continuously monitored by other users (Figure 1.6).

These influencers may use a range of social media platforms to provide curated and carefully produced content either about everyday experiences or related to some kind of niche interest, such as living in a van, doing a diet or fitness program, or using make-up (García Rapp, 2016). Such content will be somehow blended with product promotions (Van Driel and Dumetrica, 2020: 3), and such influencers can have a global reach for quite specific niche groups, which is of massive value in advertising (Sheldon and Bryant, 2016). Researchers have been interested in the strategies used by influencers on different platforms to gain attention, produce content, and communicate with followers (Burgess et al., 2009; Marwick, 2013; Riboni, 2017; Pereira et al., 2018).

The ephemeral nature of social media use

While the platforms of influencers may carry highly curated and managed content, it has been argued that much social media use is ephemeral (Ott, 2017). The idea here is that when we leave comments, we may not be entirely focused or carefully engaged. We may not examine what has already been said by others, or establish what the dimensions of the overall issue may be. We may get a sense of the general idea carried by a feed – the outrage or enjoyment about something – but we have not really carefully examined what is being proposed overall and by different users. Since we tend to encounter or be drawn towards feeds in our own particular node, it may already appear as familiar, with a recognizable narrative and expected buzzwords. This means we may be less attentive to the details (Bouvier and Cheng, 2019).

Many of the comments made on the #TwoWomenTravel hashtag discussed earlier, leaving love hearts and showing solidarity, did not appear so well-tuned to what was taking place. In particular, they mistook what perspective the hashtag represented (Bouvier, 2019). Here, we might say, in Papacharissi's (2016) terms, that they are engaging at the 'affective' level. Specifically, here they are aligning with the broader idea of the difficult position of women and the injustice of the law, not to the exact niche points of view, or the strategy of this particular hashtag. Therefore, users post love hearts and say things like 'solidarity sisters' or 'brave warrior women'.

In the fourth chapter, we look at hashtags where users criticize the woman captured on film being xenophobic. A quick glance at the stream of comments as it was trending gives a sense of people showing their anger about racism. It seems coherent. Yet a

Figure 1.6 A Weibo post from a fitness influencer:

Recently the temperature has dropped, suddenly very cold

Such time (I) want to comfortably enjoy a cup of coffee, put on fluffy clothes, cold days become warm

Maybe it's coming to the stage that [I] like to seek for things with higher quality; in daily life [I] like to work out and sometimes [I] have to look after the baby, [so] I choose a watch as the accessory, simple and versatile for styling.

Sharing with you a new DW new style, black with gold, new material is high-end quality, rubber band and watch face, complementary with rose gold time markers and hands, low key but eye catching, can be styled well with both exercising and business occasions.

You can get your hands on your Christmas present~

closer look reveals little coherence in ideas across the posts. A close reading of the sequence of posts reveals them as carrying much contradiction among them. As we noted earlier, some saw her as 'white trash', while others thought she was 'uneducated', arrogant, or a white supremacist that could be placed in the same category as Nazis or the KKK. For many race theorists, all of these misrepresent racism to some extent. We are either individualizing it or collapsing all kinds of different racism, belonging to specific unique times and places, together (Lentin, 2014; Bouvier and Machin, 2021). This view depoliticizes and decontextualizes racism (Gilroy, 2012). This means that we need to understand why this woman expressed herself in this way at this time – a woman who may otherwise be very ordinary (Gilroy, 2012). As such, the racist becomes a kind of demon and antithesis to the 'us' in the 'affective community'.

> That's too much logic. We all know or have met a #KellyPocha. We've dealt with them or seen them on video. Aggressive, disrespectful, ignorant, bigoted white women posturing with entitled superiority they believe can't be challenged or consequence.

> RACIST RANT from a member of 'Knuckle Draggers 4 Trump' one of the many bigots, racists, skin heads, KKK members, nazis & other poorly educated white supremacist, conservative 'Christian' right wing simpletons who support and defend @realDonaldTrump

Making such observations is not to criticize those making anti-racist statements, nor those wanting to give women the right to decide about abortion, but it allows us to look at how such feeds represent issues that can in part be accounted for in terms of how users may only engage with the feed in an ephemeral way.

The short nature of posts on platforms such as Twitter and Weibo, as well as their fast-moving nature, can also foster emotionally charged posts that provoke, rather than encourage more nuanced comments (Enli, 2017; Engesser et al., 2016). It has been argued that this nature, in part, leads to such platforms creating feeds that are ideologically inflexible (Ng, 2020). Any views diverging from the main simple affective narrative will be dealt with firmly.

The posts that we produce ourselves may also be done ephemerally. They will not be the product of longer contemplation or planning, but rather our own affective response. And the initial engagement with the feed, as well as composing our own post, may be done while we are waiting for our bus or picking up the coffee we ordered. We may be posting about a series of unrelated things in sequence (Bratslavsky et al., 2019), a review on a product, or sharing a picture of a cute dog we just saw. The point is that whether posting our thoughts on a news event, criticizing a famous person, or reviewing a movie we just saw, we do not really have such a deep commitment to it (Foxman and Wolf, 2013). Social media feeds about deeply important social, political, and moral issues may be composed largely of posts of this nature (Bouvier, 2020). This means that while we are waiting for a bus, we leave a review about a new organic foods café that we thought was overpriced. We also try to organize an outing with some friends and reply to an urgent work email – and we tweet, showing our disgust at racism.

This ephemeral nature of composing posts also helps explain why we may see insults, sarcasm, and incivility on social media feeds. Of course, on one level we feel we will never meet the person we are insulting and that there will be no consequences (Groshek and Cutino, 2016). Žižek's (1997) comments on early forms of online interactions is still highly relevant in that people do not have to stand by what they say. They can intervene, make a snarky comment, and then move on. This may be because they do not like the response, because it is simply fun to stir things up and vent some anger, or because their coffee is now ready and they can head off to work. But in terms of this ephemeral engagement, since we do not invest in the actual issue with any depth, we think less about the person we are attacking or come to see them not as a real person (Ott, 2017), although it has been observed that affective communities tend to simplify narratives of good and bad (Papacharissi, 2016) with an 'us' and demonized 'other' (Bouvier, 2020). Individuals who come under attack on social media may find themselves taking the form of the shared representation of the perpetrator, formed by the needs of an affective community or node, as they share their moralized version of events (Suler, 2004).

Researchers have also shown that even where users do encounter others with divergent viewpoints, for example, posted below a news clip on YouTube, they will not so much engage with each other, or even carefully consider what is being argued, but simply reproduce their own pre-existing narratives and simplifications (Lindgren, 2010; Georgakopoulou, 2014; Way, 2015; Al-Tahmazi, 2015).

Dean (2010) argues that this scan-and-go nature of contributing to forums, as well as the new culture of engagement in nodes, had led to a kind of skepticism. It means that we tend to treat all things, or at least anything outside of our nodal network, as opinion rather than knowledge. This means that we are much less open to engage with any kind of discussion, where we always have the reinforcement and comfort of our node and affective communities where our existing views are confirmed. Dean (2010) relates such shifts to broader changes in society, including how social media have taken over from more centralized forms of knowledge provision by major institutions and professional bodies. Such professionals may be increasingly replaced by influencers and self-styled experts.

Bouvier and Rosenbaum (2020) consider these shifts in terms of the broader consequences for civic debate in society. They point to a concept from Habermas (2006), where he argued that a society relies on 'communicative rationality' for democracy to function. This means a form of communication where there is transparency and clarity about issues, participants, processes, and causalities. Some scholars would argue that the former problem was that these issues would all be defined by the elites who controlled the centralized media and other institutions (Horowitz, 2013), but we might argue that these forms of ephemeral communication, done in nodes and affective connectivities, where influencers and algorithms are always at work, creates a new threat to Habermas' idea. Krzyzanowski and Ledin (2017) argue that social media have brought about a fundamental shift in how we discuss social and political issues, where nodes, simplifications, and symbolism now dominate. For Habermas, Bouvier and Rosenbaum (2020) argue, this risks a situation where communicative rationality breaks down and we move into 'violent abstraction'. In the case of the #MeToo hashtag, we can ask what it means, where we are presenting specific issues of social inequality or injustice, that this includes memes showing a woman with a gun adding a kind of sharp humor to the issue. It is here that we see social media communication as carrying symbolism, buzzwords, and being about affect rather than 'communicative rationality'.

Social media and news

News can be one important research area for social media research. News has been long considered as one of the cornerstones of democracy, where its role was considered as being a kind of watchdog over politicians and authority structures, keeping them in check. Much research points to the many reasons why news simply fails to carry out such a role, not simply due to vested power interests and ownership, but through the very nature of news production, news conventions, making news meaningful for publics, and the simple fact of the need to attract advertising (Curran and Seaton, 2018). The Internet environment has transformed news, where the former model of a one-a-day news sheet or bulletin has become irrelevant. To survive, news media have had to adopt an entirely new business model, with requirements for constant updates (Picard, 2014: 273), and news media now operate alongside and compete with bloggers, citizen journalists, and armies of public relations (PR) workers who 'participate' on social media and fulfill a range of other new communication roles (Carlson and Lewis, 2015). News, like other content, must operate in the landscape of algorithms addressing nodes and 'what you might also like' (Doctor, 2010). It is a communications environment where most people now receive news through their social media platforms, and often through sharing (Bergström and Belfrage, 2018). The former idea of news as 'top down' must be replaced by an understanding of how news stories flow through nodes and affective connectivities. Here, news and other content, as well as advertising, must be tailored to the personal needs of users (Mortimer, 2014).

News itself has become integrated into social media in other ways. Social media are now a major source of news stories (Hermida, 2012; Lasorsa et al., 2012). This could be where news carries breaking stories taken from social media posts on disasters or conflicts, providing a kind of early warning system to be then followed by news organizations (Bruno, 2011). Or news stories can use citizen-generated content to provide on-the-ground insights into events, such as in uprisings or during state-led violence. Although in this last case, such content has been much criticized. Typical scenes of street demonstrations can imply that we are being given on-the-spot deeper levels of insights and reporting, when beyond that we learn little about the actual context, as journalists tend to rely on lazy narratives about a 'people's uprising' (Keller, 2011). Journalists with neither the time nor resources can use such content to signify truth, and take readers/viewers to the heart of ongoing events, with little to no additional research or fact-checking (Bouvier, 2019). Of course, such content appearing to users in social media feeds may be compelling and attract more shares, clicks, and advertising revenue. Algorithms will allow editors to see what kind of content is most successful, so that more can be produced with the same qualities (Doctor, 2010).

Many scholars have pointed out that these shifts challenge some of the bedrock characteristics of journalism. Under pressure to create fresh, updated, and clickable content, there is no place for researching context, verification, or checking (Hermida, 2012). This can mean, for example, that a single hashtag may come to define the nature of how an event is reported in a news story (Bouvier, 2019). Yet, closer analysis of the posts may show the usual incoherence of an affective connectivity, where users are clearly engaging only ephemerally. As we saw previously, there can be much competition to have a hashtag define and shape the understanding of an event, often pushed by influencers or those who may seek to benefit.

Here we see some news headlines that carried the #TwoWomenTravel hashtag, with no additional verification, research, or even a closer look at the tweets. On the BBC 'trending' page of their website, we found:

#TwoWomenTravel – Live-tweeting the journey for an abortion

In the British *Guardian*, we found:

> Irish woman live-tweets journey for abortion in Great Britain: Woman and a friend thank everyone for their support on @TwoWomenTravel before beginning trip at dawn on Saturday
>
> (Hunt, 2016)

The BBC, of course, signals newsworthiness by mentioning the role of the celebrity poster:

> As hundreds showed their solidarity for the women and her companion, their actions gained attention from high-profile social media users like comedian and host of the 'Late Show' James Corden.
>
> (BBC Trending, 2016)

The BBC story does provide an 'alternative' point of view, where we are told: 'Not all were supportive' and that 'Catholic blogger' Caroline Farrow criticized the women and accused them of trivializing the procedure:

> This #twowomentravel thing seems to be about using the destruction of human life for entertainment purposes. Pretty sick.

Journalists are supposed to provide the different sides of the story. In the abortion issue, there were more than two sides, but here the alternative viewpoint also comes from social media. News readers are presented with a simplified view of things where an event, a journey, which appeared to be more symbolic than real, is presented with little attention to detail. Once again, we can think about the significance of all this for Habermas' 'communicative rationality'.

The original image posted on the #BringBackOurGirls hashtag (Figure 1.7), also carried by news outlets, turned out to be a young woman unconnected to the actual

Figure 1.7 Image posted on the #BringBackOurGirls feed

events (Shearlaw, 2015). This was seen as typical of the slacktivism of social media campaigning, of which the ephemeral engagement could also be seen as one part – we make our stand against social inequalities by sending a love heart while also booking our holiday to Thailand or ordering the latest iPhone for our daughter. What does it mean when our communication about social and political issues becomes like this, and the news media simply then place this into the public domain as 'news'?

The ethics of researching social media

More and more attention is being paid to how to conduct ethical research into social media (McNeal, 2014; Wood, 2014; Zimmer, 2010). This is because of the 'easy' public availability of social media data, and researchers have to apply familiar ethical principles with this new circumstance (Hibbin et al., 2018: 149). The traces we leave online potentially make up enormous data sets that can be publicly accessed, given some technological skills. The content of these posts ranges from the trivial everyday to the deeply private and sensitive, with both extremes of this spectrum being worthy of our attention (Bouvier and Way, 2021). Because much of this information has been made and left, shared, and posted willingly, there are complex questions about to what degree the researcher can just take this information and use it in a different context. Another layer of complexity is added to this when the posts contain information about other parties (i.e., third-person information), or when the user is underaged (Fossheim and Ingierd, 2015: 10). Furthermore, the Internet is not just a source of data. It can also be a means to conduct studies or a way of distributing your research (Jones, 2011). We are not going to consider all the facets of this complexity here, but rather focus on how issues such as anonymity and confidentiality (Bruckman, 2002; Zimmer, 2010), as well as informed consent (Barocas and Nissenbaum, 2014; Hudson and Bruckman, 2004), have become more complex.

So what guidelines are already in place? Standards for social media research are in the first place linked to historical policy and guidelines for 'human subjects research' (Fiesler and Proferes, 2018). This is defined as a researcher generating data via interaction or intervention with an individual, or private information that can be identifiable under US federal law (Bruckman, 2014). However, it isn't always clear if research using public information posted on social media sites does actually constitute human subjects research. Research drawing on social media content may involve a degree of interdisciplinarity and draw on disciplines outside of those where it is common to use human subjects (Jones, 2011). Further, how persons should be treated ethically has been laid down in several policies and historical documents, including the UN Declaration of Human Rights, the Declaration of Helsinki, and the Nuremberg Code. These mainly focus on "the fundamental rights of human dignity, autonomy, protection, safety, maximization of benefits and minimization of harms, [and] respect for persons, justice, and beneficence" (Markham and Buchanan, 2012), but this is only partially helpful, as these discuss ethical issues in a different, more general context. The different academic disciplines and traditions where social media research are taking place tend to have ethical codes and approaches that understand issues such as what is public or private very differently (Thelwall, 2010; Wilkinson and Thelwall, 2010).

In sum, scholars focusing on ethical issues in research have identified a deficit in guidance for research when it comes to data extracted from social media platforms

(Taylor and Pagliari, 2018: 1). Given the amount of studies that are now drawing on these kinds of data sets, we can see there is a pressing need for researchers to become more aware of the ethical challenges inherent in what they are doing and for academia to provide specific guidelines and recommendations for ethical research practice. This section of the book puts forwards a number of ethical concerns that ought to be addressed before undertaking research that uses social media data. This covers the following sections, on the nature of consent, strategies for anonymizing data, and the opportunities and limitations this kind of data offers for social research.

Consent and information

The notion of informed consent is key to ethical conduct in academic research (Jones, 2011). This is not so straightforward in online environments because these spaces have a transient and ephemeral nature. Online interactions tend to be marked by space-time distanciation, anonymous users, and a lessening of social cues. As a consequence, some users may reveal more about themselves online than they would do offline, thereby blurring what is public and what is private (Joinson, 1998; Lash, 2001; Williams, 2006). The online environment disinhibits, which means that Internet users, while being aware of the semi-public setting, may be more likely to engage in what could be considered private (Social Data Science Lab, 2020). However, it is possible that users online may be very aware of their context and have an imagined audience in mind that they are addressing (Marwick and boyd, 2010). Further, such online environments involve networked publics, where research populations can be difficult to frame and identify. Rather, they can fluctuate and "are presented in a disembodied form" (Jones, 2011). Author boyd (2014) notes that information online may have only been intended for a specific group of peers, such as those in a certain community or support network, rather than just anyone on the Internet, let alone publics that are not Internet-based (i.e., readers of a study using social media data). We should keep in mind that such information flowing out of the context it was intended for, and being viewed by those it was not intended for, has the potential to cause harm (Barocas and Nissenbaum, 2014). In a study about Twitter and consent, researchers asked users how they felt about their posts being used for research (Fiesler and Proferes, 2018). Only a few were aware their tweets could be used, and the majority objected to this happening without their express permission. However, this all depended on the nature of the study, the topic, and where results would be published or shown (2018: 1).

In view of this situation, it seems logical that researchers should not present participants' personal information so they can possibly be identified by their communities or schools. In addition, parental consent should be sought in the case of adolescents being the respondents (Moreno et al., 2013: 712). Nevertheless, a study of university boards in the US revealed that the majority recommends it is not necessary to get informed consent if the data is publicly available (Vitak et al., 2017). In fact, Fiesler and Proferes (2018) point out that most researchers who use Twitter data do not gain consent from individual users, or give notice that they are involved in a study. Further, a study that considered several hundred articles that draw on Twitter data found that very few discussed undertaking an ethics review (Zimmer and Proferes, 2014). Since revising their policy in the latter part of 2014, Twitter's privacy policy mentions that academics are allowed to use tweets as part of research, but users hardly ever read the policy statements of social media platform (i.e., terms and conditions of use) (Fiesler et al., 2016; Luger et al., 2013; Reidenberg et al., 2015).

This does not mean that doing social media research is a free-for-all. Taking a more nuanced look, Moreno et al. (2013) argue that different strategies should be taken depending on the amount of risk involved in higher-risk studies, concomitant with a higher threshold to grant waiver of the participant consent. In a study of Research Ethics Committee members, Hibbin et al. (2018: 149) found that those researchers with less experience of using social media data tended to hold rather inflexible notions of consent and risk. These would be either to obtain direct consent or to view data that is publicly available as fair game (ibid.). However, researchers with more experience would take a more nuanced approach to how they used data as regards consent. The latter, the authors argue, was the more fruitful way of dealing with social media data and should be considered best practice (ibid.). For Facebook research specifically, it would be an option to set up a page using one's professional identity as a principal investigator. This page would allow respondents to friend the researcher while being fully aware of the professional, rather than personal, context of such a link (Moreno et al., 2013: 712). Another recommendation is for the researcher to provide contact information for questions during the consent process. In addition, putting in place or listing a privacy policy may be beneficial if it lets users know what data is going to be used and how this will be used, displayed, shared or even transferred (Moreno et al., 2013: 712). Once participants have given their consent, or are aware of being included in a study, what further ways do we have to avoid them being identified through their posts?

Confidentiality and anonymity

The Internet and social media are typified by persistence, searchability, and replicability (boyd, 2010). There is the potential of re-identification through data that has been anonymized (Fossheim and Ingierd, 2015: 10), and this may cause harm, not just to individuals, but to entire communities or classes of people (Hoffman and Jones, 2016). Indeed, the impact of the publication of a study on unwitting participants can be hard to foresee (Fossheim and Ingierd, 2015: 10), especially projects using intensive qualitative data might betray important contextual details and information that can cause the original source to be identified (Jones, 2011), and verbatim quoted posts (e.g., tweets) can be traced back to the user who created the post. Even in the case of micro-data (e.g., numbers on transactions, health info, individual preferences), someone who knows even a little bit about an individual user can easily identify this user's record in the data set (Narayanan and Shmatikov, 2008: 1).

Good-faith attempts to hide the identity of users have proven to be insufficient in past projects (Zimmer, 2010: 313). Therefore, Esomar (2011) argues that respondents should explicitly give consent if personally identifiable information in the form of quotes are used in doing market, social, and opinion research. Alternatively, Bruckman (2002), in an earlier study, suggested different levels of disguising online data. For example, a 'light disguise' could involve quoting a post but hiding the username by either not giving it or using pseudonyms. The author notes though that with some effort it would be possibly to identify the creators of the posts (ibid.). Another way to protect users in qualitative research is "through narrative and creative means, which might require the fictionalizing of aspects of the research or the creation of composite accounts ... providing generalized features based on a number of specific accounts" (Jones, 2011).

Opportunities and limitations for social research

In a sense, the Internet is offering researchers tremendous opportunities to access human activity. Culture and technology have become meshed together due to the fact that much interaction online, taking place through a technological interface, is "how things are done" (Lash, 2001). Without this technology, there would be issues of access to certain aspects of our lives or culture that are "now at-a-distance" (ibid.). Estimates put social media membership at approximately 4.2 billion users at the start of 2021, equating to more than 53.6% of the global population (Datareportal, 2021). Platforms such as Facebook, WhatsApp, WeChat, Instagram, and YouTube in particular account for a large part of this activity (ibid.). In spite of these tremendous opportunities to study human communication and culture, researchers have to be aware of the limitations inherent in social computing research. As mentioned previously, one has to be careful not to cause harm (Collmann et al., 2016). For example, Twitter users may choose to post very personal information, allowing others to identify them during crisis events, in order to get help and support (Crawford and Finn, 2015). Even big data, boyd and Crawford (2012: 662) warn, can be used for malicious reasons such as privacy incursions, invasive marketing, protester tracking, and free speech suppression.

Because social media research happens in a rapidly changing and interdisciplinary field, it is hard to propose fixed standards. Rather, established ethical procedures need constant reconsideration, revision, and development (Jones, 2011). Legally, we tend to lag behind technological developments. This makes it all the more important for researchers to take the initiative in ethics, self-regulation, and responsibility. The latter are sometimes the only restraints, in view of underdeveloped laws (Mann and Stewart, 2000: 39–40).

So what do we use?

The changes that we have seen in the research landscape have challenged existing ethics frameworks, but that doesn't mean social media research is inherently more risky than other types of research (Orton-Johnson 2010). Our research also does not take place in a fixed context: privacy concerns and the regulatory structure of research can be expected to change on a global basis (Hibbin et al., 2018: 158). There are different places to go for guidance for your specific project. Though university institutional review boards (IRBs) may have guidelines, there is often a lack of consensus from one institution to another (Vitak et al., 2017). Organizations such as the Association of Internet Researchers (AOIR) have set out best practice guides for Internet researchers (Ess and AOIR Ethics Working Committee, 2002); however, as the field evolves and new platforms become popular, these guidelines have also had to be revised to ccount for new research contexts and ways in which data is collected (Markham et al., 2012). All in all, we can say that researchers using social media data are not in agreement about norms or what is best practice in this online space (Vitak et al., 2016). This means that researchers will have to remain vigilant in how they evaluate risk in the use of online content, and monitor themselves from an ethical point of view. Central to this is seeking "procedural solutions to the protection and confidentiality of data, respect for the individual, and the personal privacy of those whose data are captured for research purposes" (Hibbin et al., 2018: 158). Each Internet research project requires an individual assessment of its own ethical issues (Golder et al., 2017), and this decision-making can happen at several stages of the research process, including during planning your project, executing your research design, and disseminating your research (Markham and Buchanan, 2012).

QUALITATIVE CONTENT ANALYSIS

TEXT AND SPEECH-BASED MATERIAL

Introduction

What do we mean when referring to qualitative content analysis of text and speech-based material and how is such a study conducted? That is the twofold question that this chapter will answer. To begin with, when applied to social media and texts, it is a method that centers on categorization and description for the purpose of providing an overview of social media content, or statements about social media, and variation therein. It can also serve well as a method for literature reviews on social media research. It consists most commonly of both exploration of new elements discerned in the content under study and testing of presumptions based on previous studies and theory. Qualitative content analysis (QCA) is thus positioned right in the middle between inductive and deductive research (see Glaser and Strauss, 1998). It is particularly suitable for researching relatively unexplored phenomena, such as a novel case or issue that has not been studied before. It can particularly assist a project in grasping and making visible stakeholder's statements, actions, and orientations in a chosen situation.

The method serves studies in many disciplines and of a variety of questions. Much has been done in research on healthcare, its workforce, and users. A couple of main areas for research questions can be discerned. Given the complex boundaries between private and professional life, research has mapped what healthcare professionals actually publish on social media (Lee et al., 2014; Mukattash et al., 2020). With the opportunity to discuss experiences of healthcare, other studies have reviewed what users share on social platforms (Shepherd et al., 2015; van der Pijl et al., 2020). Yet other studies show even more clearly that QCA focusing on social media present an opportunity for studying sensitive and important issues, something that Vaismoradi et al. (2013) also has observed in the past. Research has focused on the problem of maltreatment of women in connection with childbirth and explored the content of tweets about negative experiences of maternity care shared under the hashtag #breakthesilence (van der Pijl et al., 2020). Furthermore, reactions in the form of Facebook posts to high-profile cases of domestic violence accusations have been studied (Whiting et al., 2019), as well as differences between the scope and content of health information on boys-focused channels and girls-focused channels on Snapchat (LeBeau et al., 2020). Research dealing broadly with health and healthcare is indeed the area where QCA is used the most.

In another field, research on business administration, *quantitative* content analysis is much more prevalent than the qualitatively oriented approach (Duriau et al., 2007). Research using QCA has mapped how brands create a presence among online communities and initiate consumer engagement (Ashley and Tuten, 2015; Du Plessis, 2017) and reviewed impressive amounts of research on social media marketing (Alves et al.,

DOI: 10.4324/9780429319334-2

2016). Similarly, in political science, the method has been used to review and synthesize the literature on government use of social media (Medaglia and Zheng, 2017) and to identify the extent to which social media is used in election campaigns and what the content and related activities consist of (Macnamara and Kenning, 2011). Another area, risk and crisis communication, has primarily taken inspiration from QCA for literature reviews on social media research (Eriksson, 2018; Rasmussen and Ihlen, 2017) and case studies on crisis communication (Jong et al., 2016). Thus, although the method has become common in some fields (concerning health, nursing, and medical care), in other fields it has mainly been used for literature reviews and hardly at all elsewhere. There seems to be a great opportunity to explore and test the method to a greater extent in various research contexts.

While the prior passages show quite broad use of QCA in studies of social media, there is also a growing body of methodological literature. It consists of occasional extensive work (Schreier, 2012), which deals with each analytical step in an entire chapter, providing the reader with much information but also prompting a multitude of path choices. It also includes papers that are quite limited in scope in terms of specific method application, but thoroughly compares different approaches (Cho and Lee, 2014; Graneheim et al., 2017; Hsieh and Shannon, 2005; Vaismoradi et al., 2013) or provides information on the method's history and limited recognition (Prasad, 2019) and specific aspects of it, such as the debated role of counting and representing frequencies (Morgan, 1993). Application of the method in projects that study social media is an issue that has not been explored in this literature. In this context, the present chapter seeks to make a contribution by, quite straightforwardly, explaining what QCA pertains to and how it can successfully be applied when examining social media texts. In addition to introducing the method and how it can be applied, the chapter will also help clarify important methodological choices and premises that need to be made visible when QCA is used.

The rest of the chapter is organized as follows. The next section provides a brief historical background of the method. It also clarifies some methodological choices and concepts that are crucial for how results are interpreted and described. Then there is a section explaining the research process and the analytical tools of QCA, including examples from completed research. The conclusions summarize key points on how to conduct a QCA study and suggests some avenues for future methodological development.

Qualitative content analysis: meaning making and text

Berelson (1952) was first to define and expand on content analysis as a scientific method, as he synthesized research from 1935 to 1950 that all applied related analytical principles to review and understand various texts. Thus, it is almost a century ago that analytical procedures were first developed that can be classified as content analysis. Materials that were analyzed early on were radio programs, newspapers, campaign materials, and interviews. Common purposes of the research were to analyze the content of propaganda, news coverage, and advertising and their effects on the audience. At this time, when the method was first developed and used, it was not defined and broken down so that some researchers did quantitative content analysis and others used a qualitative approach. Indeed, until about 1950, the analysis included both quantitative and qualitative elements (Morgan, 1993). However, Berelson (1952: 18) defined content analysis as "a research technique for the objective, systematic, and quantitative description of the manifest content of communication," revealing a leaning toward a quantitative methodological understanding. Furthermore, after Berelson had described a qualitative and quantitative orientation of the method, these two methodological strands were also more clearly crystallized, whereupon the quantitative orientation became the most common for decades to come. For Berelson, the qualitative approach appeared to be less systematic, prone to subjective bias, and thus inferior to the quantitative equivalent, and something he did not really want would be associated with the concept of content analysis. The approach was reduced to being seen as possibly useful for exploratory pilot studies (Prasad, 2019). Berelson may thus have contributed to the marginalization of QCA, as his book defined content analysis for some time to come. Although not with the same impact, others came to the defense of QCA, such as Kracauer (1952), who argued that few texts that become relevant for analysis contain such simple information that it can be quickly and unambiguously categorized. Rather, the data is usually of a qualitative nature; it is created from the beginning through complex, institutional processes in a certain socio-historical context, and understanding it requires interpretation and contextual consideration. Kracauer thus concludes that, because texts are not atomistic phenomena but created and made meaningful in contexts, a qualitative analytical approach is necessary for content analysis research to be able to draw general conclusions.

From its establishment in communication studies, the method has since been further developed in various disciplines. This means that there is a certain variation in understanding what the method represents. On the one hand, it is common to come across a precise definition such as that by Schreier (2014: 170), stating that "[q]ualitative content analysis is a method for systematically describing the meaning of qualitative data. . . . Three features characterize the method: qualitative content analysis reduces data, it is systematic, and it is flexible." On the other hand, there is also an understanding of QCA as a general, qualitative approach, as evidenced by a widely cited definition from Patton (2002: 453), stating that QCA "is any qualitative data reduction and sense-making effort that takes a volume of qualitative material and attempts to identify core consistencies and meanings." Based on this latter understanding, it becomes difficult to perceive any difference between qualitative, descriptive methods, such as thematic analysis and QCA. There may thus be a point in trying to follow Schreier (2012, 2014) and develop the specificity of QCA.

The historical background and the argument by Kracauer (1952) in favor of QCA indicates that its value lies in recognizing communication as meaning making, and that the analysis allows a combination of systematic procedures and flexibility, countable categories and context-sensitive interpretation. Following Bruner (1990), we may differentiate, then, between meaning making and simpler forms of information or data. While qualitative content analysis is suitable for studying the former, a quantitative approach is better for the latter. While meaning is a cultural and interactional phenomenon, simpler information has more definite significance to suit technical systems. Bruner (1990: 69) explains that meaning is "a culturally mediated phenomenon that depends on the prior existence of a shared symbol system." He further explains that meaning, unlike information, carries normative assumptions. Meaning implies evaluation of what is going on. It can be prescriptive in terms of how things should be (or done). Likewise, it can be deterministic, or vague, or imply dilemmas. Also, it is something that is continuously done or accomplished. Meaning is shaped, re-shaped, and negotiated at the intersection between existing culture and ambitions for the future. *Meaning making* is the activity people are engaged in as they make sense of the world and of themselves (ibid.: 2). QCA thus explores meaning making in terms of the interpretations and ideas put forth in our culture and organizations about roles, processes, artifacts, assessments, and prioritizations and goals. Meaning making occurs everywhere in social media, and the approach is just as relevant when studying uses of social media in the private sector (Ashley and Tuten, 2015), by government institutions (Medaglia and Zheng, 2017), or by ordinary citizens on Facebook (Whiting et al., 2019).

In addition to meaning making, something should be said about text. The chapter is delimited to the study of text, including speech-based material. Texts are understood as coherent linguistic accounts, as Halliday and Hasan (1976: 1) say, as "any passage, spoken or written, of whatever length, that does form a unified whole." A unified whole, or cohesion, suggests that different elements when taken together represent meaningful communication. By themselves, they do not. An example could be the words strung together in poetic meter, or the classical, dramaturgical elements in a play. Again: "It may be spoken or written, prose or verse, dialogue or monologue. It may be anything from a single proverb to a whole play, from a momentary cry for help to an all-day discussion on a committee" (Halliday and Hasan, 1976: 1). With a different, semiotic approach, text is seen as any chain of signs that can be meaningfully read (Barthes, 1977; Lotman, 1977) like a series of images. For the purpose of this chapter, however, we limit the subject of texts to coherent linguistic statements, written or spoken.

Fitting QCA into the research process

As shown schematically in Figure 2.1, the research process is described along four phases: (1) research design, (2) organization of data collection and coding, (3) analysis (both guided and exploratory) along with writing up results, and (4) a concluding phase when results are related to the overall issues of the study. Slightly different from the QCA research process outlined by Elo and Kyngäs (2008), this model emphasizes the place for QCA in an entire research design, and thus details both an initial and final phase a little more than they do with their model. Another difference is that this conceptual model outlines a combination of the use of coding guidelines and open coding, rather than distinguishing sharply between the two coding procedures. It can be argued that this combination of planned and flexible analysis is a major strength of QCA, and that it would be uncharacteristic to carry out the analysis either without any premises at all or entirely based on predetermined codes and existing categories.

Before each phase is presented with examples, it should be mentioned that the demonstration of the whole process in this way emphasizes the importance of appropriate use of QCA for knowledge development and awareness of the possibilities (and limitations) of the method throughout the different phases of a study. From the beginning, the process involves designing a research problem and, based on this problem, crafting a purpose, deciding on the type of material to study, and crafting concrete

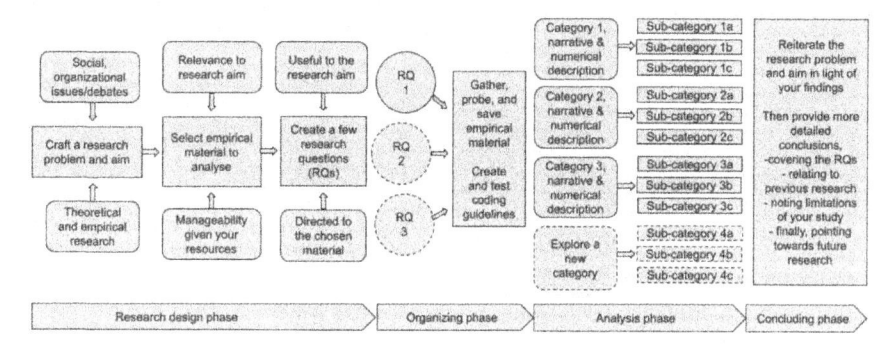

Figure 2.1 A schematic overview of the QCA process

research questions directed at the chosen material. The first phase thus contains key decisions. Without a carefully thought-out and reasonably bold research problem and purpose, a primarily descriptive method such as QCA (Schreier, 2012) risks not reporting anything new to stakeholders, and through its 'recording' of existing interpretations or realities could contribute to the status quo rather than constructive solutions. The significance of paying attention to existing knowledge and designing a study that has a good chance of rendering novel knowledge can therefore not be overestimated. The second, organizing phase includes the design of more detailed selection criteria, the practicalities of data collection, and the application of the selection criteria. In this phase, coding guidelines are also designed. What then follows is repeated reading and coding. The focus can be on understanding and organizing the material based on categories or themes (Schreier, 2012). Results are presented both numerically (frequency table/s), to provide an overview of the categories or themes, and narratively, with examples from the material and interpretations of frequency counts and examples of the categories. The main categories or themes discerned can be used as an 'organizing principle' (Chaffee and Lieberman, 2001) for the sections of the results chapter. The conclusions and the discussion then address the overall research problem, previously introduced in the beginning of the paper, but now in the context of the new findings. This concluding section then demonstrates in more detail how the purpose is fulfilled, how each research question is answered, and relates these results to previous research and, finally, to possible future research.

The research design phase

Like all research, the process of QCA begins with the identification of a research problem. A research problem should be formulated in a paragraph or two, describing an area of concern, a lack of some kind that needs attention, and which more knowledge through further studies can help to remedy. In other words, including a good research problem anticipates your reader exclaiming 'so what?' Also, it should be placed in the introduction, so that the reader is provided with motives to continue reading from the start. Moreover, a research problem should be rooted in previous research, that is, what we already know and would need to know more about. Motives for new research, to include in a research problem statement, can thus be found in previous empirical studies or theoretical literature.

> *A research problem exemplified*: Shepherd et al. (2015) present the problem that Twitter is a major platform for public debate and societal issues, yet little is known about the possibilities with the platform for communication about mental health in general and feedback on mental health care specifically. Research on communication on Twitter regarding physical health problems exists, but the lack of research about communication on the topic of mental illness forms a knowledge gap.

Without starting with what others have done, there is a risk of reinventing the wheel or unnecessarily placing one's work outside relevant research contexts. It is therefore a bad idea to try to come up with a purpose for your study all by yourself without any grounding in research. Another aspect to keep in mind is that a research problem should be relevant in society or for organizations as well. Thus, experiences in society, from private or organizational life, may inspire ideas that, when related to relevant research, can develop into a research problem. Highlighting the potential usefulness of your study is only positive. It is thus often useful to think of the research problem as twofold: that it is rooted partly in research and partly in current societal or organizational issues.

QCA is suitably chosen when the research problem asserts that more knowledge is needed in the form of (a) an overview of a well-defined phenomenon, (b) its main components or variations, and (c) positionings or orientations expressed in people's own words. Shepherd et al. (2015) can be said to exemplify this as they show that there is a lack of knowledge about Twitter content on issues of mental illness and psychiatry. They describe their own study as exploring and mapping this new area and, in addition, it focuses on psychiatric users' own feedback and messages.

With an understanding of a problem, it is then appropriate to select at least the type of material that is relevant to study. With an idea of the material to be studied, an aim and more concrete questions that the study should answer can be designed. Usually, the material is delimited and reduced, partly based on a specific issue or case, partly based on the interest in specific sources and platforms. The choice of the type of material, such as a particular social media platform, must be made with an understanding of who is using the platform and the mode of communication it gives precedence to. On the one hand, if the research problem does not signal the importance of visual communication, a platform focusing on visuals may be less suitable to choose. On the other hand, the platform's reach and degree of use among certain target groups can be important enough. A platform such as Instagram contains plenty of text material and comments alongside photos and video. That kind of trade-off needs to be made. In the case of the study by Shepherd et al. (2015) on Twitter comments regarding mental health and psychiatry, one must be aware that the users of Twitter are not an average of the population. Higher socio-economic groups are greatly overrepresented. With such a sample, the study's authors should be clear not to generalize to a population that does not use Twitter and that the results are limited as a basis for policy discussions. Moreover, the choice of a particular source, such as an institution or stakeholder, must be made with an understanding of its responsibilities and interests. Finally, this initial choice of material needs to consider resources, both time and labor. It is better to be able to say something authoritative about a limited issue than to spread one's efforts with the result ending up being broad and thin.

With a research problem in place and an idea of which material to study, it is possible to specify a purpose and preferably more concrete research questions that are distinct and readily applicable to different parts of the data. The aim should be expressed briefly and concisely, preferably in a single sentence, stating what the study should achieve and in such a way that the aim to be achieved can be evaluated (Thomas and Hodges, 2010). Vague wordings that promise too little should be avoided. *Exploring* social media content or perceptions of social media can be one such example. Exploring something can mean a little or a lot, and the result is highly uncertain. Having it as a purpose is not very binding. If such a term is still used, further concretization is needed. In a QCA study on social media, it is better to formulate an aim of mapping or reviewing a phenomenon and its characteristics and variations. A purpose should then be broken down into additional objectives (see Shepherd et al., 2015) or research questions (see Medaglia and Zheng, 2017).

For their literature review on government social media use, Medaglia and Zheng (2017) aimed to provide "an analysis of research on social media in the public sector" and derive "a framework to provide a basis for developing a future research agenda." They then provided three concrete research questions: "RQ1: What are the current foci and gaps in government social media research? RQ2: How can we frame relationships between constructs of government social media research? RQ3: What aspects of government social media should future research focus on?"

The point of crafting such objectives or research questions is to make the purpose concrete, possible to investigate, and relevant to different aspects of a particular empirical material.

In their study on Twitter messages about mental illness and psychiatric care, Shepherd et al. (2015) aimed to outline "the potential role of Twitter as a means of both service feedback and a space in which mental health can be openly discussed and considered from a variety of perspectives." This overall purpose was then addressed by studying two objectives: "1) The manner in which social media users with experience of mental disorder relate to each other and the social space during internet based interactions. 2) The potential role of resources such as Twitter for the provision of feedback on and engagement with mental health service user experience."

Organizing and analysis of data

After the focus of the study has been determined, it is appropriate to select material, obtain it, and begin to develop how the coding should proceed more accurately. In this process, we should not confuse the data collection technique and analytical technique. Indeed, the former is about what materials to analyze and the latter, like QCA, can be applied to a variety of materials (Snelson, 2016). Common data sources in studies on social media are, for instance, individual interviews (Rasmussen, 2017, 2020), focus group interviews (Fox et al., 2013), professional documents about social media use (Du Plessis, 2017), content from social media platforms (Shepherd et al., 2015), or previous studies on social media (Macnamara and Kenning, 2011). All these types of materials can be arranged and categorized based on the principles of QCA.

When assessing what kind of material one can access and collect (or help create), pros and cons are weighed based on the research aim and existing resources. For instance, interviews should be organized, and conducted and transcribed, and thus constitute a rather resource-intensive data collection technique. It usually demands less resources to collect documents about social media use (e.g., organizational policies), content from social media platforms or, if the aim is to review a field, create a sample of previous research on social media. Video material, too, is quite resource intensive since, similar to interviews, it is more readily approached using QCA after transcription. Some data reduction can be completed before transcription, though, if all the material that is central to the research aim is retained. As Schreier (2012) emphasizes, it is better for the reliability of the study to keep a little too much material than to sort out things that may be relevant to the research aim.

Given that QCA is a descriptive method that is meaningful to use for fairly large materials, comprehensive data needs to be secured in the organizing phase. Based on the purpose and questions of the research, it is important to define the population that is of interest and possibly select social channels. Furthermore, a time limit needs to be set for relevant data. Collecting data on several occasions can provide an opportunity to say something about a development and reduce bias due to special events that happen to coincide with a certain period for collection. If one wants to understand social media usage around a particular case or event, the situation may be associated with one or more popular hashtags. One way to collect data is to use advanced search functions and collect messages retroactively. Another approach is to subscribe to particular hashtags

---

Returning to the example study, we can see that Shepherd et al. (2015) managed data selection for their QCA study on psychiatric care users' feedback on Twitter by focusing on tweets under the hashtag #dearmentalhealthprofessionals. It can be reasonably assumed that those who use this hashtag form part of the study's intended population, psychiatric patients, but perhaps also some relatives and friends. In addition, tweets were selected only from the hashtag's two most active days. The data search based on these criteria led to hundreds of tweets that were de-identified and imported as text into a word processing program. After excluding retweets, 515 tweets remained.

to collect relevant messages in real time. While some platforms may be suitable for data collection via hashtags (e.g., Instagram, Twitter, LinkedIn), for others, such as Facebook it is not recommended. On Facebook, it may be more appropriate to select one or more organizations or groups that address the issues under study. A third way of obtaining data is to use software, such as Netlytic, which allows users to download links and descriptive metadata from Instagram in an Excel format (see, e.g., Laestadius et al., 2019).

If a smaller project were to draw inspiration from Shepherd et al. (2015) and design a study focusing on tweets that are posted nowadays about users' experience of mental ill-health, other hashtags that are currently in use would be chosen for data collection. With a focus on service users' own stories, hashtags such as #bipolarclub could be appropriate for data gathering, as opposed to more generic hashtags such as #mentalhealthawareness, which often features research and commercial content. For a small-scale study, a few shorter time periods could be chosen for data collection, with the delimitation that tweets focusing on experience are included. In this case, we would find it convenient to simply screen-save the selection of Tweets and gather them in a folder to then follow up with coding. For ethical reasons, posts would be anonymized, as users do not know all the ways in which their content could be used by others and might not approve of our context. Figure 2.2 shows a selection of different categories of tweets that could be included in the analysis.

Regardless of the technique used to access relevant social media content – through hashtags, special sources or groups, or certain software – it is possible to control the size of the material by adapting the study's time span, or through randomization. So, it is feasible to arrange one or more occasions for data collection, for longer or shorter periods, and also reduce the material by randomly selecting, for example, every third post. With a particular event and institution being studied, and with a focus on document or social media content, it may also be possible to make a total selection.

When the material is collected, a coding frame needs to be developed. A coding frame shows what the analysis focuses on and how categorization should be implemented. It thus contributes guidance throughout the analysis. Early on, it is important to determine what constitutes the study's unit of analysis. In one study, a unit can be an interview. In another study, a unit can be a tweet. In a third study, a unit can be an organization's Facebook page or blog. When results are added together and summed in frequency tables, these units are counted along different dimensions that have been analyzed. Once it has been clarified what a unit is, the next step is to define the main categories and, divided under these, at least one level of subcategories, sometimes two. The main categories are the most overarching aspects of the material that the study seeks to create more knowledge about. Subcategories constitute variations of the content of main categories, such as different opinions, interpretations, and ways to describe a phenomenon. In a comprehensive study, subcategories can be further subdivided through careful observation of content variation and meaning potential.

Some concrete guidelines have been emphasized in the literature on QCA. First, main categories should be so well-defined that they capture one dimension of the data. This unidimensionality implies a high degree of clarity and simplicity. Second, similar principles apply to subcategories, in that they should be mutually exclusive. If we draw a parallel to quantitative analysis, it is very clear that the values for a variable should not overlap, as it would collapse the analysis. The same applies to the subcategories of a QCA. Third, all material that is relevant for the purpose and

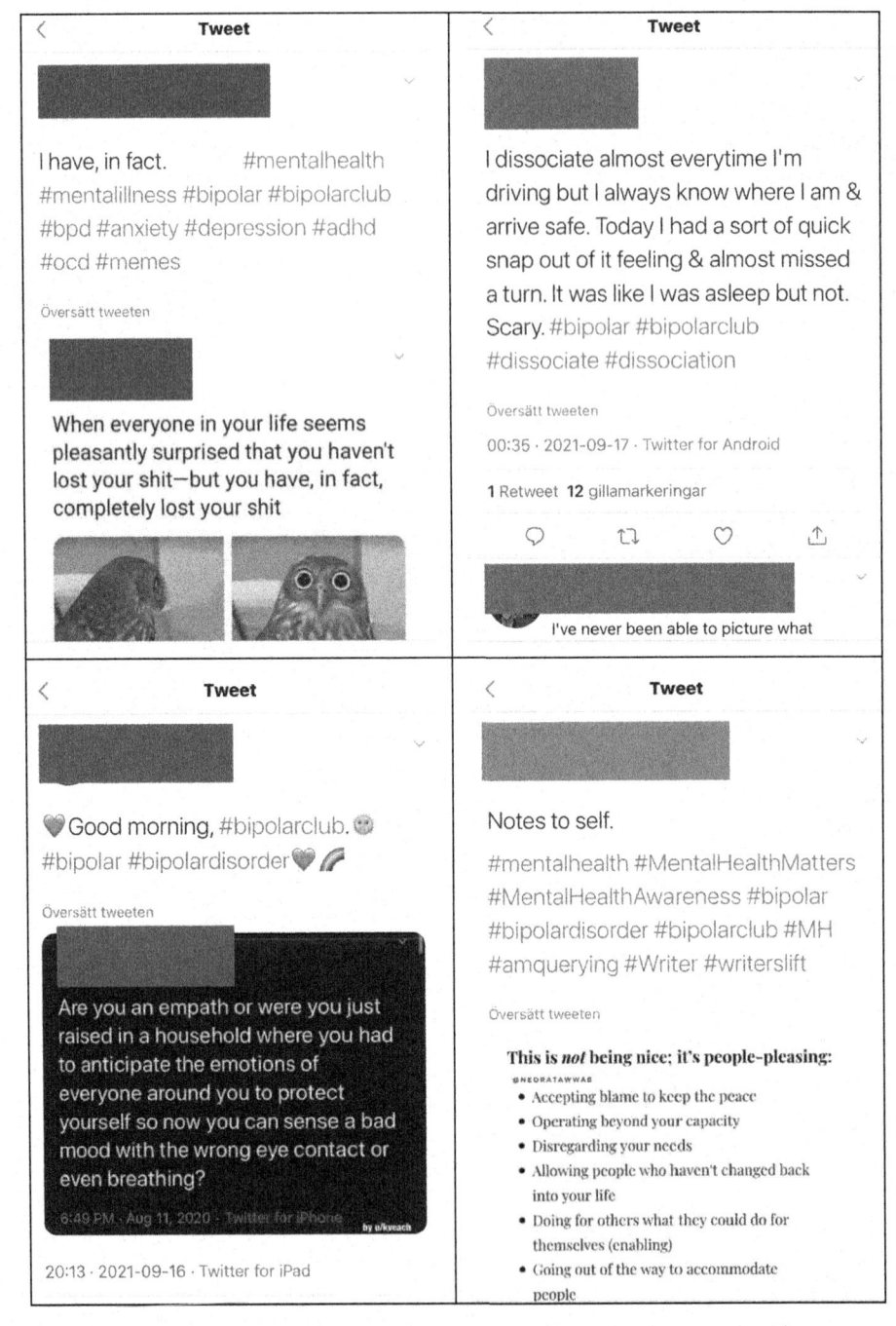

Figure 2.2 Examples of some categories of tweets that could be included in a study on tweets about mental ill-health experience: a humorous post (LU), current experience post (RU), retrospective experience post (LL), and advisory post (LR)

research questions should be coded. If the relevant material is left uncoded, aspects are left under-researched, and the mapping is incomplete. There is thus a requirement for exhaustiveness in the coding (Schreier, 2012).

However, it can be difficult to always frame actual empirical material according to these ideals of unidimensionality and mutual exclusivity, not least when analyzing speech-based material and some of its 'messiness'. People can engage in meaning making, weighing in on an issue drawing on advantages and disadvantages, without arriving at an unequivocal conclusion. This occurs in studies of a range of subjects. One way to tackle such reasoning full of dilemma is to simply establish a subcategory that captures it. Dilemma is indicative of challenge or change. Without it, human existence would be immutable (Bevir, 1999). It is helpful to use the coding framework to prepare for the studied discourse to present dilemmas. Well-defined subcategories should be created for both uncomplicated views and reflexive views.

Categorization at different levels can be *concept driven* in the sense that previous research provides direction for the coding, but the coding can also include identifying main categories through the analysis – a *data-driven* development of the coding frame (Schreier, 2012). What suits different studies depends on how well-researched the area of the study is and to what extent the author has well-founded hypotheses about the material. This choice between concept-driven and data-driven coding also determines how much of a coding frame is completed in advance, before a pilot round of analysis is undertaken.

> An example of a concept-driven coding can be found in Fox et al. (2013), which studies the importance of social networking web sites (SNSs), such as Facebook, as couples develop romantic relationships. The authors describe that Mark Knapp's theoretical model regarding different stages for the development of romantic relationships is examined in their study. The coding is described as open yet consistently related to the phases of the theoretical model, i.e., initiating, experimenting, intensifying, integrating, and bonding.

The coding frame is created by reading and encoding part of the collected material. As far as possible, the coding frame should be developed using a selection of the material, which is equally varied as the material in its entirety. This ensures that the coding frame will be possible to apply well throughout the analysis.

> A data-driven coding process is found in Shepherd et al. (2015), studying psychiatric care users' feedback through Twitter. It shows that the authors read their sample of tweets and summarized each one of them using keywords or paraphrasing. By identifying similarities and differences between the notes taken for each tweet, the material was grouped into themes. Thereby, they build from the bottom-up an understanding of all the main themes: *(1) the impact of diagnosis on personal identity and as a facilitator for accessing care; (2) the balance of power between professional and service user; (3) the therapeutic relationship and developing professional communication; and (4) support provision through medication, crisis planning, service provision, and the wider society.*

A common combination of concept and data-driven coding is that the main categories are developed through known concepts and previous research, while the properties of the subcategories are emerging as coding occurs and familiarity with the data grows. Somewhat simplified, and for those who may be more used to a quantitative methodology, one can understand main categories as variables and subcategories as variable values. A difference from quantitative studies, however, would be that the development of variables and variable values is more flexible in QCA. After observing parts of the data, a new main category could prove necessary to establish. More often, however, new subcategories emerge in the process.

Some studies build categories almost entirely from the data. When creating categories from the bottom-up, you read the material and note important concepts, sometimes summarizing with some of the words from the material, sometimes paraphrasing. In this way, new main categories or subcategories are added. When a new relevant passage is identified, it is checked for similarity to notes from previous passages. Either the passage can be subordinated to a previously created category, or a new one is created. Through continuous comparison of similarities and differences between previously read and coded material and material that is currently being read, either more material can be attributed to a previously established category or a new category is created.

When the coding frame has been tested on sufficiently varied material (concept, data-driven, or combined coding), it is a good idea to make sure that the principles of unidimensionality, mutual exclusivity, and exhaustiveness still apply. Possibly, two subcategories that are too similar to each other should merge. In another instance, the problem may be that a subcategory contains too varied material and should be divided. After careful scrutiny, the coding frame should finally contain reliable main categories and subcategories with names and brief descriptions for each. Difficult choices that have been discovered in the coding are addressed with guidance on how to solve them. If necessary, the coding frame is tested again, and after the test coding in total has covered about one-third of the material with continuous adjustments, it should be ready.

The concrete analysis can be done in a couple of different ways. We will first address one that may be called a *traditional coding protocol*. This procedure was developed when analyzing by writing on prints was the only option, but with some modifications it is still practical to use. First, your empirical material is imported into a word processing program. Then a layout is made so that, on each page, you can see both empirical material and keep notes for different categories. The empirical material to be analyzed is placed on the left half of the document. In the right half, columns are created for the main categories with their names on top. Then, documents can either be printed, for convenient reading and taking notes with a pen, or you can read at the screen and take notes in the program. While the empirical material on the left is read, subcategories and other noteworthy observations are written on the rows in the category columns on the right. When the coding is complete, you can copy all the material with a note next to it and paste it to new sections intended for each of the coding types.

Second, with a *minimalist coding protocol*, you also import empirical material into a word processing program. Then, text that belongs to one of the main categories is highlighted with a comment in the margin, either using the category name or an abbreviation or number that you have decided should represent the main category.

Furthermore, text belonging to subcategories is marked with a specific color. Then the analyst has a note in the margin for the main category and color-marked text that fits a specific subcategory. Any numbers or abbreviations as well as colors that represent main categories and subcategories are entered into the coding frame. When the coding is complete, you can copy all the paragraphs assigned to main categories and subcategories and paste them to intended, thematically divided chapters to cover the results.

Third, with a *coding program protocol*, you use special qualitative analysis software, such as QDA Miner or N'Vivo. In this case, you create the main categories and subcategories in the software, much like a folder structure that is visible during coding. Once empirical material has been imported into the program, pieces of it can be dragged and dropped into different main categories and subcategories. At the same time, the main document with empirical material remains intact. Should any coding go wrong, it can be easily repaired. Like previously mentioned coding protocols, when coding is completed, it is easy to transfer collected pieces of text belonging to main categories and subcategories to planned chapters that cover the results.

Once the coding is complete so that the material is available in main categories and subcategories, some quantification should be made. The purpose of QCA is to provide a thorough overview, and this is done in part quantitatively. When dealing with fewer units, as when qualitative interviews constitute the data collection technique, the quantification is carried out more to detect deviations from what is expected than because the figures would be meaningful in statistical terms. After all, generalizing to a population is likely not relevant. Yet, the smarter the research design, the more meaningful the figures become. A table indicating, for instance, observations of unethical stances becomes more interesting if the most ethically conscious companies are examined. Then we can infer, theoretically, that the rest of the companies are probably more unethical, even though the sample does not allow statistical generalization. Moreover, if a study aims to explore approaches to social media among professionals in a small category of employees or professional setting, information from relatively few informants has greater validity and general value for the study of the case. This is important to keep in mind when managing quantitative results. In addition to the presentation of results through tables, it is important to demonstrate results by providing examples from categories and subcategories and showing how this material is interpreted.

Presentation of results

The presentation of results needs to be adapted to the features of the method of the study. In this regard, it is valuable to emphasize some differences in comparison with historically more commonly used methods such as semiotics and quantitative content analysis. The usefulness of the latter method lies in studying few characteristics in many research units, thus applying a very narrow focus across a wide field. Since the analysis focuses on less complex features of the material than qualitative analysis does, empirical examples are of less importance. By contrast, an exploratory semiotic or multimodal analysis is used for exhaustive observations of a few units, of select webpages, for instance. Then, exemplification of actual empirical material next to analytical observations are key to convey meaning to the reader.

Thus, when using QCA, researchers need to exemplify the analyzed material more than when using the quantitative variation. The main reason is that the analysis covers more complex, information-rich segments. Analytical observations are also reported by way of writing rather than by presenting calculations. It is therefore appropriate to alternate between presenting extracts from material with analysis of these extracts. We would suggest, as a rule of thumb, to exemplify the following:

- Each category and/or subcategory
- Typical content
- Unexpected content
- Content necessitating novel understanding

First, all main categories and/or subcategories should be represented with examples that are interpreted. That is a basic requirement. Moreover, typical content, but also deviations from the norm, may be particularly interesting to make sense of drawing on theoretical insights. The typical and atypical thus form another factor to consider. Finally, it is good to keep in mind that studies are being produced to bring about new knowledge. So, observations that call for new explanations and perhaps even new concepts should have a prominent place in the results section.

Looking again at our tentative study on tweets on the topic of mental ill-health experience, which drew inspiration from Shepherd et al. (2015), we would, after having completed coding, organize results with the help of examples from the studied material. To provide transparency and an opportunity for critique of the analysis, a couple of coded examples from each (sub)category should be included, like those presented in Figure 2.1. Again, for ethical reasons, posts would be anonymized, since users do not know all the ways in which their published content could be used by others, and they may not approve of our context. The presentation of results would then go back and forth between showcasing actual tweets and presenting how they are interpreted. Readers would be able to see for themselves what kind of material has been sorted under which main category and subcategory, as well as how the researcher arrives at particular interpretations. With both data and interpretation visible, the results can to a large extent be evaluated by the reader. It provides the possibility of directly evaluating validity, which constitutes a methodological strength. Many other types of studies cannot demonstrate validity other than through the presentation of sound procedures that the reader is expected to trust.

Finally, since the literature on QCA and this chapter as well recommend the creation of neat categories to capture the meaning of empirical data, there is a risk that the messiness of actual texts and speech contains ambiguities and dilemmas, possibly ending in coding situations that are too complex. The solution to the problem that we have wanted to emphasize, is that special categories should be created for such ambiguous material, so that these results are not lost or subjected to excessive segmentation. Indeed, qualitative material often features dilemmas, which represent valuable results. Instead of ending up with only clear-cut categories, which would make more sense in a quantitative content analysis with the advantage of more elaborate statistical analysis, each project may tailor its categorization of complex material. In this process, qualitative content analysis could arguably become more *qualitative*.

QUALITATIVE VISUAL CONTENT ANALYSIS

Introduction

When social media content is shared and received, visual content is as well. When social platforms feature ever-more-rich media content, they also afford and are used for sharing various visual content. The essential offering from the major platforms, such as Instagram and YouTube, focuses on visual and motion content combined with text. Other platforms revolve increasingly around visual material, such as the proliferation of shorter videos and live streams on Facebook, in addition to image sharing and video material on Spotify. Although image and video have dominated individual platforms for a long time, these modes of communication are spreading on increasingly multimodal, rich-media platforms. In line with the fact that the visual is so important in communication, several methods have also been presented for analyzing visual features (Banks, 2009; Keats, 2009; Rose, 2012).

Of course, there has also been a proliferation of use of visuals for increased attention and commercial success. Visually based communication has long been shown to attract more attention than content based solely on text (Pieters and Wedel, 2004). This same pattern is demonstrated in the online world and on social media as well (Goodrich, 2011). Interestingly, photos of people's faces are shown to attract particularly high levels of attention (Bakhshi et al., 2014). Marketing both offline and online has, unsurprisingly, drawn on this knowledge. Even ordinary citizens who do not work professionally with advertising or other communication seem to know that they attract more attention by using visuals, as they add images to questions posted in social media forums, explicating 'image for attention', or grow social media accounts with an idea that great visuals aid effective communication. Indeed, layout and choice of fonts and colors also play a role (Goodrich, 2011).

While a certain level of expertise in visual communication and marketing has become easy to acquire and apply, and is now quite widespread, other research delves into the cultural and ideological characteristics of this visual culture. Research has argued that these communication processes involve increased individualization – that issues are expressed through and revolve around the individual – in everything from the everyday self-presentations of young adults on Facebook (Shafie et al., 2012), and the fitness trend (Deighton-Smith and Bell, 2016), to how events are communicated through the lens of social media users from conflict and war zones (Mann, 2019). There is a wide range of issues to study when it comes to the importance and meaning of visual elements in today's online communication.

While methods for analysis of visual material have been developed, the focus has not been so much on social media. The methods in general that have been adapted to social media content have often featured highly automated analysis, leading Highfield and Leaver (2016) to call for more alternatives:

> Visual social media content is an important part of everyday activity on platforms from Facebook to Vine, Twitter to Tinder, through profile pictures, memes,

information-sharing, and affective imagery, and employed to respond to any number of topics. The large-scale and automated analysis of textual social media activity has generated detailed studies into platforms, such as Twitter, but this is not the whole story of how a platform is used.

(Highfield and Leaver, 2016: 58)

With a foundation in qualitative content analysis (QCA), a method used to systematically classify and interpret the meaning of content (Schreier, 2012), this chapter comprises an account and application of qualitative visual content analysis (QVCA), focusing especially on visual materials in the realm of social media. The method is used for assessing fairly comprehensive visual data, combining an ambition to validly classify visual material and making sense of visual choices in their context. The chapter therefore caters to researchers and students who are about to study the meaning of graphics, photos, layout, vlogs, maps, illustrations, memes, tables, art, diagrams, or any other visuals in today's online communication. There is no social media without some of these visual modes of communication. So, arguably, studies of the visual are a necessity for understanding communication and media – production as well as use and reception. Moreover, the motives and purposes of studies employing QVCA may differ, just as the issues at stake in different research areas do indeed differ. Studies that use the method may ask a wide array of questions: How is climate change visually represented in social media? How do companies try to reach children through visuals in YouTube advertising? What kind of meanings are memes carrying, and what role do they play in political communication? How can social-mediated reactions to political events be conveyed visually, such as during Brexit or in regular political elections? These types of questions can be successfully studied with the help of well-designed and implemented QVCA.

The main purpose of this chapter is to explain how such a study can be planned and carried out. We hope then also to be able to contribute to the field of research that is increasingly exploring QCA, but which to a limited extent uses and explains analysis of visual content. Likewise, the chapter can contribute to the major fields of research that study visual culture and content, but to a much lesser degree appear to know about or use QCA.

The following section provides a summary of the historical development of QCA, focusing on visuals as well as a description of some of the research of recent years. This is followed by a section on key theoretical concepts, another section on research design and, subsequently, a section on tools for analysis, including an empirical case. We conclude by describing how results can be presented in an exhaustive, transparent, and captivating way.

History and current research

Before we look at some current examples of qualitative visual content analysis focusing on social media, we make a detour to earlier studies of visual material which can serve as inspiration for current projects, as well as to the development of QCA. Contributions to understanding the meaning and significance of visual content in different types of media have come from several research areas. Seminal work has drawn on and contributed to semiotics, such as Barthes (1977) on how to systematically elicit the meaning of pictures and image-text combinations. Adding another significant contribution to the analysis of visual content, Mulvey (1975) drew on Lacanian psychoanalysis and contributed theoretically and methodologically to a research agenda on and for gender equality. She conceptualized active and passive roles and the importance of the 'gaze' of the camera, actors, and the implied viewer's perspective. Soon after, Goffman (1976) showed with the book *Gender Advertisements* stereotypical gender roles in commercials, noting recurrent feminizing/masculinizing characteristics in images. In the field of journalism studies, Tuchman (1978) demonstrated how journalism portrays people (and events) using the camera at different distances with different potential meanings in terms of subjects' social roles and the significance of events. She explained that the shortest distance connotes intimacy and an emotional relationship, whereas longer, wide-ranging shots connote neutrality and social processes. Against the backdrop of these well-known studies and the canon of qualitative visual analysis, content analysis is certainly not the most commonly used or well-known method.

Content analysis is, as Rose (2012) clarifies, a method that has been used mostly to research text. In addition, most empirical studies that use content analysis on visual material are based on the quantitative tradition of content analysis, and textbooks on QCA (e.g., Schreier, 2012) mention visual analysis in passing. Therefore, it is a challenge but perhaps also a much-needed contribution to suggest something of a roadmap to QVCA, as this chapter intends to do.

To begin with, QCA is a method for the systematic classification and interpretation of meaning (Schreier, 2012), typically of a rather comprehensive communicative material. The material being analyzed should be large enough to make sense in quantitative terms. At the same time, it should not be overwhelming for focused qualitative analysis. A case study or some other delimited, topical issue is therefore ideal to study. Other methods may be more appropriate in case the focus would be on the detailed understanding of a few, content-rich artworks or webpages, or a large data set with thousands of units.

Yet, the qualitative strand of content analysis has a long history. From the early development of content analysis during the interwar period onwards, projects featured both quantitative and qualitative approaches. However, differences between the orientations came to be emphasized. The seminal work of Berelson (1952) took a stand for quantitative analysis, criticizing perceived unsystematic and subjective tendencies in qualitative analysis, whereas Kracauer (1952) responded in defense of QCA but with seemingly little effect at the time. Statistical procedures of data analysis and evaluation became the norm. Thereafter, content analysis has generally been understood as a quantitative endeavor. Only more recently has a qualitative approach of content analysis been defined (see Schreier, 2012) and spread in different disciplines, not least within different research streams of health studies. Examples of QVCA are, therefore, also few and far between.

As one of the first to define QCA and adopt it to visuals, Fields (1988) explains how the analysis of television news may be approached. The focus is on observing a variety of choices and eliciting what they mean, both linguistic ones and visual, including image choices, camera shots, angles, and more. Taking notice of humor and skepticism expressed in news, Fields even categorizes facial expressions. Overall, a procedure is described for distinguishing what a unit is, developing categorization of the units, and then a variety of literature is drawn upon to define the potential meaning of text, images, composition, and the interplay of all these elements, arriving at an "exhaustive data matrix showing the juxtaposition of all message elements" (Fields, 1988: 183). The method described is hardly a game of counting units or evaluating reliability through inter-coder reliability tests. The approach is rather rooted firmly in a qualitative analysis tradition where the interpretation of observable data is a case made statement by statement in writing rather than quantitatively.

Another early but more well-known example, Lutz and Collins (1993) researched *National Geographic* magazine through a content analysis of about 600 photographs in issues between the years 1950 and 1986, in addition to conducting interviews to understand production and audience reception as well. Coding and quantifying material along variables such as world location, urban/rural setting, male/female nudity, pose, gaze, and vantage point, they managed to demonstrate how difference was magnified, how Western culture was reflected in choices made in production, but also how gender and ethnicity were portrayed. It is an analysis that retains the strengths of quantitative content analysis, from selection to structured coding and quantification with the possibility of generalization, but which at the same time is rich in qualitative, argumentative interpretation. They argue that quantification does not exclude qualitative analysis:

> Although at first blush it might appear counterproductive to reduce the rich material in any photograph to a small number of codes, quantification does not preclude or substitute for qualitative analysis of the pictures. It does allow, however, discovery of patterns that are too subtle to be visible on casual inspection and protection against an unconscious search through the magazine for only those which confirm one's initial sense of what the photos say or do.
> (Lutz and Collins, 1993: 89)

They describe a process that ensures that selection of data is not subjective, while allowing the analysis to be qualitative.

Recent research that systematically examines and interprets visuals in social media has covered a number of areas. Among those that use systematic thematization or categorization of visuals in social media, health-related topics include the marketing of e-liquids to youth (Jackler and Ramamurthi, 2017; Laestadius et al., 2019) and content dealing with self-harm (Shanahan et al., 2019). One study that describes its method as QCA of social media visuals is Sleigh et al. (2021), which examines risk messages about Covid-19 on Twitter. The study includes 616 tweets and found that visual material in the form of photographs was used the most, and a large majority of the messages contained one or two preventative messages, such as appeals to staying at home and wearing a face mask. Furthermore, health-gain messages spread more than the more negative-sounding health-loss messages. The fact that the study does not show any qualitative material – hardly any of the 616 tweets – but only reports results in numbers, shows that the method is interpreted broadly and differently, and that *qualitative* may signify something different in health sciences than in the qualitative research tradition of humanities and social sciences.

In other subjects, QVCA is not as common. Some topics that still have been studied include aspects of political communication, such as the visualization of humanitarian action on Instagram (McCosker et al., 2020), and the use of memes in the campaign for right-wing politician Bolsonaro in Brazil (Fernández Villanueva and Bayarri Toscano, 2021). If looking beyond social media, however, more studies can be found, such as an exploration of religious messages in children's visual media (Eide, 2020) as well as the visual approaches appearing in the propaganda magazines of ISIS (Kaczkowski, 2019). Overall, it is clear that although some studies exist that use QVCA to study social media, the method is starting to get more attention, and the research method is evolving.

Defining and working with key theoretical concepts

When embarking on a study that uses QVCA, it is important to gain an understanding of key theoretical concepts, such as what is meant by manifest and latent meaning, denotative and connotative meaning, and more. These concepts are thrown around in several texts about QCA but are rarely explained in any detail. In addition, new projects need to draw on additional theory of some kind that indicates what is at stake and what may be relevant to look at in a visual analysis.

In the essay *Rhetoric of the Image*, Barthes explains that denoted material consists of elements that we consider without any higher degree of sensemaking. It can be a word, caption, logotype, color, shape, body part, or whatever elements that are part of the unit of analysis that bring unequivocal meaning. In semiotic analysis, these elements are, for the sake of a transparency and coherence, considered to be non-decoded elements. Yet it is almost impossible not to automatically engage in cultural interpretation. The denotative elements and modes of communication that are chosen and combined call for a certain interpretation, and in a more determined way the more commonly shared the cultural codes and perceptions are. As Barthes (1977: 43) puts it, "the coding of the literal prepares and facilitates connotation." Denotation and connotation are thus hard to separate. There is no connotation or communication without manifest signs.

Connoted meaning is more difficult to define because it is about the message that the viewer perceives and interprets. However, it is not an entirely 'subjective' activity. As mentioned, connotation requires a structure of manifest signs. In a message, several signs interact and call on certain connotation in a culture. Barthes (1977) thus understands connotation to be collectively produced. He also asserts that people have their own competence to interpret communication that has developed over one's life, what he calls a lexicon. These skills and patterns in interpreting communication are not value free, but draw on ideology, that is, more global systems of meaning that make sense to large crowds and across countries.

Moreover, connotative meaning can be simple or complex. The message is simple if the signs are few and limited in terms of meaning potential, and the site of reception is too. Consider, for instance, a sign posting in a homogenous culture. Then, very similar readings are to be expected from a crowd, but then the value of qualitative analysis is also negligible. If, however, a piece of visual communication contains a number of meaning-bearing elements and there are different positions to take in the context of the communication and message, the potential meanings are more complex, and qualitative analysis has more to add. Such messages are created by a communicator situated in a certain ideological, cultural context, who is inclined to choose certain denotative elements that, in turn, favor certain readings. Then, connotation also depends on the recipient's experience as well as proficiency and creativity in decoding the message. As Barthes explains:

> The image, in its connotation, is thus constituted by an architecture of signs drawn from a variable depth of lexicons. . . . The language of the image is not merely the totality of utterances emitted (for example at the level of the combiner of the signs or creator of the message), it is also the totality of utterances received: the language must include the 'surprises' of meaning.
>
> (Barthes, 1977: 47)

Furthermore, apart from differentiating between the denotative and connotative levels of meaning, Barthes also added useful insight into the relationship between image and text. The image-text relationship is relevant for analysis of visual content because almost all images are presented together with text. This is of course also often the case in social media. Barthes explains that the meaningful relationship between text and image consists either of *anchoring* – that the text helps to delimit and amplify the meaning potential of the image – or *relay* – that the text and the image add different meaning and thus complement each other. QVCA can use these concepts to investigate the connection between image and text in social media.

Also relevant for social media analysis, Barthes makes very interesting observations regarding content based on a selection and combination of elements that appear to be occurring 'naturally'. It is thus communication that to a small degree shows that it contains a process of construction. Here also are parallels to be drawn to social media:

> Although the *Panzani* poster is full of 'symbols', there nonetheless remains in the photograph, insofar as the literal message is sufficient, a kind of natural *being-there* of objects: nature seems spontaneously to produce the scene represented. . . . [T]he absence of code disintellectualizes the message because it seems to found in nature the signs of culture. This is without doubt an important historical paradox: the more technology develops the diffusion of information (and notably of images), the more it provides the means of masking the constructed meaning under the appearance of the given meaning.
>
> (Barthes, 1977: 45f)

This characteristic of seemingly authentic content is something that has been described as characteristic of social media and a part of the success of social media networks. Social media content is perceived to diverge from the high-end, polished, and depersonalized content of traditional media productions, and instead present life and people 'as they are' (Rasmussen, 2017, 2020). This appearance of authenticity is created through the selection of signs that affords perceptions of realism. These particular choices, affording the appearance of realism, can also be the focus of QVCA.

There is thus much to be gained from Barthes' theory of semiotics and rhetoric of the image, for QVCA, such as the understanding of *denotative* signs facilitating but not determining *connotative meaning* and the understanding of the relationship between text and image through *anchoring* and *relay*. Indeed, QVCA is declared a method for the elicitation of connotative or latent meaning (Schreier, 2012), and if a project zooms in on social media, it will have to deal with image-text relationships.

In addition to understanding the elements and workings of messages generally, as indicated earlier, it is also necessary that projects draw on additional theory showing what is at stake, what is particularly important to focus on, and the value of decisions regarding the visual. For example, decades of research on gender equality have drawn on Laura Mulvey's classical text *Visual Pleasure and Narrative Cinema*. The distinction she made between active and passive roles and how the roles form part of stereotypes opened the way for a number of future studies. The same was true of her observations concerning a predominant, male gaze. She argued that media content displaying events, relationships, and characters tend to be represented from a male perspective. The perspective is realized along three dimensions, from how the production calls on the viewer to (1) see the world with the gaze created by the person behind the camera, (2) identify with the gaze of characters in the visual material, and (3) adopt the particular gaze that is implied for the spectator. Active and passive roles, as well as the particular gaze presented, are all realizations of manifest content that favor connotations of power and subordination. The active/passive roles and types of gaze that are presented are possible to define, code, and quantify but also analyze in-depth. Similarly, studies adopting QVCA need to draw on theory that motivates a certain focus and perspective on visual content. Such theory can emanate from whichever field that forms the foundation of the study, be it health sciences, marketing, sustainable development, or some other area.

Finally, a difficulty that arises with certain approaches to the method that encourages analysis of latent meaning yet require analysis to be replicable (e.g., Schreier, 2012) is that the requirement for replicability runs counter to the fundamental workings of more advanced communication, as Barthes explains. In interpreting complex communicative content, different people cannot be expected to arrive at the exact same connotative meaning. If molding the analysis to this end, the value of the analysis risks diminishing along with the reductionism being provoked. Quantitative content analysis features more methodological protocol and rigor if simple meaning constructs are to be studied. So, another and more typical way of ensuring validity and reliability in qualitative research is to strive for transparency so that others can evaluate inferences drawn from a material. Indeed, you do not need to be able to perform the same interpretation to test whether someone else's analysis is solid and logical or contains exaggeration, understatement, logical errors of thought, or loose ends. Such tests of the strength of analysis can be done when both content and interpretation are available to the reader. Exemplification is therefore key in the presentation of results of QVCA. Furthermore, the connotative analysis is a matter of shaping and polishing interpretations as one writes. It includes writing up a logical story. Reporting, therefore, also represents sensemaking of high complexity. So, how the connotative analysis should be shaped in text and finally reported is not an endeavor that is feasibly replicated.

Research design and preparation

Like other studies, research employing QVCA needs to develop a problem that justifies its purpose and implementation. This is suitably done through a combination of reading literature and monitoring current issues in society. QVCA can be a great fit with research that identifies a research problem, implying there is a knowledge gap regarding a phenomenon where a certain understanding across the material would be valuable. For example, Sleigh et al. (2021), in their study of Twitter and Covid-19, explain that visual communication on social media is important to reach out with prevention messages. They then formulate a research problem including a knowledge gap that also becomes a logical transition to the purpose of the study:

> Yet to date, only little is known about what characterizes visual risk communication during the Covid-19 pandemic. To address this gap in the literature, this study's objective was to determine how visual risk communication was used on Twitter to promote the World Health Organisations (WHO) recommended preventative behaviours and how this communication changed over time.
> (Sleigh et al., 2021: 1)

Such a logical 'build up' from a research problem to purpose is a good model for other studies as well. Planning the research then includes designing the research questions. Typically, research questions for which QVCA is suitable should enable exploratory, descriptive research (Schreier, 2012). As Bell (2004: 8) mentions regarding content analysis of visual material, research questions that are appropriate are often one of the following types: (1) 'questions of priority/salience of media content'; (2) questions of 'bias'; or (3) 'historical changes in modes of representation.' These aspects that content analysis usually covers should, for our purposes, be understood in the context of qualitative analysis. The first category of question is simply about how common or perhaps dominant a certain type of media content is, such as images, a certain element of images, colors, events, and so on. The second category examines how representations in different materials differ in some way, often based on a normative starting point, highlighting whether differences should or should not exist. This may, for example, be research that shows that women in politics are monitored with a greater focus on appearance and clothing than are men in similar positions. The third category of research questions also aims at comparison but instead across time. Studies can examine, for instance, the visual representation of brands, public institutions, a group of some kind, or a type of event. Taking Sleigh et al. (2021) as an example, they present the following research questions in their study using QVCA:

- To what extent were health and government organisations present amongst the most retweeted tweets;
- What were the predominant graphic types and visual properties used . . .;
- Which Covid-19 preventative measures featured the most . . .;
- How health gain or loss framing was present and whether tone changed over time.

(Sleigh et al., 2021: 2)

As can be seen, the first three research questions belong to a category of questions that deal with the salience of visual social media content as well as prioritization, in this case regarding which measures were featured more prominently on Twitter in Covid-19 crisis communication. The fourth question belongs to the category of questions that deals with historical change, but it also includes a more qualitatively oriented how question ('How health gain or loss framing was present').

To this can be added that QVCA can cater to analysis of rather complex material, including connotative meanings. Questions that examine how messages are formed are therefore also highly relevant. The research can, for instance, explore questions about what visual means are used to shape messages in marketing, for public information purposes, health, politics, or any other area. Everything, such as choice of color, font, background, and objects and actors included in the scene, carries meaning.

With the design of research questions in place, projects need to consider which material best answers them. Visual material from a particular platform, or a combination of platforms, may be fitting. Something that is important to be aware of and read more about is that platforms are used more or less by different generations and socio-economic groups. Younger generations do not use Facebook very much at all, at the time of writing this chapter, but use apps such as TikTok and Snapchat extensively. Twitter is used more by socio-economically advantaged adults and all forms of political opinion leaders. So, the possibility of generalizing on the basis of any individual platform to a generally valid, 'public discourse' is highly unlikely (Pearce et al., 2018). Plus, the logics of social media go along with the logics of traditional media, rewarding content that personifies issues, evokes emotions, and illustrates conflict.

Questions of data collection and generalization

Given that QVCA has the ambition to both go in-depth and at least put forth solid claims regarding a case, studies need to be designed so that these ambitions can be fulfilled. With coding and quantification as well as qualitative analysis, an innumerable number of units cannot be studied. A common way to limit the amount of content is to apply some sampling technique. Kim et al. (2018) show that the most reliable way to sample social media content is to apply random sampling. However, their study still shows that 33% to 38% of the total content that a study seeks to contribute knowledge about needs to be included in the sample, or 7–8 weeks out of 21 weeks' worth of content in their case, to achieve an acceptable level of accuracy. The authors add that this is a larger proportion of content than has been required to achieve reliable results in studies of traditional news, which indicates that social media content may be more diverse than traditional news. Given that study objects can present different degrees of variation, the degree of heterogeneity of the material and the necessary size of the sample must be assessed on a case-by-case basis.

Given also how much material social media platforms can contain on just one issue, it is advisable to try to delimit the object of study so that the material does not become too small for accurate generalization or unmanageably large. So, the research needs to focus on an object of study that is so narrow that a limited number of units observed still say something general about it. This is to facilitate a project that is limited in scope but with strong claims to truth. Any of three options, to limit the scope of a project, may be appropriate for the study: (1) focus on the social media presence of a single body or actor communicating, such as a brand, agency, or region responsible for an issue; (2) focus on a study object that is limited in time, such as a short-term crisis of some kind, a specific sequence of a larger crisis, or an event in some area, such as sports, fashion, health, business, or music; or (3) focus on an issue that is limited in the way that it is new and emerging or particular to a geographical area.

QVCA also lends itself particularly well to comparative research, just like quantitative content analysis of visuals. With the element of coding material in categories and across a fairly large material, it is possible to compare outcomes between domains (Bell, 2004). However, it should be kept in mind that comparison requires a larger data set. Not only should the material of one domain (such as a channel, group, or event) be analyzed so extensively and rigorously that we gain knowledge about it on a general level, but the study should include two or more domains with equally accurate results. Comparative research can therefore better suit larger projects.

Furthermore, one does not need to focus single-mindedly on statistical generalization. Yet, this is quite often the case. For example, Bell (2004) claims that if a study examines a brand of women's magazines, it cannot generalize to other brands of women's magazines or beyond the chosen time period if not extending the sample. By consequence, only statistical sampling matters. Against this assessment, we want to point out that studies can combine different strategies of generalization. Researchers utilizing QVCA should make an effort to do so, since the method is expected to provide detailed understanding of both select cases and their context. Thus, a study can apply statistical tools to make sure the sample is sufficient to make general claims regarding the case in question. In addition to this strategy, the study may discuss transferability to other cases. In line with Campbell (1986), it is suspect to assume that difference between cases would be more plausible than similarity. Transferability is assessed on a scale and is not an all-or-nothing phenomenon, and with greater proximity and similarity of empirical data, the higher the degree of transferability of results. So, an analysis of a brand of women's magazine could be assumed to afford a degree of transferability to other women's magazines in the same genre given the principle of proximity and similarity. Whether we think it is plausible that two women's magazines in the same genre are similar or different, the rationale for the assumptions must be discussed, as in what way underlying conditions and mechanisms of content production are equal or different and therefore could render equal or different results.

A third option is to utilize what Flyvbjerg (2001) calls extreme cases. By studying extremes, the possibilities of generalizing increase in a somewhat unexpected way. For example, if one were to choose to study a social media account of a brand that can be placed at the far end regarding certain values and expressions, and the study still ends up finding 'oppositional' content and communicative choices, then we can assume that the oppositional material is larger in the communication of other brands. Similar extreme cases can be selected in the fields of political communication or health communication. If a study of the visual communication of a political group that is considered extreme in a country still shows some moderate views and compassion that others can identify with, one can assume that these values are more common elsewhere but also that there are objective reasons for less polarization. If health communication research aims to study the communication of experiences of illness, then choosing a sample of people affected by the worst disease can also provide possibilities for generalization. If these patients express some optimism and hopefulness, everyone else has reason to express hope as well. So, arguably, a combination of strategies for generalization may be ideal for QVCA.

When planning the collection of data, it is important to review the affordances and risks that different possible routes of analysis implicate (Pearce et al., 2018). A certain data-gathering method may result in bias in one's sample, for example, if limiting the selection to materials using hashtags, although the use of hashtags on the chosen platform is not prominent or decreasing, so that a significant proportion of relevant material without hashtags is excluded. Another question is whether the collection method renders text data only or visual material as well. The process often requires several steps to obtain all data that is relevant for the study. This again makes reflection on the advantages and disadvantages of data collection techniques necessary.

The data collection method that may fit smaller projects studying a few hundred units of analysis is to use search functions on the platform that the project focuses on. For example, Shanahan et al. (2019) used its central keyword #selfharm in the search functions on Twitter, Tumblr, and Instagram. One day was selected for the collection of empirical material, and the most recently published 200 images from each platform were selected for analysis. Another option in order to better capture diversity and increase the possibility of generalizing from the sample would have been to have more than one collection period (Laestadius et al., 2019) and to employ random statistical sampling. However, it is likely that a larger sample would be needed then, and first we would need to know how many possible units of analysis (the population) there are.

An issue remaining is also how posts should be preserved for analysis. An option is to print-screen each post and save them. It may be time consuming, though, at greater numbers, and thus suits smaller projects the best. For projects that examine larger amounts of data, it is common to use tools that use social media platforms' Application Programming Interfaces (APIs). The API is a back-end interface that contains a wealth of information and affords communication with other software. To the extent that the API of a social platform makes available the database of user properties, patterns of use and content, researchers and students can access them through various software services. Typically, these services make available user IDs, time and place for posts, textual content, tags, and engagement metrics. For example, Pearce et al. (2018) uses a variety of services to extract data from APIs of different platforms:

- Visual Tagnet Explorer (Instagram)
- Netvizz (Facebook)
- The Twitter Capture and Analysis Toolset (Twitter)
- TumblrTool (Tumblr)
- Google BigQuery (Reddit)

Although images themselves are not collected, they are made available by the APIs by inclusion of uniform resource locators (URLs). Then, researchers may use another service, such as DownThemAll, which is an extension for Mozilla Firefox that makes it possible to download all of the images that a project needs from the aforementioned platforms (Pearce et al., 2018). Once the principles of data collection have been established – from which platform, time period, and volume of data that should be collected – your project can adopt similar methods to automate data collection.

Coding frame and examples of analytical tools

After a project has crafted a research problem – i.e., for what reasons a particular study needs to be carried out – and designed research questions and a data collection plan, it is appropriate to design a coding frame. A coding frame is an instruction that enables the study to examine the same aspects consistently, for as long as it is needed. It provides support to the encoder in tricky encoding decisions. The coding frame thus constitutes an important step in the study's operationalization – in the process whereby ideas and theories are translated into concrete observations and measurements.

Given the purpose of all content analysis to review quite extensive materials using categories, most of the coding frame is also about defining categories. Categories can be defined in advance, conceptually, through knowledge from previous research. Then the study takes on the character of testing whether assumptions are correct, a so-called deductive approach. This is common in quantitative research. In research that uses QVCA, it is more common to combine conceptual categories, which are the result of previous research, and data-driven categories, i.e., aspects that are discovered as the project member/s learn more about the data (Schreier, 2012). A coding frame can thus contain predetermined categories but also contain instructions for observing new phenomena that still fit the purpose of the study. Furthermore, two or three levels of categories are usually used in an analysis. Easiest may be to have a few different main themes, and then one or possibly two levels of categorization underneath each theme. A project on social media use, for example, may have a theme related to the use of humor, and then subcategories in the form of different types of humor, and possibly further categorization of different attitudes toward each category of humor.

The first thing that needs to be defined in a coding frame is what constitutes a unit of analysis. When studies quantify content and present how *much* of different phenomena have been observed, units of analysis have been counted. In the analysis of visual elements in social media, it is often appropriate to consider a post to be a unit of analysis. If a post contains multiple images, it may be more appropriate to determine that an image is a unit. This is relatively straightforward in the analysis of non-moving material. When it comes to moving material, it is likely that the visuals vary. Because a unit of analysis should only be coded in one way for each category and subcategory, moving material, which may contain more complex material, need to be segmented. In these cases, a unit of analysis can be determined to be a shot, i.e., the continuous footage from one edit to another edit. Within a shot, the material probably allows the coding to only refer material to one subcategory per main category.

Furthermore, the coding frame should be created with some additional principles in mind. It is important that categories focus on one aspect of material and that they are unidimensional. Subcategories, then, should not overlap but be mutually exclusive. For example, if color is a main category, subcategories consist of different distinct colors. If clothing is a main category, subcategories consist of different distinct garments. A third principle is exhaustiveness, meaning that all material should be considered for inclusion in categories.

QCA of visual communication also benefits from drawing on analytical tools from semiotics and/or multimodality. Various textbooks (e.g., Machin, 2007) and case studies (e.g., Lutz and Collins, 1993) highlight meaning-bearing aspects involved in the inclusion and exclusion of participants, environments, and objects, based on categories developed by Barthes (1977). If we consider the analysis by Lutz and Collins (1993) of how specific cultures and peoples are represented in visual material in Western culture, some main categories in the coding focuses on participants, objects, and settings. Categories appear to be developed from questions such as the following: Is a woman or man depicted? What ethnicity is depicted? How much skin is shown? What clothing is worn? What milieu is depicted? Is technology represented and, if so, what kind? All of these main categories contain subcategories, which in quantitative research would be described as variable values. In the following paragraphs we will explain the importance of different choices regarding objects, participants, setting, color and light, typography, and composition.

Objects are crucial to the message being communicated. For instance, different clothes typically convey different contexts. A woman in a suit conveys a certain type of working life. The same woman in shorts conveys leisure or sports. A lot of visual communication in social media is referential in this way. In video thumbnails on YouTube, objects are chosen for reference to the activity featured in the videos, whether it is food for a cooking video, yoga equipment or a barbell in a training video, and so on. QVCA can compare different domains or variations within a domain, what distinguishes them, and with what meaning. Objects also have different meanings depending on how they are combined with other objects, participants, settings, and other signs such as color and font. A woman dressed as a carpenter and with a hammer in her hand conveys cultural meanings of determination and courage. A man using the same tool and wearing similar clothes and a tool belt raises less attention. But the same object in the hands of a man in a suit seems suspicious, and if he wears a ski mask, the hammer appears to be a weapon. Objects are thus linked in chains of meaning together with other objects, environments, and participants, and deviations from conventions are easily detected and can be used for certain effects.

Participants of course also convey meaning. Participants can be representatives of the organization that provides content in social media. If a leader is included, for example, a CEO, then the content conveys that what is said is important and clear. The organization speaks with one voice. If the content features the most highly educated personnel, which in healthcare could be surgeons, the communication unequivocally conveys expertise. A mix of healthcare employees would to a greater extent convey teamwork and equality. Other types of content may include children and animals to represent innocence, charm, and playfulness, while mothers with their children are a common image for care, often drawn upon in the advertising of children's products. Men are rarely included in that context, as stereotypes of fatherhood do not convey the desired characteristics of products. Studies of the representation of men and women are generally common in content analysis.

Choice of *setting* is also important for the message. Typically, open landscapes such as fields, meadows, a view of the beach and sea, convey freedom and peace (Machin, 2007). These settings can be contrasted with the clutter of cars and people in an urban environment that conveys intense physical and mental activity. The environment that is chosen to be depicted could also create connotations to already existing, cultural dichotomies of the urban versus the rural, the artificial versus the natural, or the familiar versus the exotic. As Machin points out, living and working environments with minimalist furniture, with lots of space and natural light, convey status and class. Smaller rooms full of stuff can also signal something positive, but perhaps a happy family with young children rather than material success. Likewise, it matters to the message whether the environment depicted is historical, with connotations of tradition, heritage, and ethos, or futuristic buildings questioning the old ways and connoting new thinking. Furthermore, as Machin (2007) emphasizes, settings can be documentary or symbolic. Documentary visual communication displays some context and what is going on in a realistic way. For example, in a workplace, people actually work in their offices or departmental industrial surfaces, no matter how unglamorous closed surfaces are. A symbolic image instead lacks a realistic context and places an employee in a large, bright building by the stairs, conveying that, in this organization, people are on the rise in a successful environment.

Furthermore, different *colors* are associated with different meanings, making them suitable for exploration using QVCA. Colors are used in a consistent way to create strong messages, recognition, and also to build brands that people value and

Table 3.1 Aspects of color and light and their meaning potential

Aspects of color and light	Meaning potential
Hue	From 'cool' nuances like blue and green to 'warm' shades like yellow, red, and orange
Saturation	From full saturation and high emotional intensity, demand, and superficiality to the calmness, unpretentiousness, and seriousness of muted colors
Purity	From pure nuances that signal certainty and modernity to mixed nuances that are used to signal mixed values. The more even the color fields are, the more simple, clear, and possibly superficial the world seems to become.
Luminosity	The stronger a light source radiates, the more it seems to convey mystery, divinity, optimism, warmth, or strength.
Brightness	From light that signals happiness, knowledge, love, and goodness to darkness that signals misfortune, ignorance, hatred and evil

remember. Basic, heavily saturated colors are widely used in communication aimed at children. They signal something playful, simple, but also superficial. The color red, not least together with a dashed line, signals danger and is used as a warning. Banks and insurance companies often use blue, whose meaning potential includes reliability and stability. Green is considered a soothing color and is used in healthcare. Among brands, we strongly associate Caterpillar and its boots or Kodak and its photo products with yellow, denoting sunshine and connoting optimism and happiness. Through consistent communication and color management, these brands have become easily recognizable and remembered. Color thus offers many opportunities to establish categories for coding content (see, e.g., Araujo et al., 2020). Similarly, visual devices such as color saturation and purity, brightness and luminosity have bearing on the meaning conveyed. Darkness and light carry age-old symbolic meaning, recognizable from some of culture's oldest stories. Table 3.1 covers essential meaning bearing choices regarding color and light.

Typography is about text design for optimal readability and aesthetics. Perhaps the most important component of typography is the fonts, that is, specific, consistently designed letter and number characters. In a visual communication perspective, the focus is on the semiotic potential of typography. Typography, like color and composition, is a means of enhancing a message but also for shaping an appealing and unique visual identity. While this has been the case in the newspaper industry and for brands for over a hundred years, we now also see the importance of typography in social media. A thumbnail on YouTube is not designed in any way, but with an easy-to-read and large enough font to attract attention. Boldness usually conveys strength and intensity while more slender lines signal elegance. Flourishes can be perceived as elegant, but sometimes as old-fashioned or at least traditional. Table 3.2 outlines the meaning potential of fonts that are lean, bold, straight, sloping, low, high, dense, broad, or embellished with slings.

Like color and typography, composition can help in creating clear and purposeful communication. It can help brands stand out from the competition. The various compositional choices thus constitute semiotic resources that also contribute to the message and reception. Van Leeuwen (2004) explains that composition is about arranging various elements on a surface, such as a page, screen, canvas, a square, or even a city. Similarly, in Table 3.3 we address the semiotic resources of salience, placement, and framing.

Table 3.2 Typographical choices and their meaning potential

Typographical choices	Meaning potential
Weight	From the lightness, elegance, fragility, and airiness of thin lines to the weight, bombast, and strength of bold lines
Slope	Fonts with a slope signal a direction of will forward, speed, urgency, and new times as opposed to tradition and timelessness.
Shape	Angular shapes signal something serious, rational, technical, hard, and masculine, whereas rounded shapes signal soft, natural, emotional, and traditionally feminine qualities.
Height	Extra height signals status, self-confidence, class, elegance, and lightness, whereas reduced height represents unpretentiousness, weight, and stability.
Breadth	Extra width or spacing signals self-confidence and individualism, whereas denser fonts signal coherence and intimacy.
Flourishes	Wavy flourishes signal elegance, femininity, opulence, a historical epoch, and ancient traditions.
Regularity	Regular shape, height, and width, etc. signal correctness in contrast to the spontaneity and informal attitude of the irregular.

Table 3.3 Compositional resources and their meaning potential

Compositional resources	Meaning potential
Salience	Greater and lesser salience and significance are signaled in many ways – through sharpness versus blur, large versus small, moving versus immobile, high contrast versus low contrast. What stands out relative to other elements in the composition attracts attention.
Left/right placement	Left and right – old and new, backwards and forwards, condition and opportunity
High/low-placement	Low and high investment signals reality and ideals, implementation and goals, basic versus high status.
Center/periphery-placement	Center and margin – distinguishes what is primary and secondary, and creates coherence as objects in the center and margin give each other meaning.
Framing	Framing brings together and separates elements. Clear framing connotes structure but also confinement and limitation, whereas the opposite signals openness and freedom. Overlap expresses relationship and informal attitude.

With a selection of tools like the ones we have described hitherto, a study could examine, for example, how the police present themselves on social media. In several different countries, we can see that the police are adopting a more informal communication style than is usually expected from public-sector organizations in social media. The Dover police (Ohio, USA), for example, went viral on YouTube through a video showing a police officer cruising through town singing to Taylor Swift's *Shake It Off*. On the one hand, it is interesting to note that some public authorities choose to communicate as if they were any regular dude, yet they are still different from everyone else by their powers – monopoly of violence – and beyond that, have demands on objectivity, such as treating equal cases equally, and so on. On the other hand, it is also easy to understand these initiatives because of the commitment they can gain from communities, with more recipients of their information, more tips from the public, and a better reputation.

Another example of police departments going this route is to be found in Bengaluru, one of the major cities in India. Figure 3.1 shows a selection of tweets and the profile picture belonging to the popular account of the Bengaluru City Police. Looking systematically at how they shape a new image visually, one could focus on their most popular social media account, on Twitter, and explore such aspects that have been mentioned so far, including color, participants, font, and whether images are documentary, symbolic, or perhaps belonging to another category. To encourage caution in e-commerce, the tweet in the upper right (Figure 3.1) highlights a participant from the world of Marvel – Thanos – a character who wants to wipe out half the population to solve the issue of overpopulation in his universe. It conveys that a bad purchase online may affect your mood, just like bad things make Thanos go into rage mode, which of course creates a humorous effect. The profile picture in the upper right (Figure 3.1) contains a classic emblem, the blue color that often represents the police, but also the message – arrest corona – in a large, bold font signaling strength, with corona and handcuffs in red that conveys a warning. Once again, a humorous effect is created because the appeal is real in that we should fight the virus, but arresting it is of course an exaggeration that alludes to the police department's area of activity. The Twitter message in the lower left (Figure 3.1) features a picture of India's Paralympic team and is thus drawn from a completely different context than police work. The police department thus engages in a kind of social partnering strategy, which amplifies the image of themselves as part of the Indian people cheering on their team. The final tweet to the lower right again presents a warning message that draws on the world of comic books and film, whereby the serious threat of drug use is placed alongside the threat that King Kong poses to a human cartoon character, an unexpected parallel that can create a humorous effect or at least a less burdensome meaning. Again, the color palette is saturated and simple to convey that life does not have to be so complicated – just make the right decision.

So, a study could systematically examine tweets such as these, but a much larger material, and categorize and quantify to what extent they draw on visuals that document police work, and the extent to which they use symbolic and cartoonish visuals. It could also categorize uses of color and font and explain the potential meaning that those choices create. Such an analysis could draw conclusions about what this non-typical communication from a public authority accomplishes in terms of shaping an identity or image, and with what possible positive and perhaps negative consequences. Finally, we do not see that there are ethical reasons not to show the name

QUALITATIVE VISUAL CONTENT ANALYSIS 55

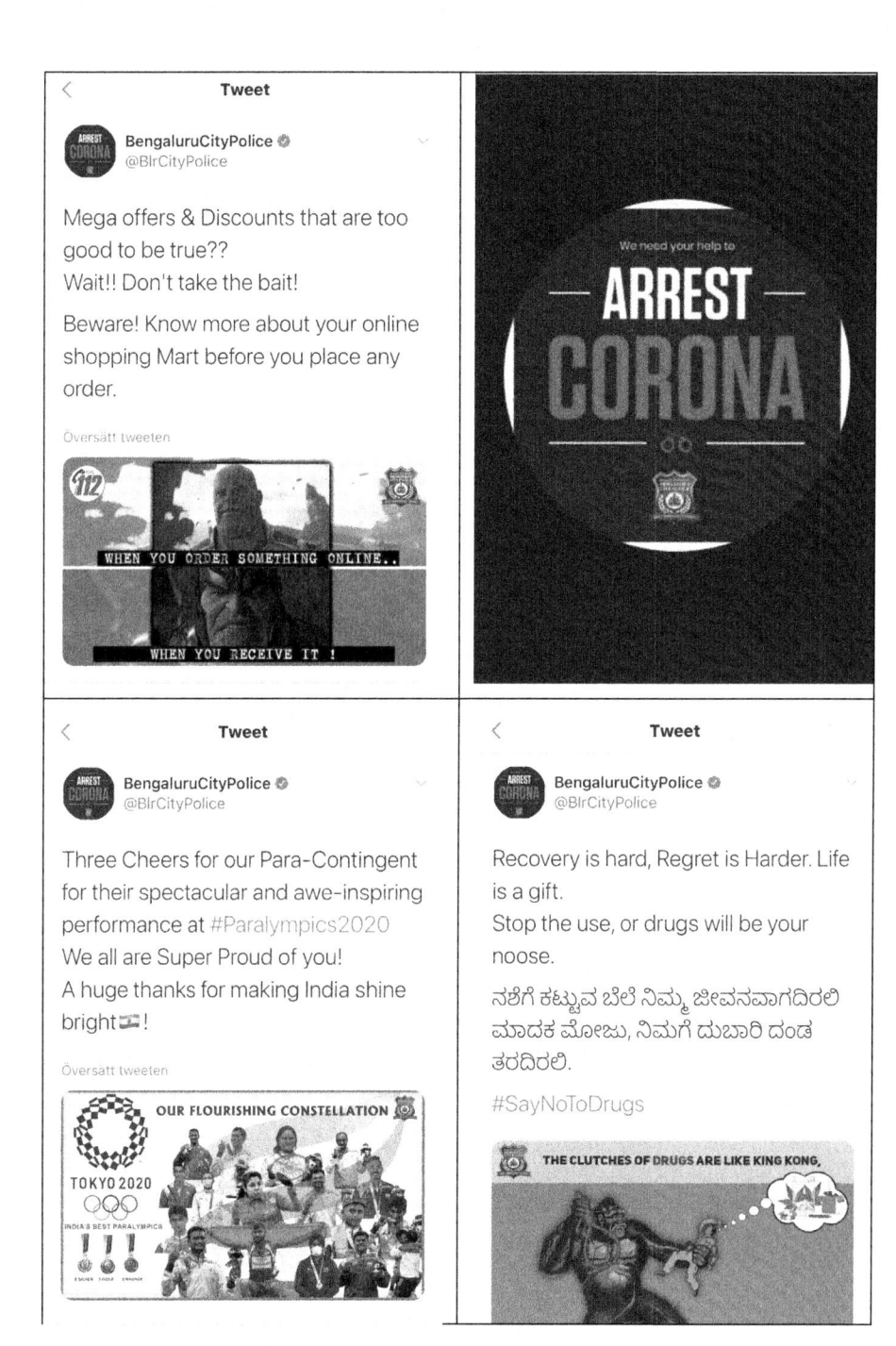

Figure 3.1 Bengaluru City Police tweets

of the account, in this case, as the object of study is a well-known organization and, moreover, a public authority with responsibility to the citizens and activities that journalism should monitor.

Presentation of results

The presentation of results should include an overview of the outcome of the completed coding. However, unlike quantitative content analysis, it is important to also show examples of categories and subcategories, interpret them, and show possible variation. It is needed because the communication being studied involves a degree of complexity and connotative meanings, such material that QVCA is suitable for. Interpretations based on literature, similar to those we have presented in the previous sections, are presented in the results chapter. If only easily observable elements with unambiguous meanings are studied, such as the presence of men and women, then QVCA is superfluous, and a long tradition of quantitative content analysis is likely going to be a better resource.

Typically, the results section features one or more tables for the general results of coding as well as exemplification and interpretation of the content of categories. For example, a study of visual communication in social media could systematize, with the help of literature, how color is used, and interpret the significance of the different choices for the meaning conveyed. This could be suitable for a case such as the one described in the previous section, about the Bangalore Police. Their account appears to feature a lot of posts with pure, fully saturated hues – a simple and clear color language that reflects a straightforward handling of reality.

Moreover, one study that contains the type of interpretive description that we consider to be fitting for the presentation of results, when QVCA is used, is a study of Shanahan et al. (2019) on the depiction of self-harm in social media. They include in the results section interpretations of content from categories established in their analysis process:

> An example of an image from this theme is a before and after shot of an arm. The before shot showed numerous cuts and scars, and the after shot showed that the scars had healed and faded. There were a number of these images across the three sites. These 'fading scar' images could be viewed as the poster feeling 'cleaner' now that the evidence of their self-harm is fading: their skin is recovering in the same way that they are. Another example of images in this theme is presentation of the number of days the poster had not engaged in self-harm (Shanahan et al. 2019: 3).

In the previous example, the authors exemplify what they have seen in one of their analyzed categories of content. It becomes clear how the analyzed images complement and reinforce the texts, what Barthes (1977) called anchoring and relay. In another example, the authors highlight the meaning of context, as well as the variation within categories and highly noteworthy features:

> Finally, there were images that subverted glamour. These images showed sexualised pictures of women which were subverted from typically western attractiveness. An example of this is women presented in dirty or ripped underwear, or

> masculine clothing. For example, one image we coded as subverted glamour was of legs in a model's pose but wearing badly ripped and bloodied tights.
>
> (Shanahan et al., 2019: 4)

By combining quantitative overview with qualitative description and interpretation, instead of focusing unilaterally on categorization, we would argue that QVCA may become a stronger alternative in the domain of qualitative analysis. Ideally, at least an image from each category of analysis is also displayed. It creates transparency in the analysis, so that the reader can partake in the analytical process, from seeing some of the content that the authors have analyzed to being able to evaluate their interpretations and conclusions. Finally, that type of presentation of results also highlights a difference from quantitative content analysis.

Following such a descriptive narrative of results, which contains both summary tables and illustrative examples, the project is ready to close the circle in a concluding section that reconnects with the overall problem, answers the research questions, and compares findings with previous research.

Chapter 4 ANALYZING SOCIAL MEDIA LANGUAGE WITH CRITICAL DISCOURSE ANALYSIS

Introduction

In this chapter, we look at how to carry out research projects on social media with what is called critical discourse analysis. This form of analysis allows us to interrogate the details found in the language use in, and across, social media posts. This allows us to carry out a sort of detective work into the meanings that are carried by language, which may be less obvious to the casual reader. Mostly, when we read social media posts as part of a feed, we may not necessarily attend to the kinds of details that critical discourse analysis (CDA) allows us to attend to.

Here is an example to get us started – before we go into this a little deeper. It is helpful to think about what we mean by the 'detective work' that can be carried out when doing this kind of critical linguistic analysis.

The following is a single tweet from a hashtag where users were attacking and 'cancelling' a woman named Kelly Pocha, who had been seen drunk in a video clip, telling a small group of migrant men to leave Canada, to go home. We will be looking more at this hashtag later in the chapter, but here I just want to begin to show why we might want to look more carefully at language and grammar, and how this is highly useful in research.

> One of the many reasons I love Canada is their respect for diversity. But every country has a #kellypocha

This tweet was posted by a person living in Canada. In CDA, it is common to ask what kind of participants are represented in any statement, and consider what words are selected to do so. We might also ask what each word is represented as doing and what intentions are attributed to them. So, at a surface level this post aligns against Kelly Pocha – every country, we are told, has one of these. And there is a positive evaluation of Canada: "one of the many reasons I love Canada." This means that here, Kelly Pocha is an exception in an otherwise lovable country. And unfortunately, it is not only Canada that has such terrible individuals. We are not told exactly which countries are those that have a Kelly Pocha (a racist). For example, does this include India, Nigeria, Malaysia, Yemen, Iraq, or countries where there are ongoing ethnic conflicts? Of course, the formulation used in the language here is typical of how people speak, but clearly, certain details are missing. And where such details are absent, in CDA, we should always ask why. In this case, the point of the statement appears to be to defend Canada. Arguably, what is actually being said here is "I love Canada for many reasons, but like other countries it has isolated bad people – Canada is not racist, isolated people are."

Another notable language use is found in the first statement – that Canadian people have respect for diversity. This is written as "their respect for diversity." This signals a simple opposition between Kelly Pocha and a general notion of all other Canadians.

DOI: 10.4324/9780429319334-4

Racism theorists have written about how popular ideas and media representations of racism tend to see these instances as individual outbursts that are unconnected, which are a matter of ignorant and extreme people whose attitudes belong to a former era (Goldberg, 2009). Kelly Pocha told some migrant men to go home, to leave Canada. In fact, such opinions, it has been shown, are fairly widespread (Scrivens and Perry, 2017) and frequently fostered by politicians from the right. These politicians will often address people whose life situation is less than good, who are experiencing increasing social and economic instability, are seeing decline and growing inequalities in their cities, or are faced with unemployment (Eatwell and Goodwin, 2018; Inglehart and Norris, 2019). Rather than being encouraged to understand the actual reasons for social and economic decline, based in neoliberal economic policies that favor reduced welfare spending, flexible employment conditions, and more privatization, they are tutored to blame migrants and ethnic minorities. From a critical linguistic perspective, what is notable here is that the pronoun *their* is used as a very broad and undefined category. Again, such pronouns are typically used by politicians as in statements such as "we Americans will not stand for this attack on freedom," when used, for example, to justify a military intervention.

There are many more things we can and will show that are buried in language, and even in this tweet. But at this point we just wanted to show how here, although we could assume that the person has good intentions in wishing to stand against racism and xenophobia, their basic choices of words call us to think more about how they are representing racism in society. In fact, we show later that such individualization of racism may even get in the way of really understanding such issues – where a drunken woman expresses her bitterness or frustration using a set of ideas that are in fact fairly common to find in news outlets, in political speeches, and in casual conversations.

This detective work of CDA, therefore, means digging around in the words and grammar used to represent a situation like a racist outburst. All instances of language use can be approached in this way. This applies to social media posts on any kind of topic. It could be something more obviously political, as in the prior tweet, but it could be simply related to more mundane issues, looking at what kinds of ideas and assumptions are carried. Later in this chapter, we look at those issues buried in Instagram-type posts about fitness on the Chinese Weibo. That calls us to think about the wider context of such language, including the nature of social, political, and economic contexts. This is because language is intertwined with all of these things. After all, we cannot plan and make sense of things without language.

Of course, this sounds like a very broad statement. In the following sections, we explain exactly what this means and how to build this concept into how we go about doing our analysis. We begin by defining CDA and then look at some of its core concepts. We illustrate these with some data from Twitter. Then we go on to provide a case study to show how CDA can be built into a research project.

What is CDA?

CDA has its origins in linguistics. In the 1980s and 1990s, a group of linguists began to take an interest in how language plays a role in the functioning of society. In particular, they considered its role in the representation of events in ways that support the views of the powerful in society. And in turn, they were concerned with how this allowed certain kinds of injustices to be maintained or to take place. This could involve the maintenance of different types of social and economic inequalities, the legitimization of political policies, of wars, and forms of international relations. While many different academic fields have studied such things, CDA showed how such motivated interests could be detected at more subtle levels in language that would be less obvious to the casual observer (Van Dijk, 1998). Using detailed observations on language and grammar found in newspaper texts, political speeches, school books, policy documents, etc., they showed these more buried assumptions could be revealed. CDA researchers, amongst other things, have shown how racist ideologies are maintained in the news media (KhosraviNik, 2017), how politicians gain support for wars that are related to gaining access to oil and resources (Bouvier, 2014), or how the terrible acts of Western global corporations are justified (Machin and Mayr, 2012). They have shown how sexism and discrimination can be highly subtle (Lazar, 2005) and how the privatization of public institutions such as schools and hospitals are presented as being in the public interest (Ledin and Machin, 2021).

This is exactly what we began to do in the case of our previous tweet. This tweet caries assumptions that racism is not infused into societies in complex ways, becoming aligned with other kinds of fears and frustrations. Rather, it is suggested this is about individuals. And since such individuals are found across societies, it is suggested that there is nothing in that specific society that needs to be further addressed, understood, or challenged. There is nothing about Kelly Pocha's speech and behavior that requires analysis. Simply, like other individuals in other unspecified countries, she is a racist. We are not called to ask why, even if drunk and frustrated, she produces this set of ideas. In this way, we might argue, the actual nature of racism or xenophobia, at this moment in time and in Canada, goes uninterrogated and unexplained. And the focus of the blame on the individual 'international generic type' serves to get Canada off the hook. Ultimately, therefore, as racism theorists have argued, this kind of formulation, in fact, serves the maintenance of racism (Lentin, 2016) and favors those who presently benefit from this situation of inequality. The close analysis of this single tweet allowed us to begin to show how language is intertwined with society and politics. The detective work of CDA allows us to reveal how this is so.

It has been argued that it is especially important for scholars in CDA to analyze social media data. Formerly, CDA has analyzed how language carries the views of dominant groups in society by looking at data from texts disseminated to a population in a 'top-down' manner by monolithic centralized media institutions, such as news, political speeches, and official documents. Such texts were seen as carriers of elite discourse, legitimizing the interests and forms of social relations favorable to this class (KhosraviNik and Zia, 2014). Social media is different. Content moves not just top-down, nor even bottom-up, but in complex and shifting ways, and users may have complex interactions across platforms. Now all users can participate in the creation and dissemination of content (KhosraviNik, 2017), but this means that we can now more easily access how dominant viewpoints are spread throughout societies. We can ask how they are reproduced, challenged, or modified. Social media platforms often feed off of and into traditional media (KhosraviNik and Unger, 2015).

One of the founders of CDA, Fairclough (1989: 28), argued that power relations in a society are always part of a 'struggle'. Put simply, this means that there are always competing ideas and points of view in any society. For example, in Sweden, where both authors have spent times of their career, there has been a dominant point of view for many years that immigration is a good thing, since it is based on a humane idea that in a stable society, relatively rich in resources, those suffering human rights abuses should be welcomed and supported. But at the time of writing this book, there appeared to be some shifting, where more conservative opinions were rising. They were arguing that immigration created a burden on society, took resources from Swedish citizens, and threatened national culture and values. Such views could be found on social media, but also in milder forms of expression by more right-wing politicians. In Fairclough's terms, there is therefore a struggle over ideas about ethnic relations. While Sweden has formerly been steered by ideas that welcomed immigrants, it appears that new points of view are on the rise that challenge these ideas. These perspectives will then come to have more power to define how we think about things, the priorities and aims that tend to shape what gets done, and why. The anti-immigrant ideas expressed by a drunken Kelly Pocha in Canada, therefore, may be best thought of less in terms of her being an individual type, atypical of the population as a whole, but in terms of being one manifestation of these rising ways of thinking.

It could be argued that formerly, CDA, with its emphasis on elite texts, has told us little about this 'struggle', but has rather thrown light on the dominant ideology. Social media, therefore, offer the opportunity to research how people in different parts of the socio-economic order negotiate with, or challenge, dominant viewpoints (Rosenberg, 2011). In the case of racism, it has been observed in CDA that the mainstream news media tend to present more negative representations of ethnic minorities (Van Dijk, 1995). The prior tweet could be said to challenge such a perspective as it is tweeted in a hashtag feed showing its intolerance to racism. Yet as we see, at the same time, the tweet plays a role in denying racism in Canadian society as a whole.

Why word choice is political

Stemming from the work of de Saussure (1983) is the idea that language and grammar are like building blocks through which people accomplish communication. Importantly here, words have no natural relationship to the world. Yet, in a language, or dialect, or local style, we agree to use the same words to mean the same things. So the word car, or *voiture*, has an arbitrary relationship to the actual thing. Saussure argued that language could be studied in terms of its use, which he called *parole*, and which would allow us to establish the underlying system, which he called *langue*. Social semiotics, which is the theory of language on which CDA is loosely based, takes a slightly different approach for three important reasons.

First, language is thought about less as a system and more as a set of available choices. Social semiotics is interested in how these choices are used in specific contexts in order to achieve our aims. The words and combinations we use come with what is thought of as *meaning potential*. This means that they have the potential built into them to mean particular things, but that how this potential is realized will depend upon how it is used in contexts.

A simple example is:

- He is a man
- Be a man!

The word *man* is used in both cases, but in the first it is used more in a descriptive sense of biology, as if in answer to the question: what gender is your teacher? The second is more evaluative and carries with it stereotypical ideas about what is proper masculine behavior. There is a sense here that the target of the statement is failing.

CDA is interested in the ideas and values carried by such choices in contexts. This brings us to the second characteristic of a social semiotic approach. All such choices are loaded with meaning that reflect the ideas and power interests that dominated at the time of their use (Caldas-Coulthard and Coulthard, 1996). We can call this the *ideology* of that particular time, meaning the broader system of ideas and values (Machin and Mayr, 2012).

Therefore, in terms of the word 'man', it does not simply label a thing/person, but comes with ideas and values about men's characteristics that will have their roots in a particular moment in a social context. One of the authors can, as a child, recall her brother having to show he was a man, by suppressing vulnerability.

Second, to give an example from a contemporary social media post, we find the following on an Instagram post by a female fitness influencer:

> Fitness is a way of life for me, a passion and a commitment.

We will look more at fitness influencers shortly, but the idea that fitness is a 'way of life' is something that, scholars have observed, has arisen especially in the late 20th and early 21st centuries (Markula, 1995; Wagner, 2017; Walseth et al., 2017). Further, fitness here is both a 'passion' and 'commitment'. The influencer is clearly using these words as a positive evaluation, but in some societies, it may appear as very odd that fitness can be a way of life. It is also of interest that she needs to state that fitness is a 'passion' and a 'commitment'. So overall, she is not simply 'keeping fit' or 'trying to stay in shape', but has a deep, almost moral investment in fitness. One of the authors recalls her neighbor would go jogging back in the 1980s, but it would have been unlikely to hear him call it a way of life, a passion, or a commitment. Words such as 'passion', 'commitment', 'striving', and 'inspired' are common in what has been observed to be a consumer lifestyle culture, where we define ourselves through commodities and activities that have accessories, clothing, gym memberships, or diet products (Walkerdine, 2003). It is now common to hear all kinds of products, services, businesses, and local public services presenting themselves in these terms. Schools strive to allow children to fulfill their potential, and they have a passionate commitment to inspire their students. Such a branding culture is typical of the ideology of lifestyle consumer capitalism.

Third, from a social semiotic point of view, language does not just represent things such as fitness or the nature of challenging racism. Rather, it constitutes these things. What does this mean? It means simply that the language that becomes established for talking about things comes to shape how we experience them, what we think they are. While in a former time we may have gone jogging in order to keep fit or stay in shape, now fitness becomes a thing in itself, bound up with ideas of passion, commitment, and success. Or we understand and experience racism as a particular kind of extreme and exceptional individual. Or we might assume that 'man' is the same thing as the ideas and values we have about that thing. These observations are important in CDA, where we are interested in drawing out the assumptions and values that are carried in language.

How words suggest models of how the world works

The tweet about Kelly Pocha carries a kind of model about how the world works. In this model, racism is not part of Canadian society, but a characteristic of a generic kind of individual found across many countries. In CDA, such a model is referred to as a 'discourse', drawing on a concept by Foucault (1972). In the case of the statement 'Be a man!', we might say that this communicates a model of the world, a discourse, where there are prescribed traits, behaviors, and attitudes for biological men, relating to being tough, not showing emotions, being assertive, etc.

Discourses are thus models of the world, accounts of how things are, and they support particular ideologies and power interests. They tell us about kinds of people and why they behave in the way they do. In our example tweet, Kelly Pocha is simply a racist type. She is not to be understood in a specific context. She is not to be seen in relation to a set of circumstances. She is just bad. We might say, therefore, that this prevents us from actually understanding her and the situation that fosters racism.

The fitness influencer presents us with a model where exercise and diet become a disciplined and managed thing, forming a part of who we are. The person doing fitness takes on a set of attitudes, of determination, focus, and passion. She uses a model to present herself, using a discourse of commitment that is common to many forms of branding. One of the aims of the close analysis of CDA is to reveal these discourses. It is like asking: what are they really saying here? In the ideology of consumer capitalism, all this passion and commitment is integrated with products and services and a highly individualistic striving for success. It is also a kind of fake world where passion, commitment, and striving can be used to describe how a coffee chain wants to give you the best service. Or where a three-times-a-week slog at the gym becomes infused with a sense of personal journey and spiritual completeness. The emphasis on ideology is important here, in the sense that we must ask 'in whose interests do such ideas and values serve'?

To help us to think about the nature of discourses, Van Leeuwen and Wodak (1999) suggest that they are rather like a kind of script. This is because discourses lay out ways of doing things, involve kinds of participants, places, times, and events. These all carry ideas, values, and evaluations about persons and behaviors. In any individual instance of communication, such as a tweet or an Instagram comment, this entire script may not be immediately apparent, but we use CDA to carry out the detective work to draw this out.

How to do CDA

In this single chapter we cannot possibly provide an account of all the analytical tools used in CDA. Those who are highly motivated to use this approach should begin to read other introductory texts on CDA, as well as academic journal papers where this is used. Nevertheless, here we can provide a set of tools and procedures that allow us to reveal the scripts in social media posts and across feeds, or that can be used to analyze the spoken part of YouTube videos.

Revealing the scripts or 'doings' of discourse

We can approach any social media data by asking what discursive scripts are carried. We can ask this question of single posts, of someone's personal account, a blog, or what we find across a hashtag or feed. In the latter case, we may be attentive to the extent to which there is coherence, variation, or contradiction across the feed. We will look at what this means practically when we come to our applied examples in the following section.

There are two basic entry points to the detective work involved in revealing these scripts. The first is to look at how the participants are represented. The second is to look at what they are represented as doing. Part of this second way involves the motivations that participants are attributed for their actions. Participants can be attributed states of mind (in terms of their experiences) and feelings.

For the first of these, we can consider the example of how some of the tweets represent Kelly Pocha in the same feed based on this hashtag:

> Now, I understand the meaning of "white trash". Too bad we can't #deport #KellyPocha to where her ancestors came from Woman who was caught on video telling group of men they're 'not Canadian' at an Alberta Denny's loses her job. thestar/Edmonton/2018/. . . #cdnpoli #racism

We can see here that the term 'white trash' is used. This tweet makes a joke of threatening to do the same thing to Pocha as she wanted to do with the migrant men. In the tweet we saw previously, Pocha was seen as a type, certainly not representative of Canada as a whole, where people value diversity. In this tweet, she is also a generic type: 'white trash'. This is a slightly different way of representing Pocha. Here, she is not so much a complete anomaly in Canada, but rather a despicable type of person found there.

In CDA, we can ask if participants are represented as individuals, where we would be given more personal details and context, possibly even insights into their thoughts and concerns. Or are they represented as a type or as a group? We can see the effect of this in the following fictional examples:

- ❏ The mob demonstrated against the government.
- ❏ The demonstrator at the front shouted abuse.
- ❏ Jiu stood as part of the demonstration, her daughter's hand held firmly in hers. She felt a combination of fear, joy, and anger.

In these three examples we can see how the first collectivized the people in the demonstration as a 'mob'. This negatively evaluates them. Here, the script encourages us to align against them. A 'mob' sounds bad. In the second, we find a generic demonstrator. Nothing encourages us to align alongside or against them. In the third case, we find individualization. We are given a name, a mother-daughter bond, and also insight into the woman's thoughts. Immediately, we feel we align with her. Of course, we are not told what the demonstration was about. Once we were told this, we might feel much less alignment. People demonstrate about all kinds of things relating to abortion, migration, civil rights, fascism, etc.

Returning to the meaning of the representation on the Pocha tweet, we can say that there seems to be a kind of middle-class elitism underlying this statement, where racism is accounted for in terms of lack of education, stupidity, and also reference to particular impoverished regions of the country. Scholars have shown that this dismissal of racist attitudes to simply being down to the ignorance of lower-class people has been a common feature in society (Richardson and Wodak, 2009). Racism theorists have in fact warned about this kind of representation of racism (Gilroy, 2012), which, again, prevents us from asking what actually lies behind the kind of outburst produced by Pocha. Those tweeting may have good intentions by mocking racism for its stupidity as something related to primitive, uneducated attitudes.

> Damn right that is who #KellyPocha is. She's just upset she was exposed for the racist POS she is. An obnoxious racist. As parents we teach our children how to behave & treat others. This is lesson for my child on how not to act, I wonder how here children view this?

In this tweet, we see that Pocha is a 'racist POS' and 'an obnoxious racist'. This indicates that there is less of a sense of aligning her with a type of person, but here other participants are introduced: parents and children. Clearly, the person tweeting presents herself as a good parent and Pocha as a bad parent. In this case, racism appears to be more about individual attitudes and good upbringing. This is slightly different from the other tweets, which were more about racist types. But again, there is no context, no sense of asking why, perhaps this otherwise normal woman produces this outburst.

It is also of note here that it is not considered that Pocha could still be a committed parent, even though she was filmed giving a drunken rant using a discourse about racism commonly found at the time. As Van Dijk (1998) points out, discourses can involve what he calls an 'ideological square'. Here, a script can carry sharp binary oppositions, contrasting a 'we' to a 'them'. In this opposition, all things positive about the 'them' will be mitigated and interpreted as bad, whereas all negative things about the 'us' will be mitigated and interpreted as good. The result is that the script creates an antithesis of good and evil. Suler's (2004) point is also useful here in regard to how hashtag users appear to create a kind of shared mental representation of a perpetrator. The perpetrator is over the boundary of the ideological square, and therefore can have all manner of evil traits and associations loaded onto them through the mental representation of them being the antithesis of their own morality.

In this last tweet, we see this use of 'we' clearly: 'as parents *we* teach our children'. And then earlier: 'too bad *we* can't deport'. Those tweeting may not have a consistent or clear sense of what Pocha's outburst means, but they are clear that racism is very remote from who they are as good parents, as Canadians who value diversity. Further, they are also clear that there is a distinct, identifiable 'we' who are not racist and have no part in it.

In CDA, it has been shown that pronouns such as 'we', 'us', and 'you' are typically used in the expression and manipulation of social relations (Van Dijk, 1998: 203). These can be used to create compelling, yet undefined, categories of shared purposes, interests, and identity, which can conceal much difference, complexity, and contradiction.

We see another representational strategy of Pocha that plays an important role in the hashtag:

> #KellyPocha your excuse was that you were drunk and what you said really isn't you? You do realize that alcohol brings our [sic] the inner you, you racist son of a bitch. Be a better person #FFS

Many of the tweets address Pocha as 'you'. They speak to her directly. Of course, they have no idea whether she is following the hashtag or reading the tweets, which is rather unlikely anyway. But here the use of 'you' allows the 'we' a sense of fearlessly and uncompromisingly addressing Pocha and the racism she represents.

A feature of this emphasis on 'inner you' and 'true self' relates to observations on the importance of authenticity as a routine basis for evaluation of others in the context of social media (Shane, 2018). Any claim that the racist behavior was out of character, or even where a long apology is given with deep regret expressed, are dismissed as inauthentic. Those tweeting act as 'authenticity detectives', refusing to be led by the inauthentic claims (Salisbury and Pooley, 2017: 7). This inauthenticity also becomes further evidence of a flawed and despicable nature.

Many of the tweets using this hashtag were about the relative good and moral actions of those tweeting. Here is another example:

> Brilliant . . .
> #KellyPocha
>
> [retweet] I'm in the Timmies line at the Royal Alex. Two gentlemen of African descent in line behind me, laughing & speaking in a language I do not understand.
> I'm not arrogant enough to assume they are speaking about me. And as they are physicians, I'm pretty sure they pay taxes.

We can see the elite position here. The Timmies line refers to waiting to buy a coffee at the Royal Alex, which is a hospital. Here, the person tweeting overtly contrasts the grim, base, drunken, and bigoted tone taken by Pocha with the bright reference to two gentlemen of African descent and calling them physicians. The person tweeting acts in a manner that is respectful and not at all arrogant.

On the one hand, the tweets on this hashtag are less than coherent in terms of the discursive script they form to represent the nature of Pocha's outbursts. But on the other hand, as scholars have argued, there is a coherence at the level of affect (Papacharissi, 2016). In other words, the coherence in not to be found in terms of agreement about a clearly formulated point of view, but rather around an emotionally charged position of rallying against Pocha. Overall, we can summarize what representations of participants and actions appear as a kind of script.

The participants here are Kelly Pocha, addressed directly in first person as 'you', and called 'white trash', 'racist POS', 'racist son of a bitch', and 'obnoxious racist'. She is also classified as a type of racist who is common to many countries. The other participants are the 'we' who are tweeting. There are no terms used to classify them as not being white trash, or overtly as not being racist. This is implied and also communicated through actions. Thus, a person can be represented through their actions.

In terms of actions, just in the small sample of tweets we have looked at here, Pocha reportedly acts in an arrogant manner, is upset she was exposed, gives a fake apology, makes excuses, and acts in a manner that constitutes bad parenting. As we see here, the script does not account for Pocha's outburst at all. This feed is not so much about what Pocha has done, but about who she is. It is rather about attacking her character, her overall integrity and authenticity. She is denying what she did, looking for excuses. When she apologizes, it is evaluated as insincere. In contrast, the 'we' tweeting represent themselves as good parents, as showing respect for 'people of African descent'. They also show their smartness by making jokes and using sarcasm at Pocha's expense.

These observations are not meant as any criticism of those tweeting, but we can see that the discursive script about racism is of a nature that has been highly criticized by theorists. Racism is presented here as being about extreme individuals, personal dispositions, lack of education, or the lower classes. In one sense, it has been argued (Lentin, 2016) that this depoliticizes racism. It strips it of context. And by demonizing the racist in this sense, we lose the meaning of what is actually taking place. What was more striking in our societies at the time of writing was the increase of anti-migrant sentiment in people around us, who were otherwise nice people, good neighbors, and those capable of kindness in other ways. Here, as has been observed, anti-migrant attitudes can sit alongside other ideas, such as that political institutions no longer care about ordinary people yet favor minorities, also allowing society to crumble (Eatwell and Goodwin, 2018).

Summary

Participants
- Individualized – names, details, situation
- Collective – racists in different countries, all people in Canada, collective 'we'
- Generic – white trash, good mothers
- Anonymous – 'their', 'they'
- Absent participants – such as people who are far from being folk devils, who hold racist or anti-immigrant ideas

Actions
- What actions and processes are represented?
- Who is the agent of these actions?
- To what extent are these represented clearly or through abstractions and symbolism?
- What actions and processes are missing?

Doing a project with CDA: fitness influencers on Chinese Weibo

In the following section, we show how to use CDA as part of a simple research project. Here we use a research question, show how we must place this question in the context of existing scholarship and how we select data, and then demonstrate how CDA allows us to answer this question. We show how the analysis might be presented.

The example used here is from the Chinese platform Weibo, China's version of Twitter and, to some extent, Instagram. The case study involves women fitness influencers. Such influencers can have many hundreds of thousands of followers. Fitness is an interesting topic, as it is something new to China. There is a growing interest, and the idea is imported from the West.

Like Instagram, Weibo is very visual, though it is possible to post something without adding a picture – much like Twitter. We carry out the analysis of the visual part of these posts in the next chapter. In this chapter, we can look at how we would deal with the language.

Research question

CDA should be used to answer research questions. This can be formulated in terms such as asking how a text represents a particular topic, such as a riot, a war, climate change, etc., to draw out the discourses. As with the Twitter example, we would look for what kinds of identities, actions, and evaluations are involved. Alternatively, a research question can be formulated in relation to an existing body of research literature. Although in both cases, good scholarship places its analysis against a thorough search of existing work on the topic. This draws on the collective established knowledge for help to ask the right kinds of questions and to understand what we are seeing in our data. Here is the research question we use in this case:

> How do these young Chinese women understand the newly arrived fitness culture? In terms of CDA, what discursive script do they have for talking about this?

As you will see, this question is formulated in relation to existing research. This helps us to frame the question, but also provides points that allow us to draw out what is going on in the posts.

Literature review

We looked for literature that would help us to understand some of the cultural shifts in China, of which fitness culture is one part. We were also interested in what had been written on shifting cultures of fitness.

There is literature showing how in China there is a newly emerged middle class. This group of people is attracted to, and has the spending power for, Western-style products and fashion. Products such as wine, coffee, and clothing, and lifestyle choices such as fitness, hiking, and high culture can signify being modern and chic and bring with them high cultural capital (Peng, 2019; Henningsen, 2012; Brunner, 2019). These people are the main users of Weibo and certainly characteristic of those posting on this topic (Anagnost, 2008).

In particular, younger middle-class women participate in this new culture. It is also accompanied by a form of Western individualism, and it comes with what are called 'neoliberal identities'. Neoliberalism is where the state withdraws from supporting citizens. They are all free to compete, to strive for success in the jobs market. All parts of life come to be treated in this way through a market logic, where all aspects of life are to be managed with commitment and competition, to create happiness and success. Scholars have observed that fitness culture aligns with this neoliberal idea in Western societies. People no longer just casually keep fit, but they focus on managing their bodies, through regulated workouts and diet. In the case of women, this has led to a new kind of 'muscular femininity', part of a culture of 'power femininity' (Toffoletti, 2014) with a sense of 'go-getting', 'assertiveness', and 'being successful' (Walkerdine, 2003). In this sense, health and fitness become another symbol, in neoliberal ideology, of self-control, self-discipline, willpower, and mortality (Crawford, 2006).

This individualism has been attractive for these young women, who struggle with the persisting ideas and values of traditional Confucianism, which sees women in family roles, as subservient to kinship and knowing her place. It has been observed that through globalization, Chinese values that intertwine Confucianism, Marxism, and Maoism are making way for the promotion of Western consumer culture and neoliberalism (Feng and Karan, 2011). This includes a marked presence of individualism, self-fulfillment, and hedonism – traits and themes that were not formerly found in China (Chen and Machin, 2014).

Choosing and gathering data

Approximately 5,000 Weibo posts were collected in 2020–2021 from the accounts of female fitness influencers. This included some who had many hundreds of thousands of followers and those where this count was more modest. The important thing in such decisions is that you are clear about what you have collected and how this information allows you to answer your research question. Given what we found in the literature review, the aim was to understand what discourses we found in these posts about fitness.

The posts were imported in NVivo software, but also simply pasted into a Word document. This is merely about getting to know your data, so it can be browsed while traveling, while in a café.

The data at this point is analyzed using what Van Dijk (2009) would call 'semantic macro-analysis'. This means simply looking for the main themes found in the data. Individual instances of data may carry different elements and combinations of such themes.

In the examples we gave in an earlier section in regard to the tweets about Kelly Pocha, one theme would be that those tweeting very often represent themselves as 'we', as a group who can be simply opposed to Pocha. Another theme was that they often assessed Pocha on the grounds of her being uneducated, inarticulate, and 'white trash'. Such observations come through looking at the data through the lens of CDA. Getting to know the data and placing it into discovered thematic categories allows us to move progressively into revealing the linguistic details. This process can lead to revealing the discursive scripts that may, at first glance, be less obvious.

Other researchers point to how we can use the hashtag as the basis of sampling. Hashtags present terms that we can search such as #fitness. Such hashtags, Zappavigna (2015) tells us, comprise linguistic convention for the communities in which we have interest.

Shifman (2012) suggests a two-phase sampling process using hashtags to help us to find those most used in a community. First, using our main hashtag, such as #fitness, we could then create a list of, say, the top 20 influencers. Second, we then screen the posts that are trending on each of the influencer's profiles and find the most-used hashtags. This collection of hashtags gives us excellent access to the kinds of themes that best characterize those most visited by the fitness community. So we can then create our sample by taking the top set of posts from each. Remember in qualitative analysis the point is to generate the best possible sample that allows us to then examine what is taking place. We need to narrow down a sample to something manageable because on a platform such as Weibo we may be dealing with literally millions of posts on a hashtag. In Zappavigna's (2015) terms, we viewed the themes provided by these hashtags as interrelated and as constituents of the ongoing discussion within Weibo mother's community.

The analysis

As we did earlier with the Kelly Pocha tweets, we can approach this data by looking at the participants and their actions. How are people represented here? What actions are included or excluded? How are these evaluated and what states of mind do we find? As follows, we look at these under a number of the themes identified in the first stage of analysis.

Being independent
One theme among these posts was that the women comment directly about others controlling them, where fitness is part of a challenge to this control. We see this in Figures 4.1 and 4.2. In Figure 4.1, she comments: "other parents always disrespect and disparage me, now no one can discipline me." This is in regard to making her own clothing choices. This is striking in the Chinese context, where scholars observe the conflicts and criticism that can arise where young women do not follow more traditional behaviors and obey their elders, often meaning they have to juggle different identities in their professional and private lives (Ji, 2015).

But in Figure 4.2, we see nevertheless a lack of confidence where she comments: "hope no one will ask me to be thinner anymore . . . after all my appearance is mainly for pleasing myself, and, perhaps please my husband." Here she mentions "the white young thin beauty standard", noting that she rejects this and the pressures to conform as she likes her 'six-pack'. Hovering in the background, nevertheless, is this sense of social pressures, where, scholars note, such newer female identities can be disparaged in the media and by kin, it is suggested as a reaction to these shifts (Sun and Chen, 2015: 3).

Choice
The idea of 'choice' is a prominent theme in the sample. This relates to the women being able to make their own choices, as in the prior examples. The concept of choice has also been observed as being central to Western notions of individualism, and additionally, as a fundamental component of consumerism. The ideas of free choice and

ANALYZING SOCIAL MEDIA LANGUAGE 71

Figure 4.1 A fitness outfit as a challenge to discipline

My outfit on the way to ballet class: body suit + shorts, before the class, I only have to change to short tights and start dancing. When I wore a camisole when I was young, other parents always disrespect and disparage me, now no one can discipline me

成33JANE
2020-10-10 来自 iPhone X

希望没有人再要求我更瘦一点了……
毕竟我的外貌主要是为了取悦我自己，
以及，顺便取悦一下我老公，
而且我从来不曾追求过 白幼瘦 向的审美。
各自的审美留着要求自己就好了，
毕竟6pack的快乐....
不能强求所有人都懂....哈哈哈哈哈哈

Figure 4.2 Fitness as related to new female identity

Hope no one will ask me to be thinner anymore . . .
after all my appearance is mainly for pleasing myself,
and, perhaps please my husband,
moreover I never pursue the white young thin beauty standard.
Save your beauty standards for expectations of yourself,
after all, can't force everyone to understand . . .
the happiness of 6pack . . . hahahahahaha

the right to self-determine, both for businesses and individuals, become core moral values (Wacquant, 2009). But in CDA we would ask: in language, what things are listed where choice is important? What are the women making choices about?

In fact, what is chosen in these posts is rarely specified. In the previous example, we find one rare example in regard to clothing. Rather, choice tends to be represented as a thing that is desirable. In Figure 4.3, we find that she becomes a person who has 'the right to choose'. This is something she earns because of work, fitness, and effort.

In CDA, where processes or verbs, such as *choosing*, are treated as nouns, as things, we call these 'nominalizations'. This means that things such as 'choice' or 'the right to choose' can be talked about without saying what the subject of the verb is.

One criticism of the idea of choice in neoliberal societies is that there is the idea that everyone can have choice. Everyone making the right choices and working hard can have success. Yet people simply do not have the same opportunities for success and happiness. Such a view conceals deep inequalities of opportunities in societies, which

【掌握感】

刚在整理专访合作案的细节

里面有一个问题是：

『Ashlee之前发的影片为什么用"做个有选择权的人"这句话？是否曾遇过没有选择权的时候？』

我思考了一下…

当然我经历过很多没有选择权的时候!!

我不是富二代，
也不是生下来就拥有很多技能，
长相不是校花类型，
更不是天生比基尼麻豆身材…

在面对没有选择权的我，
甚至不知道自己是因为没有选择权而不快乐。

我觉得自己幸运的地方是
我的工作让我吸引到共同价值观的人 😊 (94妳)

而我希望能利用个人影响力去传递我所领悟的，

就好像在提醒过去那个不知道自己是因为没有选择权而感到不快乐的自己…

妳认为"有选择权的人生"是什么样子？

#心情##選擇權##人生感悟# 收起

Figure 4.3 Fitness as related to the right to choose

I was editing the details of an interview of a collaboration project
There was a question: "Ashlee, why did you say 'be a person who has the right to choose' in your video? Was there a time there was no choice for you?" I pondered . . .
Of course, I experienced many times that I didn't have the right to choose!!
I am not a trust-fund kid, neither was I born with many skills,
My appearance is not the school-babe type and I do not have a natural bikini model type of body. . . . When I faced no choice, I didn't even know I was unhappy because I had no choice.

means many people do not have the same kinds of choices to make (Abramovitz and Zelnick, 2010). In this way, we can see how the women on these posts embrace this neoliberal idea of choice. Yet it is used, not to actually discuss concrete specific choices in life, such as how to manage modern and more traditional social demands, but in relation to a less specified sense of being successful and happy.

Thus, she becomes a person who has the right to choose because of her work and because of fitness, and this comes from her personal effort.

Self-management

Making the right choices is bound with another main theme. This is perhaps the most striking across all the posts. It is the need to systematically manage all parts of life as part of attaining success. We see an example in Figure 4.4.

For middle-class Chinese women, either those who work or those who take responsibility for child management, there are issues of negotiating modern and traditional roles. Parenting can be intense as children have to deal with massive pressure at

Bella金贝贝
2020-9-2 来自 HUAWEI Mate30 Pro 5G
""开学啦！"
""我妈妈比你妈妈好香"。
开学季最近看到最多的一段话。体会过当妈的辛苦才能理解麻麻这个角色扮演是最累的；母爱伟大为孩子付出也不要全然放弃了自己，麻麻可以合理安排碎片时间，管理自己的形象。
父母也是孩子最好的老师，父母的言行也时刻影响着孩子，自律且自信！可以给宝宝 ... 展开

Figure 4.4 Fitness as a management project

"Back to school!"

"My mum is better looking than your mum"

The talk I see the most recently during the new term. Only after experiencing the hard work of being a mother (one) can understand the role of being a mummy is the most tiring; mother's love is mighty devoted to children but don't give up on yourself, mummy can seasonably plan pieces of fragment time, manage your own image.

Parents are also children's best teacher, parents' words and deeds constantly influence children, self-discipline and confident! Can give baby a better environment of growing up.

school, often requiring extracurricular schooling or taking complex alternative journeys to private schools, as well as a huge array of out-of-school activities to help make children competitive later in high school, at university, and in the job market. Scholars also point to the intensity of life in modern Chinese cities. There is much need for such management. But here is a discourse where all things become small management projects. As we see in this post, managing childcare is placed alongside managing one's appearance and image. In many posts, this management encompasses fitness, work, commuting, and shopping. Yet what is never mentioned is managing the extended family and husband. Largely, these participants are absent from this discursive script.

Striving

Another highly salient theme is that of striving. This is in regard not only to fitness, but also as a way of approaching all aspects of life. Figure 4.5 provides an example.

The observations and advice given in this post are presented in a one-size-fits-all maxim-type manner: 'Push the limit. Push yourself'. And this striving, as with the management, is used for all domains of life: 'When facing small challenges in life and work'. Again, actual details are never given.

This post also uses pronouns to address the readers/followers as one: 'Understand yourself objectively and rationally'. It creates a collective 'we' and 'us', as in: 'maybe they are too small, they don't make us take them seriously, it is our instinct to avoid them'.

Salient across the posts is the notion of 'knowing yourself' and 'understanding oneself', as part of a discourse of self-reliance. But what these things means is never explained. In CDA, such taken-for-granted ideas are referred to as 'presuppositions'. It is never clear what should be 'understood' or 'known' about ourselves. There is no acknowledgment of actual situations and dispositions, such as addressing family issues, practical matters, pressures of marital relations, lack of actual choices, access to wealth, and job opportunities. These are substituted by more abstract notions of 'we avoid challenges'. The idea of the entrepreneurial self, who gets ahead in society, conceals deep inequalities of opportunities in societies, which means that many simply do not have the same kinds of choices to make (Abramovitz and Zelnick, 2010). We are told in this post to not waste time on others. Yet who these people are is not clear.

The comments are written in a form dominated by the indicative and imperative mood. This is a combination of statements of fact, such as 'Where your limit is, is where it's worth pushing', and instructions or empowering statements, such as 'Understand yourself objectively and rationally'. They make for an empowered, confident style of language.

The personal qualities of self-discipline were highly valued in Confucianism and have been argued to be central to understanding work ethics in China (Low, 2012). We find this too in these posts, but here it becomes colonized as a kind of freedom of choice and empowerment, shifting away from the former emphasis of this self-discipline, being related to obligations to others. In this neoliberal form, there is no sense of group, or wider collective wellbeing, as we all look after our own interests (Duggan, 2002).

Figure 4.5 Fitness as part of one's everyday life

Fitness | Push the limit Push yourself
Where your limit is, is where it's worth pushing
Understand yourself objectively and rationally,
you will then find the breakthrough point of life,
No matter when, you should improve yourself

Fitness | Small challenges VS the big picture
When facing small challenges in life and work,
maybe they are too small that they don't make us take them seriously,
it is our instinct to avoid them

Fitness | Weekend home workout
Rather than spending time complaining, hating, envying,
Spend time to train yourself,
After all life is short,
That kind of time is wasted on others,
While training is investing in yourself.

Consuming Western products

Finally, all of the influencers showcase their use of Western-type products and fashion.

Scholars have documented how consumption, particularly of Western brands and Western-style products such as wine and coffee, have become central markers of status and identity amongst the emerging Chinese middle classes (Peng, 2019). In particular, this has been related to gendered identities, where women are able to communicate empowerment, modernity, and good taste through consumer choices (Leung, 1998).

In Figure 4.6, we see reference is made to Western designs, with the visit to the Vogue café and the use of the English word 'appetiser'. The comment here adds:

Figure 4.6 Weibo post focused on Western products and lifestyle

Happy Christmas
Made a reservation for VOGUE café Christmas set menu a week in advance
It's the first in East Asia, I am tasting it first
A happy surprise from the sherbet in the appetiser made me not able to stand still
Minimalistic low key and heart-warming atmosphere
Perfect with a glass of wine
Rosy cheek
Toast for this year
Hat/Cos
Jumper/Baserange

'minimalist low key and heart-warming atmosphere. Perfect for a glass of wine', to note the awareness of both Western design styles and wine consumption as a marker of distinction. At the end of the post, she adds 'Hat/Cos, Jumper/Baserange', overtly referencing Western products and accessories.

Drawing conclusions

So, what is the discursive script here? And most importantly, how have we answered our research question: How do these young Chinese women understand the newly arrived fitness culture? And have we made a contribution to the literature?

First, let's summarize who the participants are in this script. We know there is an 'us' and 'we', and there are 'others' who waste our time. 'You' and 'yourself' are used a lot. There are children who need to be managed and inspired, and there are the mothers who are mentioned only in regard to this, not to say love, providing support, comfort, or in terms of domestic obligations. Very rarely, there is the mention of a husband or parents, as we saw in Figures 4.1 and 4.2. But in the language, there are very few participants. The women, apart from their children, who are a management issue, appear to be in a vacuum. The very people who may provide the restrictions on their choices, with whom they may have conflicts over independence and modern identities, are not present. This is silenced here. Another participant is a person who has 'the right to choose'.

So what are the participants doing in the language here? As we have seen, they are making choices, although what these choices are exactly is not specified. They are managing all things: work, leisure, children, and fashion. There is no sense of where contradictions, clashes, and stress may lie in this situation. There is an overall lack of detail. Choice and striving are often nominalizations. In other words, they are things we aim for and value, but as things in themselves, rather than as concrete outcomes. And the women enjoy Western-type commodities. There is a sense that a model for a successful life, for us women, is being communicated in these posts. But a closer look at the language reveals something else. It is more about an attitude of rejecting being controlled, or at least fantasizing about this, carried in a style of positive can-do language.

Finally, we can add that we have contributed to the literature. Scholars have been interested in how Western ideas and values interact with more traditional ones in China. The analysis here suggests that the discipline of Confucianism becomes transferred to the striving and commitment of neoliberalism. Choice and self-focus become almost overdetermined as the women seek to find a way in the merging of the two sets of values. These feeds provide little in practical terms to allow them actual resources to understand and discuss their situations.

MULTIMODAL CRITICAL DISCOURSE ANALYSIS

Introduction

Multimodality is a broad field that has developed out of linguistics. The basic idea is that it is possible to bring the same kind of attention to details in our analysis of things such as images, visual designs, and sound as we can to our study of language. Emphasis is also placed on the idea that communication must always be seen as involving more than one 'mode'. So, language can be thought of as one mode and, say, gestures another. In practice, these modes are always interwoven, but it is useful to separate them for analytical purposes.

This suggests communication is always multimodal. Even in the case of writing on a page, the meaning of the words can also come from the kind of typeface used, the texture of the paper, and the colors it carries. We see this, for example, on product packaging where the same basic item will use different fonts, color, and composition to target different consumer segments such as children, teenage males, women in their thirties, and so on.

While the observation that communication is multimodal may seem pretty obvious to those working outside of linguistics, it has three clear benefits that are important to us in this chapter. First, it encourages us to pay close attention to the smallest details in all modes of communication. Second, it means we ask how, even in the same instance of communication such as a tweet or an Instagram post, different modes may be used to 'say' different or even contradictory things. Third, it calls for us to understand how things such as causalities, processes, and classifications of things can be symbolized, rather than clearly stated, in the way that different modes work together.

As with all chapters in this book, those who have a particular interest in multimodal analysis should read specialist books and journal articles that use this approach. The aim here is to provide a model and tools to show how it can be used in a research project, and to show what kinds of questions it can be used to answer. In this chapter, we are interested in the visual part of social media posts. The nature of this can be varied. It can include photographs that have been edited to different degrees, or drawings, icons, uses of artwork, and homemade Photoshop compositions. This chapter will be looking at how to analyze this kind of social media content. This method can be used alongside the ones presented in other chapters in this volume, for example, the previous chapter, where we take a highly related approach to look at the language in social media posts.

Multimodal critical discourse analysis (MCDA) allows us to ask what kinds of worldviews are represented visually in social media posts. It allows us to look at how people, actions, events, processes, and places are communicated about, and how they are evaluated. The example in Figure 5.7 shows a post from a fitness influencer on Weibo. In the previous chapter, we looked at the language used in these posts, asking how this leisure activity, which is relatively new in China, was being taken on by young women. These influencers provide content about fitness and diet programs, but also about products and shopping. In the language part of this particular post, we can see that the user is presenting ideas for gifts, for which there will be some small

DOI: 10.4324/9780429319334-5

commission. As usual on Weibo, we find a set of images. Using MCDA, we can ask what kinds of ideas and values are being communicated about this type of fitness activity across these groups of images? We can start to draw out how it is given meaning. What kinds of identities and evaluations do the images carry? Here, we see the influencer looking good and being busy and active in many different settings. At the simplest level, it seems she has a successful and multifaceted life that includes relaxing, having fun at the beach, doing yoga and intense workouts. But looking a little deeper will allow us to see more about the role of these images in the meaning of fitness.

The example in Figure 5.1 shows a tweet from the hashtag #KellyPocha where users were attacking, or 'cancelling', a woman. A video clip of her, in which we see her drunk and angrily telling a group of migrant men to 'go home' and leave Canada, had been widely shared on social media. Following this, tweets called for her to lose her job and to be publicly shamed for being racist. The posts call her 'white trash', 'uneducated', and a 'white supremacist', among other things. She was seen as an exceptional case in an otherwise non-racist Canada. While Pocha made an apology on Twitter, as is usual, other users rejected this apology, particularly as she said the outburst was not a true reflection of who she actually is. The Twitter users argued that it was. Here, we see that one user has taken an image from one of her social media accounts. It shows her drunk on a different occasion. The user has pasted the image over her apology. Again, in MCDA, we would ask what kinds of identities and evaluations does such an image carry?

This kind of photograph can be easily found on many people's personal accounts – a joking reference to a shared evening out, for example. But here, juxtaposed to the apology and with a sarcastic comment at the top, it takes on a very specific meaning. While Pocha's outburst was unpleasant to watch, to say the least, it of course could be possible that otherwise she is a hard-working, good mother. Perhaps this incident, some racism theorists would suggest (Gilroy, 2012), calls us to consider how ordinary, everyday people come to take on such anti-migrant, racist ideas – even if these are uttered in a drunken rage. Arguably, these ideas are present in her social environment, in order for her to have picked them up.

Figure 5.1 Reshaping the meaning of the apology

[retweet] #kellypocha Sad. This hard working mother of three. Can't even write an apology for her actions just excuses. #stopracism

MULTIMODAL CRITICAL DISCOURSE ANALYSIS   81

MCDA would approach such an image in terms of how it communicates about anti-migrant sentiment or racism. In addition, its deployment here would allow us to consider the forms that 'challenging racism' takes, as found in these tweets. So what ideas about racism, racists, and xenophobia are communicated here? To do so, an analysis using MCDA would ask how participants are represented, what actions they are seen taking, and in what settings. In this case, Pocha is represented as being passed out, by a toilet. Therefore, this is how we understand racists and racism – as something not about society in general, but in the form of extreme and appalling individuals.

In Figures 5.2, 5.3, and 5.4, we see three very different kinds of images posted to the #MeToo Twitter hashtag, which had huge international attention at the time. The hashtag related, at least in its earlier period, to sexual misconduct against women in

New Wave Collective
@N_W_Collective

Come join us at our next meeting on Feb 12th 7:00 pm at Highland Park Apartments

The meeting will center the #MeToo 💃 movement. Come prepared to share and learn.

It's never to late to join the wave!!!

9:47 AM · Feb 6, 2018 · Twitter for Android

Figure 5.2 A call to action

the film industry and later more broadly in the workplace, where men have abused their power and positions. In fact, the research of one of the authors showed how very soon the hashtag became much less focused in terms of what problem was being addressed, who was suggested to be at fault, and what was to be done (Bouvier, 2020). This was, she suggested, no criticism of the hashtag per se, but simply what tends to happen on social media feeds. As many scholars have shown, they do not really form a coherent dialogue. Rather, people chip in, aligning with the emotional tenor of what they feel is taking place (Papacharissi, 2016). Hashtags will tend not toward logical analysis of situations or issues, but toward symbolism, buzzwords, and simplified good-versus-evil narratives (Bouvier, 2020). And those posting may not exactly be deeply engaged with what has been posted by others, as they tweet while waiting in the queue at the coffee shop or as they are at the same time engaging with other social media feeds and platforms (Ott, 2017).

In a research project, we might want to find out how problems and solutions are formulated on feeds that have a social justice nature. In this case, we may want to ask how the images carried on the feed play a role in this. MCDA, put simply, helps us to look at the details of such images and reveal what model of the world they represent. Figures 5.2 and 5.3 here are what we might describe as highly symbolic. This means that we are to understand this struggle in reference to the meanings offered by a kind of revolutionary art, where we see workers carrying a flag. So what kinds of meanings does this bring to #MeToo? And are they all useful in terms of what might be the hashtag's aims?

In Figure 5.3, the costumes and banner align suffrage for women's votes at the start of the 20th century to the #MeToo movement. This is of interest in MCDA: we communicate about a thing in terms of symbolism from the past and not in terms of the concrete details, issues, and causalities of the present. We saw this problem in the case of #KellyPocha. In the end, we do not talk about racism, but rather create kinds of demons that we can throw responsibility onto. Of course, symbolism can motivate, but on social media feeds, while this may work very well as part of the outrage, as in the revolutionary art in Figure 5.2, or the image of Pocha by the toilet, it may be part of how more nuanced accounts are blocked (Bouvier, 2020). In MCDA, we would be interested to identify which parts of an account of things are represented symbolically and which parts are discussed in more transparent detail. In the case of the symbolism here, what is foregrounded, arguably, is the coming together, the 'just fight' of noble, simple workers against an exploitative elite, rather than considering the actual core of the matter involved in this case. Or by referring to the suffragettes, it draws a former broadly acknowledged fight for justice into the online 'debate'. How these are the same or different to the present problem is not clear.

Figure 5.4, also from the #MeToo hashtag, is different from the others. It does not symbolize the meaning of these events by reference to the past. So how does it communicate? MCDA would be interested in how people represent themselves in such an image. Why do they stand in a row, all wearing black? Would it have been different had they been wearing different bright colors? Is it important that they stare straight at us, rather than looking off to the side? And is it important that we see no background here?

It is common on social media feeds to find businesses and individuals who are posting in order to align themselves with the moral capital of that feed. This is not to say that those posting are not committed to the actual cause, but what these types of posts actually contribute is less clear, and may rather be symbolized by postures and direct full-on stares out of the image, where color coding suggests unity of stance.

MULTIMODAL CRITICAL DISCOURSE ANALYSIS   83

> **chloe ingram** 🎈
> @chloe__i
>
> Don't forget how far we still have to go.
> #MeToo 🎀 #100years
>
> [Photo: Three women dressed as suffragettes wearing sashes and hats, one holding a sign that reads "SAME SHIT, DIFFERENT CENTURY"]
>
> 10:32 AM - 6 Feb 2018
>
> 42 Retweets 132 Likes

Figure 5.3 Suffragettes

As with all the examples we have considered so far, MCDA is a way of helping to look at how an image, or a collection of images, represents persons, events, processes, actions, or places. MCDA assumes that images can be used to shape how such things appear in ways that can serve specific points of view. What is symbolized, rather than accounted for? What is positively or negatively represented, and how? MCDA offers a model and a set of tools to ask such questions.

Figure 5.4 #IWillSpeakUp

What is MCDA?

MCDA is an approach to communication that looks at the finer details of what is taking place to understand *how* they create meaning, with the ultimate aim of revealing exactly *what* they communicate (Machin and Mayr, 2012). This is because all instances of communication carry versions of the world, evaluations of things, which ultimately become part of how we act, plan, and make our reality. Ledin and Machin (2018) give the example of two burger menus by way of illustration. One is for a fast-food restaurant and the other for a much more expensive organic burger café. The names given to the burgers in each menu are very different, but also different are the fonts they use and the color scheme. One menu uses bright, rich colors and the other more muted colors. One has a smooth, glossy texture while the other is pastier and rougher. One is more cluttered and busier while the other is spacious and orderly. The point these authors are making is that the meaning of the meals that we can get at the two cafés is coded into all of these things. Marketing invests extensive resources into loading products and services with such meanings in order to steer us, or shape our experience of something. To understand both *how* these menus communicate and *what* they communicate, we need to look at this level of detail. One burger, through a more tasteful color scheme and spacious composition, becomes something of greater quality, less rushed, less processed even. Textures can suggest something more natural. This kind of analysis entails a sort of detective work, where we show how something communicates rather than simply accounting for it in terms of adjectives, such as it looks 'high quality' or 'more natural'. In doing MCDA, our aim would be to show exactly how such meanings are communicated. When we look more carefully, we may find something different.

The same assumptions about the need to look at the details goes for the images we find on social media. We need to consider how they communicate to understand what they communicate.

Visual communication involves choices

The notion of choice is important in how MCDA approaches communication. To illustrate what this means, we can think about the choices made in the #MeToo tweet in Figure 5.4 to use black and white, rather than color; to stand in a row, rather than as a cluster; to look out of the frame, rather than down; and to show the men with folded arms rather than holding hands. Each of these choices and the alternatives changes the meaning of what is communicated. Imagine the same image done in bright, saturated colors, a wide palette of yellows, reds, and blues, where the men are of strikingly different heights, they look off in different directions, and each strikes a different pose. Such choices clearly come loaded with possibilities for making meaning. MCDA seeks to identify these choices in instances of communication.

MCDA is based on a theory of language called social semiotics (Halliday, 1978). This theory sees language not so much in terms of a rigid grammar, but as a system of choices that are available to us. For example, we might have a choice to say "today is hot" or "today is warm": these statements bring with them evaluations of too hot or pleasantly warm. These choices allow us to give accounts of things, but also shape how we represent them to others. In MCDA, which follows the groundbreaking work of Hodge and Kress (1988) and Kress and Van Leeuwen (1996), we can approach all forms of communication in this manner. We can think about the communicative choices made in the tweeted image in Figure 5.4. We can also think about the choices made in the font in Figure 5.3 and the colors in Figure 5.2. We can ask how different choices in font and color would change the meaning. If this is the case, then we can be certain that this is significant in regard to a particular instance.

The choices we make are political

Words do not simply describe things, persons, or processes. The very simple difference between saying a day is 'warm' or 'hot' may not simply be a description, but rather an interpretation, used to serve particular aims. We might say to a friend that "today is hot, we should go to the beach". More significant are the word choices we use to account for kinds of people such as ethnic minorities, as either being national citizens or primarily designated in terms of ethnic origins. When one author first applied for a job in the UK, they were surprised that applicants were called on to state they were 'Asian', even if they were, say, third-generation British. Such words do not simply describe us, but classify who we are, evaluate us, and shape our opportunities. And words are infused with meanings and associations of the time they came into being (Kress, 1989). 'Asian', as it is found on UK equal opportunities monitoring forms, relates to a historical view of the world embedded in Britain's colonial past (Machin and Van Leeuwen, 2007). The same kinds of process are also true of visual communication. Here, too, choices in representation will be loaded with meanings, and such visual choices define and shape how persons, events, things, and processes are represented. These choices, as with the word 'Asian', will invite us to evaluate the people we see. They can draw attention to some parts and distract from others, just as the word Asian may conceal complex personal experiences and alignments to make salient a connection to a huge and diverse part of the world in which a person may have neither interest nor knowledge.

Therefore, we can ask how the detailed choices in colors, postures, settings, etc. seen in images seek to shape how we experience things. This could be the identities of racists, not as ordinary people but as generally bad people who get drunk. It could be the choices of colors, lighting, and activities shown on Weibo to tell us the meaning of fitness regimes.

How choices tell bigger stories about the world

In MCDA we pay close attention to these smaller choices made in communication, as we are interested in the broader way they add up to provide versions of what events and situations mean. We want to know how we are encouraged to understand things. MCDA draws on the notion of 'discourse' (Foucault, 1978) to capture this process. Discourses are models of the world. They are ways of thinking about how things work. One discourse would be that immigrants are a good thing for a country, providing fresh ideas, enriching culture, and opening our minds. Another discourse could be that immigrants are a burden for a country, creating a drain on welfare and a threat to the national way of life. This means discourses are not related to 'truth' but to the kinds of understandings that we hold as true. At different times, different discourses may become more established as the truth of how things are, where those who question them will face some kind of sanction or criticism.

In the examples we have considered already in this chapter, we can think about the way the Kelly Pocha tweet in Figure 5.1 is part of a discourse that understands racism in society as being about extreme cases of persons who are otherwise bad and immoral. While those tweeting in such cases may have the best intentions, it could be argued that this attitude helps to misunderstand racism (Bouvier and Machin, 2021). Ultimately, it may not help to address the kinds of structural inequalities faced by ethnic minorities who live in poorer areas, where access to good education, work opportunities, and quality housing are terrible (Wilson, 2011).

Van Leeuwen and Wodak (1999) suggest that discourses can be thought of as 'scripts'. In other words, they are composed of elements such as types of persons, actions, settings, ideas, values, times, etc. Such elements may not all be present in an instance of communication, but they can be signified. In the Pocha case, we have a script about racism in society. The script to the feed using this hashtag is one where racists are immoral, arrogant, uneducated, white trash people with bad attitudes. In fact, through the hashtag we learn little about racism in itself, as the emphasis is rather placed on demonizing Pocha. This means that this script in particular is one that foregrounds types of persons (of flawed character), rather than actions and causes. In CDA, we would be interested in identifying what is foregrounded and what is backgrounded or absent.

In MCDA we are interested in revealing these scripts and discourses in terms of how they may help to introduce, maintain, or legitimize particular ways of thinking about the world. These may favor the interests of one group over those of others. Such broader interests are captured by the term 'ideology' (Fairclough, 2000). Racism is an ideology that seeks to maintain the power position of one ethnic group. Capitalism is an ideology that seeks to have societies organized principally around private ownership of property and the facilitation of profit generation: everything is about "production, distribution and consumption" (Fairclough, 1992: 207).

Discourses tend to support different ideologies. Importantly, discourses are not simply found in instances of communication, but are embedded in our activities and in the logic of our forms of social and institutional organization. So, we might find all parts of society, such as sports, news, romance, education, healthcare, relationships between people, and so on, become shaped by the discourse and logics of capitalism and profit making. A closer analysis using MCDA may find that such logics and priorities are carried by instances of communication, which have all sorts of aims.

Codification and classification

Two more concepts are important for doing MCDA (Ledin and Machin, 2018). The first is 'technologization', taken from Fairclough (1992). This simply means that there has been a gradual increase of the technical manipulation and management of semiotic resources (such as color filters) over the past few decades. This first arose in branding techniques and marketing, but has now found its way into more everyday kinds of communication. This means that many of us have become familiar with a more careful management of the semiotic choices in our forms of visual communication, as we seek to signify discourses. For example, to what extent do we alter and enhance Instagram shots through filters? This managing of semiotic resources has also arisen as software now makes this so much easier to do. But the term technologization also captures the drive to do so, the fact that we see this as important, and that we inhabit worlds where this takes place. As Ledin and Machin (2018) argue, it is not that communication has become more visual, as many assume, but that it has become more technologized. Ultimately, this all leads to a process of standardization of communicative resources. These become more similar as we all use the same software. This software allows certain kinds of manipulations of choices as certain codes become more aligned to specific uses.

The second concept is that of 'integrated design' (Ledin and Machin, 2020). These authors were interested in how instances of communication, which, for example, combine chunks of texts, images, and graphic shapes set in types of composition, present things not as running text where participants, processes, relationships, and causalities might be clear. Rather, causalities might be symbolized through graphic shapes or uses of tables. Participants may be represented by photographs and drawings set apart from accounts of actions. In Figures 5.2 and 5.4, participants are symbolized by reference to past events and the meaning of events by using artistic styles. In Figure 5.4, the identities of these men and their states of mind are not explained, but rather symbolized through their pose, gaze, and how they are positioned in a row. The color scheme, as well as being stylish, suggests a more somber mood. That they all carry the same color and form of pose symbolizes that they share the same set of attitudes. At the time, it could have been good that men were supporting the #MeToo hashtag, but at the same time, what they think and how they will act is communicated only symbolically. Kress and Van Leeuwen (2001) argued that visual communication, such as with typeface and color, were increasingly coming to take over tasks formerly accomplished through language. Ledin and Machin (2020) have also looked at the increasing systematic use of a range of semiotic resources, such as found in food packaging, interior designs, and computer software.

How to do MCDA

Multimodality offers a huge wealth of tools for analyzing an array of elements and features of visual communication. As is the case for other chapters in this book, researchers who are highly motivated to use this approach should begin to read dedicated introductory texts, as well as academic journal papers where this is used. Here, we can provide a practical framework for how to do MCDA. The other tools you encounter in your reading can be added as extras to this framework.

Revealing the scripts or 'doings' of discourse

We can approach any social media data by asking what discursive scripts are carried. We can ask this question of single posts, someone's personal account, a blog, or what we find across a hashtag or feed. We may also be interested in the extent to which there is coherence, variation, or contradiction across the feed. We might be interested in how images and language play slightly different roles in terms of how the discursive script is communicated. We will look at what this means practically when we come to our applied examples in the following section.

There are two basic entry points to the detective work involved in revealing these scripts. The first is to look at how the participants are represented. The second is to look at what they are shown as doing. This second part involves the motivations that participants are attributed for their actions. Participants can be attributed states of mind (e.g., looking bored) and feelings (e.g., appearing cold). To these two basic entry points, we can also ask about the settings in which people are depicted and what kinds of objects they hold, which suggest things such as activities, domains, and identities.

Analyzing participants

This is to do with who is included in the script at the visual level, and also with how they are represented.

We can ask the following questions:

1 *Are people represented as individuals and groups?* People can appear in images as individuals or as being a group. We can see in Figure 5.1 that Kelly Pocha is individualized. Of interest is that the language in the tweets, as we showed in the previous chapter, does much work to represent her also as a generic type of racist: 'white trash', 'uneducated', etc. In Figure 5.5, from the #MeToo feed, we see a celebrity, here individualized. We are given her name, see her alone, and are told some of her opinions as she speaks out. The women in Figure 5.3 are collectivized as a group. They wear the same clothes and little encourages us to see them as individuals. In Figure 5.4, the row of men is represented as a group, collectivized, yet the fact that they strike slightly different poses allows some individuality to come through. Should they strike the exact same poses, this may suggest conformity or posing, rather than a group of men thinking also as individuals to show their support for #MeToo. We can see in Figures

5.4 and 5.5 that there is a degree of homogenization as they resemble, act, or pose in the same way. In some cases, this may have a negative meaning, but in the case of #MeToo, it can suggest 'standing together' and 'ready for change'. This may be so, even where such images are more opportunistic, where companies and persons seek to align themselves with the moral capital offered by a hashtag. The point here is that 'sameness' of identity or attitude can be connoted or symbolized visually.

2 *Are people shown closer or farther away from us?* Distance in regard to positioning in a scene can also play a role in individualization. Close-up shots can create intimacy in the sense of physical proximity. We are given a close-up shot of Kelly Pocha in Figure 5.1. The group of men appear at the front of the frame in Figure 5.4, which also creates a sense that they are closer to us in regards to proximity. Here, we may be encouraged to consider their expressions, reactions, and states of mind. Other people might be represented in the distance, where we are less encouraged to consider their states of mind.

3 *Do images represent people as a generic type?* This can relate to things such as 'cultural types', relating to clothing or settings. A Muslim woman wearing a more traditional form of dress may be used to represent such a 'type'. The images of Kelly Pocha, drunk by the toilet, are not used to represent a rather excessive night out, or the dangers of alcohol, but to represent a type of 'white trash' racist who is also a bad parent. The men holding the flag in Figure 5.4 are generic fighters for the people. We see this in their artisan-type clothing. Representing people as generic types in this fashion can be used to simplify matters.

4 *Are people in images anonymized?* This is the case when the identity of people is concealed to some degree. We see this in Figure 5.6, again from the #MeToo hashtag. On this hashtag we find many images of people staring directly and

Figure 5.5 Confidently staring out of frame

confidently out of the frame, as in Figure 5.5. But in Figure 5.6, there is the sense of the other women out there, also affected by the issues raised by #MeToo, who may yet be silent. Nevertheless, here these women are not represented as alone, but together collectivized as a group. Of course, this image may have been unrelated to #MeToo when it was taken, but here it is recontextualized, both by the use of text and by being posted in the hashtag. Like the men with the flag, the women dressed as suffragettes, and the men staring out at the viewer, this becomes part of the symbolism and affective meaning of social media feeds. The actual issues and precise aims may be much less clearly found within the language in and across posts. It is what Papacharissi (2015) called the affective connectivity of such feeds.

5 *Are any people missing or not represented?* We show how this is of particular importance when we come to our research case study in the next section, but at a simple level across a hashtag, for example, we might ask what kinds of people we do not see. On #MeToo, we see many professional-type women, but we tend not to find working-class and poorer women. This reflects the user profile of the platform, but it also links to criticisms made at #MeToo: that it offered little change or visibility for poorer women around the world.

Analyzing actions

This is to do with what people are represented as doing in images. Following Ledin and Machin (2020), we can look at these in terms of 'processes'. Still images cannot show actions or processes, but they can carry things that index them or point to them, such as someone holding a tennis racket as if in a moment of swinging it, or a person sitting with a glass of wine in front of them (Figure 5.7).

Figure 5.6 #ChangedByMeToo

MULTIMODAL CRITICAL DISCOURSE ANALYSIS 91

赵依侬_
2020-12-17 来自 侬的iPhone 12 Pro(海蓝色)
#侬的好物发现#
最近礼物季收到很多提问！
"送家人、爱人、好友什么礼物？"

推荐#apple watch# 送健康！

今年生日我送了我妈 以后，每天都能看到她的运动数据（督促她多散步多拉伸），随时同步关注她的心率，再也不担心妈妈找不到手机（ 一秒找到 ）~更多功能可以查收图~

当然其他八张图，就是我各种和Apple Watch在一起的每一天

（夸 百搭夸我好看 收起

Figure 5.7 Processes in a Weibo post by a fitness influencer

Recently the temperature has dropped, suddenly very cold. Such time (I) want to comfortably enjoy a cup of coffee, put on fluffy clothes, cold days become warm

Maybe it's coming to the stage that [I] like to seek for things with higher quality; in daily life [I] like to work out and sometimes [I] have to look after the baby, [so] I choose a watch as the accessory, simple and versatile for styling.

Sharing with you a new DW new style, black with gold, new material is high-end quality, rubber band and watch face, complementary with rose gold time markers and hands, low key but eye catching, can be styled well with both exercising and business occasions.

You can get your hands on your Christmas present

There are three basic kinds of processes that we can consider:

1 *Material processes*: here we see people carrying out concrete activities that have some kind of outcome. This could be playing sports, buying a coffee, or taking part in a demonstration, as in Figures 5.2 and 5.4. In such cases, we might ask which participants tend to be represented as being active and doing things. And we can ask what actual actions these are, and might anything be excluded? In Figure 5.4, there is a sense of alignment with #MeToo, but it is less clear what material processes this involves. In Figure 5.1, we see 'Kelly Pocha the racist' in the process of vomiting after heavy drinking.

2 *Emotional processes and mental states*: we can look for what kinds of moods and mental states are indexed by facial expressions and postures. In Figure 5.7, the fitness influencer appears highly focused in each of her images, whether keeping fit or drinking a coffee. This feed is all about striving, go-getting, and being successful. Here we see her in the process of doing these activities. In Figure 5.4, the men appear confident, certain, unflinching. Such images give us a sense of the state of mind of those men depicted. In Figure 5.2, the men with the flag appear not in an uprising where they are murderous, but rather as calm, together. The man in the middle appears optimistic.

3 *Verbal processes*: people can be depicted as communicating. We see this in Figure 5.5. In such cases, what is being said may selectively be provided or interpreted in the text. We can also ask what kinds of people we do not see speaking. On the feed of the fitness influencer seen in Figure 5.7, we never see her communicating, but she is always busy doing things, while in the written comments she gives us advice. We can ask here who is represented as communicating and who is not. We can also ask what ideas, states of mind, and emotions may be aligned with this communication. In Figure 5.8, we see that 'verbal processes' are not being heard, but rather are symbolized along with being sarcastic, by posting an advert seen in a shop window. On social media, we need to be aware of how even such playful images and memes can be interrogated for how they are signifying states of mind, values, and situations in terms of wider discursive scripts.

Shaping viewer engagement

How we engage with an image will depend on our own interests and dispositions, but we can make several observations to see how engagement might be steered. This relates, basically, to perspective and has long been standard in film camerawork and in photojournalism.

Personal address

We can ask if the person depicted looks at the viewer or not. Are they telling us something, challenging us, aligning with us, pleading with us, looking down upon us? In a sense, such things invite a response, as when people look at us in real life. So in Figure 5.4, the men look out at us showing they are engaging with us, perhaps aligning with some and challenging others. The image would have been very different if they were each looking in different directions off frame. In contrast, in Figure 5.7, the fitness influencer does not look at the viewer. While in her post she continually addresses

Figure 5.8 Symbolizing verbal processes in a shop window advertisement

'you', who she advises, in the images we are invited to look on as an observer of her busy, go-getting life. In each case, we can ask what role such images play in the meaning of the discursive script.

Perspective
We can be given the viewpoint of the persons depicted. This can be found in Figure 5.6, as we see the women looking out over the city. Although in this case, the

setting has been taken out of focus to indicate that they are the subject of the image. We can also look up or down at people to different degrees. As we see in Figure 5.5, we look up at the presenter who talks. In Figure 5.6, we look down on the group of women, which here has the consequence of making them appear slightly vulnerable.

Distance

We can be given a sense of intimacy with a person through them being represented in close proximity, or they can be represented as distant and remote. The #MeToo hashtag carried some images showing close-ups of women in the film industry. It helped to communicate emotional intensity, opening up, sincerity. Where accused men were shown in extreme close-up, taken from Hollywood publicity shots, the effect helped to heighten a sense of disgust.

Settings in images

Ledin and Machin (2018) draw on Roland Barthes to look at the connotations of objects and settings seen in images. We can think about how the settings chosen in images on a social media account or feed communicate discourses about a person, event, or process. For example, do we see beautiful, gentle, relaxing natural settings or more rugged nature? Do we see modernist office spaces? On the #MeToo hashtags, we did not see images of women working in sweatshops or generally working-class women in more impoverished settings. We could ask if this is relevant to the discourse of women's empowerment that is communicated. In Figure 5.7, the fitness influencer is depicted in modern urban scenes, brightly lit empty fitness studios, and in nature. We do not see her in more mundane, scruffier city spaces, grocery stores, or on public transport. The pleasantness of these settings is a part of communicating her success. In Figure 5.6, we see the women in what may be a park in a city, but this is a winter scene that looks slightly dark and even bleak, rather than a nature scene that suggests freshness and relaxation. This brings a sense of the women being slightly huddled together. The collectivization communicated by them wearing the same hats also adds to the sense of them being a group.

Important in Figure 5.6 is that the setting is out of focus. This decontextualizes the image and helps raise the symbolic role played by the setting. We see a different kind of decontextualization in Figure 5.4, where the row of men have cropped their own image so that the background is simply an empty space. This allows the image to appear more stylized and chic, which is important in branding. It also allows it to work more symbolically.

Images in compositions

In social media it is common to find edited images, with comments added, or where several are combined or pasted in. We see this in Figure 5.1 where Kelly Pocha's image has been pasted over her apology. Memes can also work in the same way, where photographs are recontextualized or thematized through captions. In such cases we can still look for the discursive scripts communicated, even where this involves humor and where photographs combine with artwork and emojis. There are two particular aspects of the use of images in compositions that we want to draw out here. Once again, we take inspiration from Ledin and Machin (2020).

Images can create hierarchies
Images or parts of images can be larger and more salient. They can also overlap other components. This can suggest hierarchies of importance. Therefore, we ask which images have been posted in larger size. Have images been overlapped by text in order to change or subordinate their meaning? We can see in Figure 5.1 that the image of Kelly Pocha by the toilet is used to shape the meaning of the apology that appears beneath it. Or are images represented as the same size and in the same way, suggesting different things are actually of the same status? This can especially be the case on Weibo, as we see in Figure 5.7, where tiles of images can be used to suggest 'activities of the same order'.

Images can be coordinated
We can use qualities such as the size and shape of an image, or color linking, to suggest that they are linked, aligned, or of the same order. In the images in Figure 5.7, the fitness influencer has used a color palette to edit her tiles of images to give them coherence. This helps to bind them together and creates this coherence. On the Kelly Pocha feeds, one tweet included newspaper articles about different forms of racism, fascism, and indigenous land rights posted together, suggesting that these were of the same order and a thing to which Pocha's actions were a part.

Of course, on social media feeds such as those on Twitter, images can be bound together by the affective flow. So the men staring out in Figure 5.4, the joking use of the horse in Figure 5.8, and the anonymous group in Figure 5.6 – even if it's less clear on closer inspection what kind of coherent worldview they represent as a 'movement' – may be seen as part of the 'rising up' and the anger of that flow. The posts about fitness on Weibo include different ideas and contradictions, yet they are bound together by a sense of good taste and go-getting. Scholars have observed that on feeds, such as a comments section under a YouTube video, there can be quite contradictory sets of ideas presented, with little close attention being paid to the details of what is being said. Nevertheless, we find a coherence in the sense of anger or resentment about a particular thing (Breazu and Machin, 2021). Analyzing images means also being careful to deal with these levels of contradiction and coherence.

Doing a project with MCDA: fitness influencers on Chinese Weibo

In the following sections we show how to use MCDA as part of a simple research project. Here we use a research question, show how we must place this question in the context of existing scholarship, show how we select data, and then demonstrate how MCDA allows us to answer this question. We show how the analysis might be presented.

Our example is drawn from the Chinese platform Weibo, which is China's version of Twitter and Instagram. Like Instagram, Weibo is very visual. The case study involves women fitness influencers. These influencers can have many hundreds of thousands of followers, and fitness is an interesting topic as it is something new to China, growing in interest, and imported from the West. In the previous chapter, we looked at how we would research the language part of the posts for these Weibo fitness influencers. The aim is that these sections can be used together. This can be important in research to show how images and language are used to communicate different things. We present the project here in a way that it can be a stand-alone piece of research, for those only interested in dealing with visual analysis, but also provide some linking comments for those interested in both. We use the same research question and place in it the same literature review.

Research question

MCDA should be used to answer research questions. As explained in the opening sections of the chapter, it allows us to look for the models of the world or the discursive scripts that are represented or suggested. So, in terms of images, how do things such as racism, sexual violence against women, or keeping fit become represented? What scripts are communicated? How do images represent kinds of people, actions, settings, causalities? What reactions are represented? What kinds of priorities and solutions are included or implied as part of this script?

Of course, on social media feeds such scripts may never be clear. As we know, feeds can be contradictory, messy, involving mainly short comments formulated by buzzwords and symbolism. Our job as researchers is to nevertheless pin down what script or scripts are carried. Our aim may be to reveal the contradictions as well as the coherence.

A research question must always be formulated in relation to an existing body of research literature. While something may appear as 'new', there can certainly be research on related or similar things. Connecting with this research allows us to draw on already established knowledge. This will help us to ask the right kinds of questions and to understand what we are seeing in our data. It will help us to avoid asking questions where there is already extensive knowledge and previous discussion. Here is the research question that was used for this particular project:

> How do these young Chinese women understand the newly arrived fitness culture? In MCDA terms, what discursive script do they have for talking about this culture?

As we see in the following section, this question is formulated in relation to existing research. This helps us to frame the question, but also provides points that allow us to draw out what is going on in the posts. However, this research question was designed for a project that included an analysis of language and images. We find the analysis of the language in the previous chapter. In a project, it is possible for our interest to only be in the use of images. Such a question could be phrased as follows:

> How do Chinese female fitness influencers use images in the process of self-branding?

Again, we would be interested in using MCDA to reveal the discursive script. Were we to use this research question, we would have to be certain that such an analysis of images alone would provide a solid contribution to the literature. We would have to make this clear in how we present the research. This might be the case, for example, where there was research on social media feeds that had missed something important due to not including images in their analysis. Or where, for example, comparing images between platforms or accounts or over time has a clear purpose. Or simply where we could show there was value in doing this research, given what is already known. In the introduction to our research report, we would say what is known and how we are able to make a contribution.

In the following case study, we will focus on the research question in relation to the images alone, but this will be placed in relation to the findings of the language analysis that we will summarize shortly.

Literature review

We looked for literature that would help us to understand some of the cultural shifts in China, of which fitness culture is one part. In addition, we were also interested in what had been written on the shifting cultures of fitness more broadly, in the US and Europe.

There is literature showing how in China there is a newly emerged middle class. This group of people are attracted to and have the spending power for Western-style products and fashion. Products such as wine, coffee, and clothing, and lifestyle choices such as fitness, hiking, and high culture can signify being modern, acting chic, and having high cultural capital (Zhang, 2020). These people are the main users of Weibo, and they are certainly characteristic of who is posting on this topic (Anagnost, 2008).

In particular, younger middle-class women participate in this new culture. It also comes with a form of Western individualism, and it comes with what are called 'neoliberal identities'. Neoliberalism is where the state withdraws from supporting citizens. They are all free to compete and to strive for success in the jobs market. All parts of life come to be treated in this way through a market logic, where different aspects of life are to be managed with commitment and competition to create happiness and success. Scholars have observed in Western societies that fitness culture aligns with this neoliberal idea. People no longer just casually keep fit, but rather focus on managing their bodies, through regulated workouts and diet. In the case of women, this has led to a new kind of 'muscular femininity', as part of a culture of 'power femininity' (Toffoletti, 2014), with a sense of 'go-getting', 'assertiveness', and 'being successful' (Walkerdine, 2003). In this sense, health and fitness become another symbol in neoliberal ideology of self-control, self-discipline, willpower, and mortality (Crawford, 2006).

This individualism has been attractive for these young women who struggle with the persisting ideas and values of traditional Confucianism, which sees women in family roles, as subservient to kinship, and knowing their place. It has been observed that through globalization, Chinese values that intertwine Confucianism, Marxism, and Maoism are making way for the promotion of Western consumer culture and neoliberalism (Feng and Karan, 2011). This includes a marked presence of individualism, self-fulfillment, and hedonism – traits and themes not formerly found in China (Chen and Machin, 2014).

Choosing and gathering data

Approximately 5,000 Weibo posts were collected in 2020–2021 from the accounts of female fitness influencers. This included some who had many hundreds of thousands of followers and those that were more modest. The important thing in such decisions is that you are clear about what you have collected and how this allows you to answer your research question. Given what we found in the literature review, the aim was to understand what discourses we found in these posts about fitness. In this analysis, we will look at how they use images to do this.

The posts were imported in Nvivo software, but also pasted into a Word document. This is simply about getting to know your data. This way, it can be browsed while on the go, while in a café, and so on.

The data at this point is analyzed using what Van Dijk (2009) would call 'semantic macro-analysis'. This means simply looking for the main themes found in the data. Individual instances of data may carry different elements and combinations of such themes. In the chapter, so far, we have been pointing to some of the themes found in images posted on the #MeToo hashtag and on a Twitter hashtag attacking Kelly Pocha for her racist outburst.

Other researchers point to how we can use the hashtag as the basis of sampling. Hashtags present terms that we can search, such as #fitness. Such hashtags, Zappavigna (2015) tells us, comprise linguistic convention for the communities in which we have interest.

Shifman (2012) suggests a two-phase sampling process using hashtags to help us to find those most used in a community. First, using our main hashtag, such as #fitness, we could then create a list of the top 20 influencers. Second, we then screen the posts that are trending on each of the influencer's profiles and find the most-used hashtags. This collection of hashtags gives us excellent access to the kinds of themes that best characterize those most visited by the fitness community. So we can then create our sample by taking the top set of posts from each. Remember in qualitative analysis that the point is to generate the best possible sample that allows us to then examine what is taking place. We need to narrow down a sample to something manageable because on a platform such as Weibo we may be dealing with literally millions of posts on a hashtag. In Zappavigna's (2015) terms, we viewed the themes provided by these hashtags as interrelated and as constituents of the ongoing discussion within Weibo mother's community.

The analysis

As we have been doing for the examples considered earlier in the chapter, we can approach the data by looking at the participants and their actions. How are people represented here? And we can ask what actions we see, what emotions and states of mind? We can also ask what kinds of persons or actions are excluded.

Our linguistic analysis of these fitness influencer Weibo posts showed that there are a number of themes that add up to a discursive script. These are: being independent, having choice, the need for self-management, and striving to achieve success, consuming tasteful Western products. The discursive script is one of women being modern, go-getting, very busy, and active. All parts of life are to be managed strategically to be successful. The right choices must be made. It is not clear what these choices are to be, beyond working out, and in regard to consumer items, although it is clear the freedom from control is important. The overall discourse is one of being a fashionable, in-control person. Yet this is largely signified as an attitude rather than connected to the concrete life situations of these women, who will be caught in more traditional family and kinship situations.

So how do the images play a role on these Weibo posts? What kinds of identities, actions, and settings are represented? What views of the world are offered, and how are the images used in the compositions afforded by the platform?

A decontextualized world
At a basic level, these posts resemble the world as it is represented in advertising. It is idealized. This is a very specific form of photography, which has been distinguished as the difference between more documentary and naturalistic styles that have typically characterized former amateur pictures and more symbolic styles typically associated with advertising and commercial, generic images (Machin, 2004). These images have specific qualities that allow them to play a very particular communicative role. This can be accounted for in terms of the representation of settings, objects, persons, and composition. Such images are designed to be able to be used in multiple contexts and to be easily incorporated into designs.

In regard to settings, this is a world stripped of context. It is a world where settings are included, not so much to depict actual places or moments in time, but for what they connote. The symbolic use of settings is something that has been well-established in scholarship of advertising (Ledin and Machin, 2020). Nature can be used to communicate innocence, simplicity, and adventure. European villages can connote authenticity and traditions. Modern glass cityscapes symbolize modernity, cosmopolitanism, and success.

We see such uses of settings, for example, in Figure 5.10 in the form of an urban scene. It is not clear where this scene is. The image is slightly washed out with morning sunlight. In Figure 5.7, we see a range of other fragments of settings – a beach where the woman and a friend are surfing, to represent fun and leisure; a rural farmland scene where she relaxes; a modern, urban, glass window connoting 'modern', 'busy', and 'cosmopolitan'. These settings do not document actual places but show fragments to connote specific ideas.

Importantly, in none of these images do we see clutter, random papers, empty used cups, worn towels, or random colored children's toys. As Machin (2004) argues, such settings are often stripped back and relatively free of artifice, which allows them to better fulfill clear symbolic roles. They come to signify the places where modern, active, successful women go about their lives. If we saw cluttered, more realistic images of stressed mothers dealing with children, in messy rooms or places of work, with random improvised fitness clothing, things start to look different. Or if we see them in a busy park with litter on the grass, or with a range of family members looking on, there is a shift away from order, successful management, and optimism. This is a highly managed, ordered, and codified representation of the world.

Coordinated life domains
These images use filters and color carefully. On one level, this serves to idealize and bring vibrancy to scenes. We see this in the sky above the ocean in Figure 5.7 and in the pure, saturated white in Figure 5.9. On another, perhaps more important, level here, this allows images to be presented in compositions that are able to coordinate

and appear as integrated (Ledin and Machin, 2018). This is something that has become increasingly common in commercial media design from the 1990s (Chen and Machin, 2014), but here it is found as part of everyday social media communication.

This involves adding and modifying colors to create links and overall consistent and coherent color palettes. We see this in Figure 5.10, where a filter has been used so that the woman's turquoise top carries the same color as the buildings. Here the woman becomes integrated into, and rhymes with, the setting. This can then be used to create links and harmony across images. We may find a very limited palette is used, for example, in Figure 5.9. Here the white of the top, the wall, and the cup work together against the black of the coffee, her hair, the vest, and the picture.

In Figure 5.7, we see a use of vibrant colors to create a color palette that allows all of the images to sit together. We also see that the images sit in an overall design where those in the central column are much more muted in terms of color and content, compared to the more dynamic and color vibrant images to either side.

Ledin and Machin (2018) have argued that color, along with other semiotic features and qualities, can be used to create systems of classifications. This is an important element of contemporary communication that they call 'integrated design'. Elements in designs can be coded as alike or different by color, size and form of graphic shapes, fonts, etc. How they are similar or different is not explained in clear running text, but is symbolized. Actual differences, complexities, and contradictions can be glossed over. In the posts, color is one resource used to create links across the images and

Figure 5.9 Coordination in a post by a Weibo fitness influencer

Figure 5.10 Decontextualized settings

therefore to classify different domains such as play, relaxation, consumption, work, and childcare as being of the same order.

At one level, the coherence created by color harmonization, across images and domains, creates a sense of a well-managed, ordered, regulated whole. It is chic and feel-good. But the symbolized sameness silences the contradictions and tensions among leisure, family obligations, and work. This is important in neoliberal ideology, where all parts of life are to be treated in the same way: as projects to be managed, where the right choices are to be made, and where the results can be success and happiness.

The people and actions in the images
We can also ask what kinds of persons populate these images and what they are seen doing. We mostly see the woman, alone. These posts are not documenting social connections and social interactions, but individual activities. We occasionally see friends depicted as one image in a configuration, as seen in Figure 5.7, where the rest depict the individual woman or products. We seldom see groups of people, never crowds, family members, or coworkers. Small children appear often, as part of successful managing in the multi-domains of modern life, but seldom husbands.

The women are represented often in close-up, communicating relative intimacy, as is the affordances of selfies. This is important for the close, personal form of address used with followers and the intimate knowledge of 'inner-self' and 'inner-you' used in the advice and guidance that is given. We also see the women, as in Figure 5.7, in the middle distance – as we might see in a fashion shoot.

We tend to not see the women engaged in concrete activities. Again, these images are not so much documenting events as moments in time, but symbolizing ideas and values. Poses are key here (Ledin and Machin, 2020). These are used typically in commercial stock photography and advertising as a way to symbolize wider ideas and values (Machin, 2004). Freedom from worries and from anxiety can be symbolized by someone jumping with arms open on a beach. Spirituality and peace of mind can be symbolized by a person in a meadow striking a meditation pose. Confidence can be symbolized where a person stares squarely out of the image with their arms folded across them. 'Attitude' is where they strike a pose that might be associated with a rap artist.

We see this in Figure 5.10, where the woman is stretching in the urban space wearing an expression of confidence and focus. This pose gives a sense of both freedom and agency. In Figure 5.7, we see poses that suggest movement and being dynamic. We also see 'on-the-go' and 'purpose' to the bottom left as she walks out of the scene with her take-out coffee. We see 'cute-and-chilled out' to the bottom right and the spirituality and balance of the yoga at the top center. In this composition, this woman can be all of those things as she makes the right combination of choices in a happy successful life.

We also see poses come from those that are mandatory in fitness photography, designed to show narrowness of waist and to give the impression of longer leg length involving slight twisting postures and rocking shoulders to one side. We see this in Figure 5.10. Here, the woman strikes a confident pose.

Drawing conclusions

In sum, this is a highly decontextualized, feel-good visual world. It is clean and ordered. It carries its own morality of happiness, being busy and successful. It is represented in a form that is highly integrated, where domains of life form a coherent whole. These feeds appear to be about fitness and diet, but clearly are about so much more than this. They are about the lifeworld of the women who do fitness, and here we begin to get a sense of the discourses about women's identities that are being communicated. These are not demure, dutiful Confucian women who know their place. These are active, lively, fun-loving women, who are busy in multiple domains that are infused with happiness and success. The nature of these images is highly important to grasp the nature of what is written.

MULTIMODAL NARRATIVE ANALYSIS OF VIDEO CLIPS

Introduction

In this chapter we show how to carry out a research project on the shorter kinds of advertising and promotional clips we tend to find across social media platforms. This includes the kind of self-promotional clips made by social media influencers. Social media as a whole carry all kinds of film clips. Platforms such as YouTube carry full-length movies and event streaming, as well as people playing games or unboxing products, half-hour collections of fatal car crashes, clips from news bulletins, and so on. But here we focus on two forms of shorter clips.

The first of these is the short advertising clip. On our social media platforms, we continually come across short promotional clips. These tend to have a number of forms suited to the shorter format. The second is the personal diary-type posts of a social media influencer. This latter type of film clip can have a range of purposes and can cover a vast range of topics: a visit to the gym, making food, trying out make-up. Given the way that advertising has now shifted to access the large and often very niche followers of social media influencers, these two kinds of film can share many of their basic functions. In this chapter, we show how the same framework can be used to analyze both of these kinds of film. This approach is also applicable to any other kinds of film.

To analyze these clips, we draw on some of the theory and tools presented in the previous two chapters. In those chapters, we were looking at how we could answer research questions relating to how an issue, persons, events, processes, or settings were represented in language and images on a personal account, across a hashtag, feed, or even across platforms. What is different in the case of film clips is that we also need to deal with the fact that we find sequences of scenes and shots, placed in relation to each other. This juxtaposition and sequencing will also play a role in the meaning of what is being represented. For example, in this chapter, we look at how fitness influencers on Weibo present themselves, not only in relation to keeping fit, but also as part of showing who they are as people and as part of selling a kind of identity that may have appeal for the younger Chinese middle-class women who follow them. In this case, our research question relates to how fitness regimes, which are relatively new and emerging in China, are given meaning, so that influencers can gain followers needed to attract product endorsements. In other cases, we may be interested in how such clips represent 'being beautiful', 'eating healthily', or even very different kinds of topics where people complain about immigration or another social or political issue.

Telling stories about the world

The approach we give to analyzing film clips here draws on multimodal critical discourse analysis (MCDA) (Ledin and Machin, 2018), and in particular builds on Ledin

DOI: 10.4324/9780429319334-6

and Machin (2018). MCDA is an approach to communication that looks at the finer details of what is taking place to understand *how* they create meaning, with the ultimate aim of revealing exactly *what* they communicate (Machin and Mayr, 2012). Here, communication is never assumed to be simply about the sharing of information, but always presents versions of events and things in the world in ways that evaluate them. How we represent an evening out with friends or colleagues will be evaluated by the words we choose. For example:

> The club was full of wild people partying; it was great.
> We found the club was too full and frantic. We could not find a table.

These two statements provide different accounts and tell different stories about the same event. One account also includes a specific viewpoint, saying what 'we' experienced. In MCDA, we are always interested in the versions of events and processes that are carried in any instance of communication and the kinds of perspectives offered by them. This may be less obvious on first viewing. A film clip on social media, posted by an influencer, may at first glance seem to be just about them having fun, perhaps going shopping with a friend. It may seem to be simply information about a thing or activity. But a closer look allows us to think about what kinds of ideas, values and identities are being positively evaluated by what is said, what scenes and things are shown, and also the way that the sequence of editing brings these together.

Film clips and models of the world

MCDA assumes that all instances of communication carry versions of the world. Such models of the world are thought about using Foucault's (1978) notion of 'discourse'. A discourse is a type of loose framework that people share, which provides an account for how things are and why they are so. An example of a discourse is that we can all be successful in life if we are dedicated and work hard. Another discourse might be that society is unequal, where some people simply have better opportunities. This may be based, for example, on if their family have relative wealth, or might go to better schools, etc. Discourses should not so much be thought of as true or false, but as models that we use to give accounts of things. As we see in this instance, one discourse suggests that society is open and fair, and the other suggests that it is not so. MCDA would, however, be interested in understanding how discourses are used, whose interests they serve, and how. The view that society is open and fair as it stands would clearly support the interests of those who gain from the status quo. Research shows that people in poor areas, with long-term unemployment, poorly performing schools, associated social problems, or high incidences of crime and drugs, tend not to have the same chances of life success as others from middle-class areas (MacDonald et al., 2005). We might argue that, given clear official statistics of things such as how poverty relates to life opportunities, the discourse that represents society as open to those who work hard supports what we call a particular 'ideology' (Fairclough, 1992). In this ideology, we see society as comprising competing individuals where the best of those will rise to the top.

Discourses are not the same as stories. A story may be about a detective who is trying to solve a crime, but the discourse would lie in the worldview that may be implicit in the story. This would be the model of the world and how it works. Machin and Mayr (2012) show how crime television has shown crime, sometimes, more in terms of being embedded in social problems, where those involved may be shown as caught in a set of circumstances. Such a model of crime, these authors show, is very much in line with that of criminological research. As a consequence, violent crime and theft may be more prevalent in areas where there is high unemployment, weak social infrastructures, and few life opportunities. In relation to other areas, crime might be shown as being about bad people who act against innocent people. News media, as well as movies, tend to foreground the evil and twisted nature of exceptional individuals. In this latter case, crime is more about individual character than social context.

Social media clips are bound to tell us many different kinds of stories. Later we look at examples from a promotional clip selling software, which helped a manager solve all their business problems. Another is where a social media influencer recounts a trip to a nature resort. The discourse in each case relates the kind of model of how things work. What kinds of situations and outcomes are valued? What kind of causalities do we find? Such questions can also be asked, even in the case of more instructional-type film clips, such as where we are told how to make our own organic health drink. Here, there may be a discourse about managing the planet's problems through making the right kind of shopping decisions (Ledin and Machin, 2020).

Important in the view that MCDA takes is that discourses exist not only in communication, but are infused into what we do, how we organize things, and how we evaluate people. Discourses that come to dominate tend to have a huge impact upon what our societies come to look like. Carrying out research on film clips means revealing the discourses that they carry. This means looking deeper into what the clips say about how the world is. In the case of promotional film clips on social media, this means looking at the kinds of worlds, ideas, identities, and values alongside which products are being placed to make them meaningful to consumers.

As mentioned, this chapter uses some of the same tools for analysis as those used in the previous two chapters. We begin the chapter by looking at how we apply these in the case of film clips, but we need something additional here. Film clips present sequences of action. We see movement and interactions. Scenes are juxtaposed with each other in different ways. They can be edited into different kinds of sequences to give them meanings. This is important in terms of how they make meaning. The structures of film clips play a part in what is included, foregrounded, and excluded. It communicates temporality, processes, and causality. Eriksson (2015) has shown how in reality television, all of these can be manipulated for the purpose of simplifying issues, and making people and situations appear in a favorable or unfavorable light. Minor moments, when decontextualized, could appear as defining features of stories.

Breazu and Machin (2020) have shown how film clips on YouTube about Roma people may avoid being openly racist. Yet the ways in which footage and language are combined, edited, and re-sequenced help create a discourse that the Roma are all criminal and untrustworthy, and choose to live a marginalized existence. Implied, and taken up by those commenting, is that ordinary, law-abiding, tax-paying people suffer because of the Roma.

Identifying the discursive scripts in film clips

Van Leeuwen (2008) and Ledin and Machin (2018) show how we can go about drawing out the discourses found in instances of communication, such as film clips. This follows what we showed in the previous two chapters for CDA and MCDA. We would suggest that those readers wanting to work with film clips also read these chapters. Film clips are, of course, also special as a form of data, since they present unfolding actions or scenes. They also bring different possibilities of combining different scenes and language. We look at how we can analyze the sequences and structures found in clips in the next section, but here we can think about how to start looking for the discourses.

Participants
We can look for who is represented in a film clip. As in the CDA and MCDA chapters, we can ask if these people are shown as individuals: are they named, are we encouraged to relate to them as specific persons? Or are people collectivized or represented as a type (worker, student, ethnic, etc.)? Are some participants that we might expect to see not represented? In one of the clips we look at later, three friends visit a nature resort in China. One feature of these resorts is that wealthy, middle-class visitors are taken care of by a range of different levels of worker, for entertainment, food, and comfort. Yet we see none of these workers. Rather, we see close-ups of the friends. We can ask why this is the case.

Here we can also ask whether the representation of persons in the scenes is different from what is being said in a narration or voice-over. Breazu and Machin (2020), using MCDA to look at news clips posted on social media about the Roma in Romania, show how we may simply see Roma people in a village, but they are described as 'them' in language, for example, suggesting that they are not like 'us', the viewers. Close-ups are used in particularly unflattering ways, along with editing to make their replies to questions seem evasive. In other words, it is through the combination of what we see and what is said that the Roma are represented negatively.

We can also ask to what extent juxtaposed scenes create connections between participants. Breazu and Machin (2021), again using MCDA, show that in a film clip blaming the Roma for spreading Covid-19 in Romania, a clip of a Roma man making a joke posted on his Facebook page had been placed next to footage of a police-enforced quarantine of a Roma village. The man therefore becomes de-individualized, decontextualized, and another 'Roma type', irresponsible in the face of the pandemic.

Social action and social interactions
As we showed in the last two chapters, we can ask what kinds of actions are represented. In other words, who is doing what, and how are these actions evaluated? One of the clips we look at later is a promotion film for a university. It is not at all clear what the students are doing in the different scenes where they hold objects and interact with technology, but it is clear that they are entirely immersed in what they are doing and that they are busy. The voice-over talks about your vision, imagination, and strength to be part of this collection of minds, as there is much to be done on our way to becoming a leader. What is signified is that students will not so much have to study, learn, work hard, and show self-discipline or humility, but that they are already special people who will be part of something incredible: a moral journey, where cool technology is a major part of the journey.

When accounting for actions and interactions in language, we can shape what we draw attention to and what we hide. We can say 'fifty angry women shouted at the manager'. Film footage might show that there were only 12 and one was talking rather than shouting. Nevertheless, we can design and shape footage to also hide or foreground. As mentioned, in one of the clips we look at later, a fitness influencer goes on a trip to a nature resort with two friends. She presents the film as showing what good friends she has, which can be seen as part of her self-branding. Yet the most salient action in the clip is that they dance a lot. They seem to do nothing related to the natural setting. We can ask why this is the case. We can also consider how this may diverge from what might be accounted for in the voice-over or captions. We will see how to use such observations to carry out an analysis of the following examples.

Settings

In the previous chapter, we considered the importance of analyzing settings. Promotional film clips will likely choose settings carefully. In the university promotional film that we consider later, we do not see big lecture theaters with a large number of students. Rather, we are shown labs or large open spaces where there are one or a few students. The only class/teaching scene that we are shown takes place outside, where a small number of students sit in a circle. Spaces tend to be empty and uncluttered. Arguably, the settings here perhaps misrepresent how teaching tends to take place across universities. We would want to ask what discourse, therefore, is being drawn on through this representation of settings.

In another one of the examples we look at later, we find a short promotional clip for software that is marketed as being a user-friendly replacement for spreadsheets. We see a manager speaking to us from her workplace, which is open plan, dominated by a large sofa. It is a color-coordinated space that appears highly modernist, creative, and informal, yet at the same time employees appear to work in a dedicated and happy fashion at their creative work. This setting helps place the software in a discourse, not so much of administration and processes, but of a modern, fashionable kind of management style.

Film clips can also, as Ledin and Machin (2018) show, juxtapose settings, such as rugged mountains and a modern city, for example, where a car for sale is both being related to the freedom of adventure and being cosmopolitan. The university clip carries scenes of students sitting in a garden, where there is classical architecture, but also a scene in a poor Global South setting where women and children appear to be in wonder at a water-carrying device, presumably created by university students. Both settings here suggest possibilities and high values.

Language, narration, and captions

Also important is what is said or represented in captions, versus what is shown. Breazu and Machin (2020) were particularly interested in how the meaning of a clip and its ideological position can only be revealed by looking at how narration, captions, and footage play slightly different roles. We will attend to this as we look at the following examples. We would here recommend that those interested in language analysis read the chapter on CDA.

The stages in film clips

It is useful to approach these film clips as a kind of storytelling. Scholars have long thought about how humans use stories in order to share not just experiences, or as entertainment, but in terms of conveying personal experiences as ways of coping with life (Labov and Waletzky, 1967). There are also ways whereby cultural values and forms of social organization can be tutored to new members of society (Lévi-Strauss, 1963). These may to some extent be less visible where stories on the surface appear to be about fantastical or mythical characters, but nevertheless, they carry evaluations of kinds of actions, forms of social order, and behaviors (Barthes and Duisit, 1975).

Scholars have shown how stories that on the surface appear to be about the same kinds of issues, such as about battles, detective work, etc., tend to have deeper and subtle differences, carrying underlying ideas and values dominant in a society at any time (Wright, 1975). For example, at one time, detectives and criminals in novels might be more alike to each other: imperfect, flawed characters. Yet at another time, there is more appetite for simpler good-and-evil types of characters. We might ask why this is the case and how this links to broader ideas about character and morality.

Other authors have shown how children's stories, whether about fairies and dragons or humanized animals in domestic situations, will be underpinned by evaluations of kinds of actions and situations: they will carry messages about social relationships and morality (Bettelheim, 1976). In MCDA, we would think about such evaluations as being one component of 'discourses'. Therefore, our aim would be to reveal these discourses. Here, we have the distinction between a 'story', which may be 'hero catches bad person', and a discourse that involves the kinds of persons, causalities, and worlds that the story lays out and evaluates. Are we, for example, encouraged to understand crime in relation to social contexts of poverty or in terms of the moral deficit of individual persons?

Ledin and Machin (2018) show how a starting point for drawing out the discourses buried in film clips is to identify the basic stages of what takes place. To do this, they adapt the basic narrative stages used by Labov (1972) to analyze written and oral stories. These are very easy to identify in any film clip. Here are the stages:

- Orientation – Who is involved and what is the time and setting?
- Action – What is next?
- Complicating action – What is the problem?
- Resolution – How is the problem resolved?
- Coda – What is the evaluation or ending thought?

As Ledin and Machin (2018) show, these stages are easy to apply yet can be very revealing as to what is taking place. Promotional film clips found on social media tend to have one of three basic structures. Each draws on these basic stages in different ways. They tend to always have some kind of orientation and coda, but not all have complicating actions and resolutions. Using these stages to reveal the structures of clips provides a first step to allowing us to draw out the underlying discourse.

The problem-solution structure

In this kind of clip, as the title suggests, a problem is presented, which is then solved. This is very typical of advertising, where the problem is formulated in a way to allow the product to provide the solution.

MULTIMODAL NARRATIVE ANALYSIS

This example, which we use to illustrate the structure of a short clip, can be found on a number of social media platforms. It centers on a software package for administrating a business, for keeping track of resources, tasks, staffing, finance, etc. Here is what takes place in terms of the narrative stages.

A note on how we present this data here: we are not showing all of the scenes, due to space limitations. Here we only show the salient ones. In a full analysis, you would want to create a transcript that showed all the scenes, along with the language related to these scenes.

00:00 Orientation:

If you're managing a team, you have to try Monday.com.

Monday.com is a platform to track everything your team is working on. We use it for all our projects.

Figure 6.1 Film clip from Monday.com, using the problem-solution structure

00:00 Problem:

I tried managing everything we were doing with spreadsheets. It was a nightmare.

00:00 Solution:

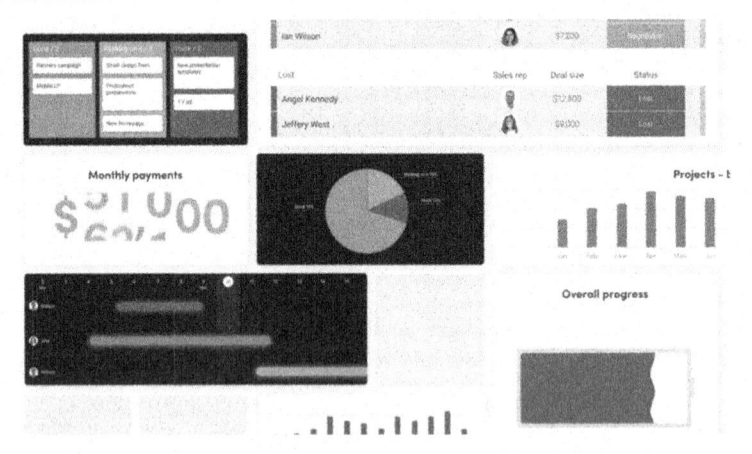

Now we have a tool that's easy to use. It's given us the confidence to take on more complex projects.

Figure 6.1 (Continued)

MULTIMODAL NARRATIVE ANALYSIS   111

You get a sense of everything falling into place.

00:00 Coda:

Seriously, if you manage a team, you need to use Monday.com.

Figure 6.1 (Continued)

Orientation:
In the orientation stage, we see two very rapid shots of office buildings. The nature of the setting here is important. One of the buildings appears to be in a classical style, while the other is modernist and appears slightly industrial. Together, they suggest a prime urban business area in a larger city. We then cut to see a woman sitting on a sofa in a creative, modernist office workspace. What she says informs us that she may be a manager, as she tells us about the software. It is a small business set in a city. The workspace is modern, open plan, which appears very designed with color coordination and has a sofa. The relaxed manner of the manager, her casual clothing and posture, help tell us about a kind of situation, so this provides orientation for the viewer. It tells us the who, where, and what.

The next scene introduces the problem. She says: "I tried managing everything we were doing with spreadsheets. It was a nightmare." She does not explain why it was bad, which particular things were less good, or what went wrong. As she tells us this, she carries a bleak expression, and a rather incomprehensible spreadsheet appears behind her, taking over the scene.

Then we see a series of scenes where we are presented with the solution. Smiling now, she tells us that the software has "given us the confidence to take on more complex projects." So here she talks not as 'I' where she had the problems with the spreadsheets, but as 'us' of the team. We see a screenshot from the software, which carries the same colors as the office scene. It is also rather incomprehensible, but the parts carry very simple kinds of graphics. We also see a series of scenes where there appears to be creative work going on. There is a sense that this is a creative business, where we see the man drawing with a camera in the desk – in an open-plan layout. Such activity, placed in the solution section, serves as evidence of a smoothly operating, successful business.

We are told that: "You get a sense of everything falling into place." Four smiling workers appear in turn on the sofa next to their manager. They are sitting closely together, suggesting an informal, friendly, and open team. Here, she shifts from talking about 'I' and 'us' to 'you', including the viewer in the experience.

Coda: As we cut to the logo, the woman says: "Seriously, if you manage a team, you need to use Monday.com."

Software administration systems are becoming increasingly used in institutions. Here this product, as with many consumer products, is sold as a solution to a problem presented in a manner that makes that solution suit the product. Another example might be a new washing powder that is designed to deal with the problem of three different kinds of dirt.

Research shows that many institutions now take on software to administrate a plethora of things, including staff, resources, processes, and finances. This is done as digital technologies carry connotations of being modern, increasing efficiency, transparency, accessibility of information, and also monitoring workers and quality control. Yet such software can take much time from staff to populate the screens and to input data. The templates and flows presented in the software do not simply record what gets done in a workplace, but shape what gets documented, measured, and managed (Ledin and Machin, 2021). We should remember that the more software provides templates to make things easy, the more we deal with 'one size fits all' products.

So this is the 'story'. The software solves the problem. The discourse here is communicated in part at this level, but it is also communicated by the persons, the settings, and the actions that are used to align the product with kinds of identities, ideas, values, and a discourse about business. This is a smallish business, which is modern and confident, as we can see in the easy and self-assured attitude of the boss. It is cosmopolitan. There is ethnic and gender diversity in the workforce. It is open plan, and work is creative. This is reflected in the color-coordinated interior.

In problem-solution structures, it is important to question how a problem is formulated. For example, Ledin and Machin (2020) show how in a short promotional film clip, a brand of milk alternative, called Oatly, presents itself as somehow addressing climate issues and as being part of sustainability. Yet, how this is the case is never clearly explained. This company sends its products around the planet, engages in marketing, and dresses up packages of contents that comprise mainly water with small amounts of grain content with expensive and difficult-to-recycle packaging. Such companies, Ledin and Machin (2020) note, can colonize consumers' worries about social and environmental problems. There is wider scholarship and research on what is called 'political consumerism', where marketers align their products with some kind of social or political issues to allow shoppers a sense that they are making a difference (Mukherjee and Banet-Weiser, 2012).

These problem-solution structures can be used to create more entertaining clips. Typically, in advertisements, this is where a person might encounter a problem, or see a problem, which the product allows them to solve or rise above. There can be a mild comedy aspect to this. Ledin and Machin (2018) give such an example in the case of an advertisement for The Bank of Ireland. Here two flatmates look up mortgages from the bank to buy a new flat, when a third flatmate moves in his geeky girlfriend. In this case, the bank seeks to increase its loan portfolio by aligning with the safety

MULTIMODAL NARRATIVE ANALYSIS 113

and familiarity of a sitcom setting. In the case of social media influencers, we can ask what kinds of problems and solutions they present.

Recounting events

Some film clips don't have a problem-solution sequence. In such cases, we will still have an orientation phase where we are told about who, where, and when. And we will find a coda where the meaning of the sequence is given and where the product will appear. Where this is a promotional clip for a product, a service, or the identity of a social media influencer, it is not that these things (e.g., a bankcard, a washing powder, or diet program) solve a problem. Rather, the product becomes aligned with kinds of people or places, and certain ideas and values become loaded onto those things in the process of recounting. Ledin and Machin (2018) give the example of a credit card advertisement. We see simply a sequence of events starting from seeing a businessperson in a large office getting a phone call. We then see him get on a large motorbike, ride through a city, and arrive at a restaurant where his beautiful wife and friends await. In the coda, we see the credit card and the slogan: 'Life without Limits'. Going into debt on a credit card here is placed not in terms of its consequences, but as a highly appealing world of attractive people, the individualism of the man who arrives slightly late on his motorbike, which can be understood as a sign of his individualism and youthful spirit, arriving not to scowls from his wife, but a loving kiss. As we see the slogan on the screen in the coda, we see the friends still deep in light-hearted conversation.

Here we look at an example of such a recounting clip. This example is a fitness influencer posting on Weibo. This is a young woman who has many followers and posts fitness and diet programs. She gives this post the title of 'Are all girl's friendships "plastic"?' The term 'plastic friendship' (塑料友谊) in Chinese is a typical social media buzzword used to describe a friendship that is rather fake and superficial. The clip recounts a trip to a rural tourist resort with two of her friends. We see them having fun and relaxing, and she speaks about their friendship.

0000 Orientation:

A saying goes, 'Women's relationships are always fake and plastic.' This might be the case for other people, but not for us, not my girls and me.

Figure 6.2 Film clip from influencer, using the recounting events structure

(Dance music begins)

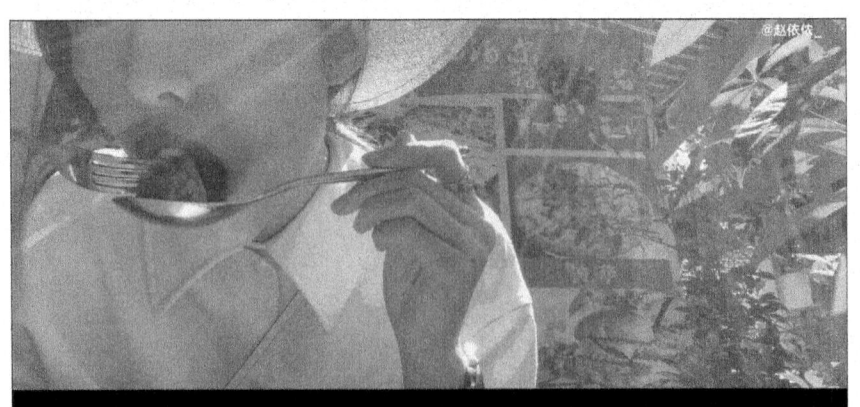

Figure 6.2 (Continued)

MULTIMODAL NARRATIVE ANALYSIS   115

We can meet each other without make-up but stay comfortable.

(And she speaks in the clip saying) Two female celebrities with their staff (referring to the only guy in the camera)

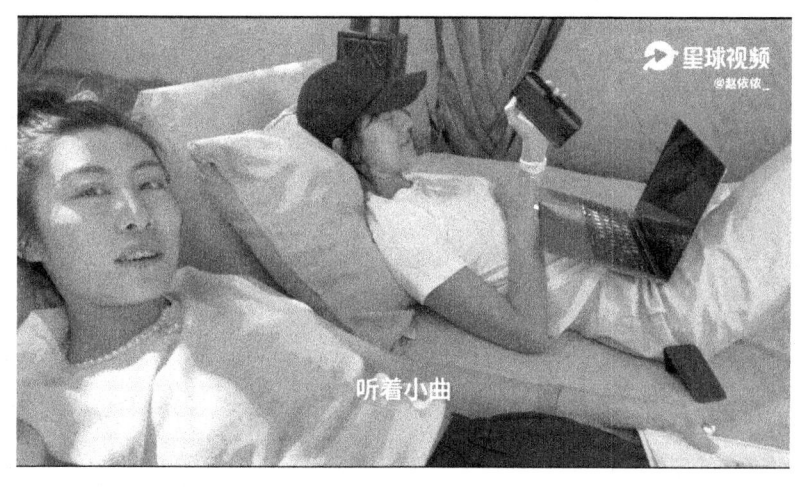

(They both laugh)

(Voice-over) We can just stay with each other, enjoy the silence.

Figure 6.2 (Continued)

(In the scene she says) There is a small pool in front of us. Listening to the music, reading books, enjoying the sunshine . . . (The friend says) if only we can do this every day.

Seen dancing and then the shot is frozen while information is given

(Voice-over) Zhu and I were friends growing up. It's been 30 years since we've known each other.

Yoyo used to be a senior student to me, and we've been real sisters for 16 years with different biological parents.

(Voice-over) We can dance anytime if we are in the right mood. We are also here for each other, during many rituals of life.

It's me who is always out there for her, but not her parents or her (Beep). (her boyfriend's name).

00:00 Coda:

(Subtitle) To all the girls: wish you be independent and be free

(Voice-over) Before we left Xishuangbanna, we were sitting in the yard of our place. We started to think about what we will do, if one day we have enough money and

Figure 6.2 (Continued)

time, to live our lives to the fullest. Yoyo said she will live by the sea, so that she can hear the waves every day, and she can lie down and relax whenever she is tired. Zhu said she'd like to be a guitarist in a small town. Meet new friends and booze in the clubs every night. For me, I just want to stay at home, enjoy the sunshine, the books, just like what I've been doing for these past days. If I get tired, I will take out my camera to take interesting photos (Singing).

(Voice-over) We walked our own paths to get here, to be who we are today. We met and became a pack. We share happiness and sorrows. I think this is what a woman's relationship looks like.

Figure 6.2 (Continued)

In terms of structure we have an orientation where we are told that the influencer has true friends, certainly not plastic, artificial ones. She then recounts a trip to the countryside where they have fun and relax together. No problem is solved, but recounting the events communicates a discourse as part of her self-promotion as an influencer. As on all her posts, she looks beautiful, and her friends are beautiful. She is always active and energetic or enjoying a moment of eating or relaxing. The recounting is done to dance music that starts after the orientation, and as she says, they dance whenever they can. Even walking through a forest, they are happy and dancing. Here fitness and her identity as an influencer are clearly part of a lifestyle. It is not simply about bodily health, but linked into beauty, consumer products, and pastimes, as well as success: in good taste, beauty, as well as friendship.

In this film, the setting serves a particular purpose. In China, researchers have observed shifting attitudes toward nature, at least among the newly emerged middle classes (Leggett, 2020). This is influenced in part by concerns over pollution, but also, as in Western culture, involves a new romanticization of the countryside as a kind of commodified reaction to anonymous, stressful city life. For many decades in China, the countryside has been associated with backwardness and poverty, the very antithesis of everything modern and fashionable (Su, 2010). But this attitude has shifted where it is now fashionable for middle-class people to visit the countryside and stay at the resorts now appearing around the cities (Zhu and Zhu, 2017). These resorts often offer carefully packaged experiences that involve hiking, relaxation, and idealized rural life, along with good cuisine and entertainment (Brunner, 2019). In this sense, the setting for this clip helps to signal this kind of lifestyle. Other indicators are also present, where we are told they read books together. High culture in the form of reading novels as a leisure activity is also part of signaling success through distinction and good taste. Posts by Weibo fitness influencers typically involve reference to Western products, such as coffee, wine, and clothing.

The social relations in this clip are also important in terms of the discourse that is communicated. Scholars have observed that authenticity is an important basis for evaluating others on social media (Shane, 2018). Salisbury and Pooley (2017: 7) argue that followers of influencers or product brands act as 'authenticity detectives'. Lack of authenticity can call into question all other kinds of claims to offer reliable knowledge or services. Here the fitness influencer, as well as showing she has the right kind of middle-class lifestyle – going out into nature, hiking and relaxing – is also able to make a claim to authenticity through having 'real' friendships, not those that are plastic. So we see them having fun together and indulging by the pool, notably, being able to be together without make-up. In the coda we are told that friendship is to "share happiness and sorrows," although of course the film, nor any other posts by this influencer, does not raise what form those sorrows might take. Fundamentally, the world she represents is upbeat, can-do, and go-getting.

At the end of recounting this trip, the coda is important. This ties the scenes of nature, reading books together, and dancing more explicitly to the discourse that runs across the account of this and other women fitness influencers. We can draw out this discourse by looking more closely at the representations of participants and their actions. The posts of this fitness influencer, for the most part, represent only her. In the chapter on CDA, we looked at some of these posts. In this clip, we find extensive individualization of the three women, as we see them in close-up and hear about their feelings. In particular, this is the case for the influencer herself, who we are able to dwell upon in lingering close shots.

In the CDA chapter, we saw that these posts tell us about facing challenges with a certain attitude, about making the right choices, but we are never told exactly about what these choices are. In the coda here, the influencer tells us that friends share their sorrows, but not what these are. In MCDA, we might ask why such challenges, choices, etc. are so often alluded to without specifying what they are. In this clip, the only other participant we see visually is a young man who appears more working class, notably there to guide them and do things for them. When the camera points at him, he does not smile, pose, or dance. He remains a generic man there to help them and suit the story that puts the three friends at the center. He is not individualized. Here the huge divide between city and rural areas – in terms of access to resources, wealth, and life opportunities (Fu and Ren, 2010; Wu and He, 2018) – is not mentioned, yet would be utterly evident to the man. We are told that one of the friends has an ex-boyfriend, but again, across these posts there is little sense of wider networks of social relations.

In MCDA we can also ask what kinds of actions are represented and positively evaluated, as well as which are either absent or negatively evaluated. Dancing is salient throughout the clip, and underlined as important in the statement "we dance anytime." Life here is fun, positive, and active, and such physical movement can also symbolize a kind of freedom of spirit and abandon. As we saw in the analysis in the MCDA chapter, the images posted by these fitness influencers emphasize 'striving' in all domains of life. They work hard, train hard, and also perform at leisure and relaxation. We might ask here if the young man, seen in the clip, might make such a statement in regard to dancing at any time. In a Chinese rural village, more basic priorities related to immediate economic survival may be more salient.

What is evident in the clip is that the salient actions are dancing and relaxing by the pool. Nothing is said about the actual resort, and no actions relate to nature per se. In one scene, we see them walking in what appears to be a wooded area, but they dance as they walk. The scene tells us about fun, not interacting with the natural environment. As analysis, this tells us that recounting the trip to a resort is not about the resort itself. It simply plays a signifying role as part of middle-class taste.

In the coda, other actions are mentioned in regard to future life plans. One friend wants to simply "live by the sea, so that she can hear the waves every day," and "she can lie down and relax whenever she is tired." Another wants to "be a guitarist in a small town. Meet new friends and booze in the clubs every night." The influencer herself states: "I just want to stay at home, enjoy the sunshine, the books." The discourse here, as we saw in the chapters on CDA and MCDA, is one captured in the subtitle at the end of the coda: "To all the girls: wish you be independent and be free."

These Weibo posts and this film clip do not talk about the contradictory demands that are placed on young Chinese middle-class women in society. These remain shaped by the traditions of Confucianism, knowing one's place, kinship obligations, and the woman's place as a carer in the family (Zhang, 2020; Xu, 2007; Child and Warner, 2003; Hong, 1997). At the same time, modernization brings individualism, new kinds of career possibilities, and social pressures and additional burdens on the women who end up trying to do both. This film clip and the coda present a discourse of women having fun, outgoing lives, being successful and beautiful, but with an underlying sense of needing to break free and make choices for oneself. Men or family relationships are certainly not dealt with openly, nor are any of the other issues driving this need to celebrate individualism and the need for choice.

In fact, there is one more aspect to this video clip that also tells us much about how it works. It is not only a film that recounts an event. There is a section just after the beginning where there is a sequence of fast edits, in no particular order. To understand this sequence, we need to look at our third structure, because clips can combine elements of the three forms we present here.

Projection narratives: possible worlds

The third structure does not recount events or solve a problem. It has an orientation stage. There is a kind of coda stage, but this can be more of a 'reorientation' than a conclusion or evaluation. In between, we have a sequence of scenes that are not presented in terms of order of temporality or causality, nor the kind of problem-solution basis found in our first example. In this structure, we find a rapid series of scenes. There may or may not be voice-over providing some kind of commentary, but this can be more poetical in style than narration, or a pop song may provide the coherence. The scenes can be used to present a kind of possibility or symbolize a broader grand idea or vision, which will not be explained in clear and transparent terms. Ledin and Machin (2018) call this kind of sequence a 'simulation'. We will show why later. These structures are typical in branding clips about universities, airline companies, or where there is some kind of less clearly defined ethical message – for example, an oil company taking care of the future. This structure too, as we show, can be found routinely in the clips on social media and constitutes one embedded section of the film by the fitness influencer we looked at previously.

Ledin and Machin (2018) illustrate this kind of structure with the example of a promotional clip posted on Facebook, for a university. This is typical of how educational institutions tend to seek to brand themselves, and the structure will be easily recognizable once its nature is pointed out to us.

There are 27 scenes in this film clip. We have not included all of them here due to space, but what is clear is that this is not a logical case for why you may want to be at a university or what being there involves. Much university work is not like this. There is much arduous study. It is unlikely that students will be creating new knowledge, new medicines, or fixing easily identifiable problems for villagers in the Global South. But the kind of activities represented here are about go-getting, being active, striving. This is represented right from the start where the students are seen running across the grassy space, and then the pace of the activity and speed that the projection unfolds. And we are told "come because there is much to be done and to be undone."

The scenes do not all work in exactly the same way. Some are more linked to the university, whereas others are more about broader ideas such as social justice in the world – such as helping poor people in the Global South. Equality is symbolized in

00:00 Orientation:

00:00 Projection:

Create and calculate

Figure 6.3 Film clip from University of Michigan, using simulation

MULTIMODAL NARRATIVE ANALYSIS 121

Shatter both records and stereotypes

Build improbable machines

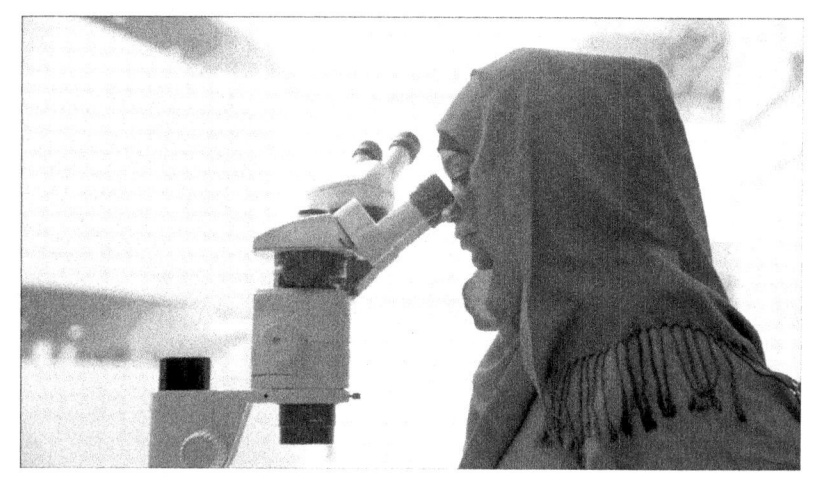

And impossible medicines

Figure 6.3 (Continued)

Unleash masterpieces

and birth theories

Come because there is much to be done out there and undone

Figure 6.3 (Continued)

MULTIMODAL NARRATIVE ANALYSIS 123

Come find out everything of which you are capable

Come believe in something greater than yourself

An experience unlike any other awaits you here

Figure 6.3 (Continued)

Here dreams are in need of your voice

Fragile ideas that need

your strength

Come answer this call

Figure 6.3 (Continued)

MULTIMODAL NARRATIVE ANALYSIS 125

Join this assembling of minds

Put your grand imagination to work

Come let your visions rattle these walls

Figure 6.3 (Continued)

and help move the world forward

Come join the leaders and best
The victors valiant
00:00 Reorientation:

Come to Michigan
Figure 6.3 (Continued)

terms of gender roles and ethnic diversity, which may or may not bear resemblance to the actual student profile at the university. The coherence of the clips is also provided by the use of the yellow color, taken from the university logo, which is included in most of the scenes: on the car, an object in the background of the microscope scene, the liquid in the tanks, and the water carrier in the Global South.

Salient here, Ledin and Machin note, is that the university is mainly about technology that seems to be the savior of humanity. Even in scenes where we see dance and music performance, this is related to some kind of technological research.

In two scenes in the film and in the coda, we do see some reference to history and the tradition of learning and scholarship in the form of the classical architecture. But this appears to play a role only in connoting grandness, greatness, and higher knowledge, more than to any clear sense of the meaning of learning. In this film clip, study is a kind of go-getting that brings immediate and tangible outcomes. It is not related to arts and humanities, for example. But together, all the scenes lay out possibilities. The classical buildings symbolize the grandness of these – as is made salient in the poetical narration that mentions fulfilling visions, building improbable machines, and creating impossible medicines. Typical of much university branding, the emphasis is not on learning, gaining knowledge, but on making you into a leader, fulfilling your vision, unleashing your potential.

In MCDA, we can ask how the participants are represented. Here, they are never individualized. We see them only in snatched moments. They are a collective of persons who are clearly signaled as diverse in terms of gender, ethnicity, and nationality. Universities use such representations to help attract high-spending international students, but this also allows them to represent themselves as part of a global future. Ethnic diversity here is positively evaluated, yet we nevertheless find one scene where the complexities of political and economic problems in the Global South can be easily solved by the simple ingenuities of those in the Global North, where we see a white woman presenting the solution. This scene is unique, because while the others represent 'progress', this actually represents a solution. Yet in such a projection structure there is no need to account for how such parts work together, and social justice is easily portrayed as a thankful group of villagers far away and not, for example, more local socio-economic matters, such as children in the US with no access to regular food, good health care, or quality education.

The collective in the film are united both in being dynamic and also by their absolute commitment to the positive world they are creating. Several members of the collective carry the same facial expression of absorption in the moral journey as they create the future. Reactions are clearly important in this film, so the journey, the moral worthiness and the commitment, the positive view unites these scenes. How such faith in technology and advancement relates to drought or to the economies of the Global South does not need to be dealt with. The language, where the verb 'come' is repeated, suggests a kind of moral calling. It talks about 'your strength'. We are told to "Come believe in something greater than yourself." It is not clear what this thing is exactly, yet it is symbolized by the projection of this 'feel-good', go-getting use of technology to somehow build a better world as part of this world family.

Overall, therefore, we can ask: what discourse is represented here? Scholars have shown that education at all levels, including schools and universities, has become more and more treated as a commodity to be bought and sold and branded (Shumar, 2013). Institutions are required to compete for students and resources. Levels of 'success' may be measured by changing forms of quality assessment such as 'student satisfaction', 'internationalization', numbers of research outputs, 'social impact', or numbers of graduates in employment. Institutions from kindergarten to universities can find themselves in league tables where they are ranked nationally and internationally. This whole process is highly criticized. At one level, the measures tend to less represent actual levels of quality. At another, it leads to institutions becoming more focused on outward presentation than on content (Shore and Wright, 1999). At the same time, there has been an increasing process of privatization of education in many societies, where companies are able to take over the running of schools. Such companies understand the role of branding to attract better students to help them maintain quality, even at the cost of staffing and resources (Parker, 2011). The discourse here is therefore one where we find a marketized model of education. In this model, the student is not addressed as a learner, where the institution is the carrier of important knowledge. Rather, they are addressed as a customer who is already special, with visions of an incredible imagination, strength, a potential leader. The university offers these customers an 'experience', where there is intrigue, fascinating shapes, and juxtapositions, and where everyone becomes absorbed in a moral vision of a better future where they are the agents – deploying their imagination, strength, and vision.

Projection sequence in the fitness influencer clip

In the Weibo film by the fitness influencer, we saw an example of a recounting events type of structure. The woman recounts a trip to a nature resort as part of showcasing the relationships she has with her friends, but before she does the recounting, following the orientation, we find a very short sequence that runs for about 10 seconds and contains 10 scenes that flash past. It starts with the longest shot in the sequence, looking up at the treetops. Then rapidly we see the influencer eating an ice cream with mineral water, and in another eating a strawberry. We see her getting a make-over in a salon; we see some exotic birds; and then we see her friends dancing, which, as we showed earlier, runs through the whole one-minute clip.

Labov (1972) explains how one part of story structures can be that there will be a kind of 'abstract', which can form part of the orientation. So there can be a kind of summary at the start that lays out what happens and what might be learned. For example, we are told that a girl sets off on an adventure and finds out the importance of family after she meets what she at first thinks is her perfect romantic match. After this abstract we get immersed in the actual story, characters, and settings. In our fitness influencer film clip, we can to some extent think of this sequence as having this function. At the end, the scenes rapidly rewind, and the actual events are then shown. But we can also think about this sequence as a projection. We see scenes that are not connected by the logic as we might expect in an abstract. The purpose of the clip is about branding the fitness influencer, much in the fashion of what we saw in the University of Michigan clip.

In the coda, the caption tells us: "To all the girls: wish you be independent and be free." What is clear from an overall analysis of the accounts of these fitness influencers is that fitness and diet programs are made meaningful, not so much in terms of body health, but as part of a lifestyle where young middle-class Chinese women express their freedom from the constraints, control, and obligations of traditional Confucian values that are embedded in family expectations. This lifestyle is infused with the idea of making one's own choices, with go-getting, with individualism, but also with consumerism and being modern and cosmopolitan. This sense of freedom and choice is the discourse that is being communicated in the film clip.

MULTIMODAL NARRATIVE ANALYSIS

Just as the university offers a projection about the possible future of go-getting moral worthiness delivered by technology, the sequence in the influencer film clip provides a projection about independence and freedom. We find consumption – of the ice cream and water, Western style; the newly romanticized and commodified experience of nature, complete with imported wildlife, a swimming pool, beauty salon, and Western products in the café; and the friends dance at all times, physically symbolizing freedom and abandon from worry. So we can imagine a life of friendship, fun, and independence, signaled as modern and individualistic through the Western-style consumption.

Figure 6.3 (Continued)

Figure 6.3 (Continued)

Doing a research project using film clips as data

In this chapter we have already given a sense of how the analysis of individual clips can be related to broader issues. To carry out a research project using film clips, we will need to do this as part of answering a clear research question and in relation to a body of research literature. This will mean that if we are interested in the branding of education, selling technology, or social media influencers, we will first need to explore all the research on these topics. This does not mean only research relating to films, but overall. We will need to make a summary of the main findings in this body of research. We can then be sure that we are not simply repeating what is already well known or what has been demonstrated to not be the case. Research can help us to formulate our own ideas. We may want to carry out a case study that simply adds to existing knowledge, exploring it in a new area.

Creating a literature review

Let's say as an example that we are interested in looking at the promotion of universities. We may have noticed that different institutions have what, at first glance at least, seem to be different-looking films. From an MCDA perspective, however, we may want to look a little deeper at identities, actions, and settings to assess if there are actual differences. Before we picked our exact research focus, we would find and summarize the research on marketing education.

Collini (2012) asked what it means if we also expect our educational institutions to either make money or be financially independent. In other words, if they are not supported by the state. Universities, he points out, have been formerly seen as valuable in themselves as places where knowledge could be developed and where education was viewed as interrelated with civilization, the quality of civic society, and human development. We now seem less certain about what purpose universities serve. Certainly now, we expect them to play a role in the economy and produce employable graduates, but this suggests that what universities do is not about knowledge per se, but more about training based on the needs of businesses. This marks a radical shift that is not really talked about.

In addition, it has been shown that there are problems in teaching students as customers. Learning can mean being challenged, struggling, and experiencing humility. But to what extent do such things clash with the idea of customer satisfaction? In the film, the students are not being challenged or pushed, but rather courted. They are told that they have vision and ideas, and should do special things. How does this align with the notion of education as an opening up of your mind, where it may take many years to come to grasp just the mere beginning of a set of ideas?

What does it mean where we no longer have teachers and learners but customers and providers? And where providers must risk-manage in the face of a possible complaint? Research also shows that students become more focused on the availability of books, access to e-learning, feedback, and grades, rather than on their personal development and learning within the subject (Hemsley-Brown, 2011).

There is also a rather simplistic idea of how we make students employable and through which subjects (Alevesson, 2013). It may not be the case that businesses need more mathematicians or engineers. Rather, university education can give people skills to think, act, assess, and evaluate.

Where universities are run as businesses, they must deliver good education but also cut costs. In order to balance the books, they may take on more students, employ cheaper less-experienced staff, or depend on part-time workers (Molesworth et al., 2011). Here they can run the risk of decreasing student satisfaction.

Overall, researchers such as Alevesson (2013) see such film clips as part of how institutions become more and more focused on self-promotion, places in league tables, and financial stability, rather than on the quality of teaching and research. Student satisfaction may also be worked upon, not in the sense of making courses better, or oriented to employability, but in regard to things the students demand, which may in reality run counter to these issues.

Researchers from around the world have carried out more localized studies offering comparisons. For example, Wang (2013) has looked at privatizing education in China. Ledin and Machin (2021) give an overview of the situation in Sweden, where large corporations come to run schools for profit, again operating on the basis of cost cutting, and often using technology to offset other forms of money-saving cutbacks.

This represents only a fragment of the existing research, but here already we begin to understand some of what we are seeing in the film. A more complete literature review would allow us to give a clear thematic sense of what is known and be clear about how we intend to make our own contribution. In this case, a research question may be something like:

> How do universities in two countries promote themselves in film clips?

Or we could ask:

> How do universities targeting different market sectors promote themselves in film clips?

In many countries, universities seek to attract quite different and specific demographics that may relate to age, socio-economic status, or geography. Such research projects can help us to understand the discourses of education and learning now being created by institutions, but can also be used to simply understand and compare branding strategies. We could include an analysis of film clips with an analysis of other promotional material, such as websites and still advertisements using images.

Gathering and managing the data

Which film clips you collect and how many will depend on your project. Remember that for a qualitative form of analysis, the aim is not to have massive amounts of data in order to seek to say things of statistical relevance. Rather, it is to look closely at a smaller number of examples in order to carry out a more in-depth analysis. For an analysis of university promotional films, you may want to gather 10 from a particular country. Or if the aim is to carry out a national comparison of how students are targeted, then you would need to first carry out some background research to look into the profile of each institution, so that you can be sure to have examples with which to compare. If you are interested in films made by privatized schools, you may seek to collect as many as possible, up to around 10, although a larger project may seek to make a collection of all available films. In all cases, what is most important is simply that you explain in clear language why you chose these examples and how they help you. The analysis of the University of Michigan video does not tell us about all universities, but it allows us to show what kinds of discourses it carries, which are understandable in the context of the literature. We might, in a project, look at three more such promotional clips to show how we may find some variations on this theme, but nevertheless the same underlying idea about what education means.

For other kinds of research with film clips, it would be advisable to gather more examples. For example, when dealing with the films made by fitness influencers, we may want to gather 40 of these. In this case, there may be less research literature clearly laying out the kinds of idea and values that are likely to be carried by such influencers. Therefore, after looking at the clips, we will get more ideas about what kind of literature and research may be helpful. In the CDA chapter, we reviewed some of the literature that helped us to understand the Chinese fitness influencers. This explained about the emergence of the Chinese middle-class consumers who are attracted to Western products and ideas, to modernity. We also learned that scholars have observed tensions between traditional Confucian roles of women and newer neoliberal ones, based on independence. Here we had to undertake a kind of detective work to find the research that could help us to understand the nature of the representations found on the social media posts, and this approach is key to doing MCDA. The tools may allow us to show patterns in instances of communication, but the existing literature can help us piece together the meaning, the social and political relevance.

Carrying out the analysis

You will see that analyzing even a short video clip can take up a lot of space, word count-wise. We need to make full transcripts. Even in the analysis, we did not include all scenes due to space, but it is important to do so in order to clearly see how they unfold, which sequences follow on from each other. If there is an interaction or action, we can see better how it is sequenced and edited. A project may simply want to investigate, for example, how one kind of action or interaction is represented. The transcription also allows us to clearly see the relationship between voice-overs with the images. So how do the two combine to give us a sense of what is going on? While making the transcriptions is time consuming, it can open our eyes to what is taking place. We may not need to transcribe all of our sample, if it is large, but transcription should be done wherever possible.

We should go through each transcription asking about participants, actions, and settings. In each case, note how these are presented in images and language. We can even present these, in the first instance, as a table. Being systematic in this way means we can see things that can be easy to miss. For example, in the fitness influencer video, it is easy to miss the fact that their actions do not involve doing things in nature other than dancing, even though the film recounts a trip to a nature resort. In the university film, it is easy to overlook that we always see the students alone or in small groups, never in larger numbers. We see them in larger spaces rather than filling large lecture theaters.

Presenting the findings

Given the space required to analyze a film clip thoroughly, we might choose to look at one or two in depth, as case studies. Remember that MCDA seeks to show how instances of communication carry less obvious models of the world buried in it. We might refer to our sample as a whole as we go along, but would relay no key examples. So we may include the entire transcription in an appendix. Then in the analysis, we may include scenes or extracts of sequences as we make our observations.

We would also use themes to present the findings, rather than talk through each clip. You can see how this might be done for the fitness influencer in the CDA chapter. For the university clip, themes might be:

> *What does the university offer?*
> A chance to make the most of your vision, ideas, and strengths. A place for the coming together of minds.

> *What is learning?*
> A kind of deep moral immersion in making a better world through technology, creativity, and innovation. We see tradition, but only in buildings to connote 'higher ideals'.

What does the university look like?
Small groups and individuals doing exciting things in empty, spacious, intriguing settings.

Before we present these themes, using scenes from the clip to make our case, we can explain how it is a projection structure, where it is never clear what is actually taking place or being achieved. Yet this structure is useful for avoiding such things, for presenting a vision or general sense of commitment, or striving for an idea in the manner of branding.

Drawing conclusions

So, what is the discursive script here? And most importantly, how have we answered our research question? Have we made a contribution to the literature? In the case of the university promotional film, it helps to show just how students as consumers are not encouraged to see learning in relation to self-development, being challenged, as a kind of apprenticeship, gaining skills from those with more experience. It is not about engaging in traditions of knowledge. It is about developing their visions, having their ideas realized. Such ideas will change the world in obvious and exciting ways, and university looks pretty much like good fun. What this glosses over is funding, where universities have to remain cost-effective, where the latest technology and best staff may be expensive. It also conceals the realities of the hard work, the slow pace of actual learning, and the humility and self-responsibility required to allow oneself to be open and be challenged.

ONLINE ETHNOGRAPHY

Introduction

This chapter seeks to explain and exemplify what online ethnography is and how it can be applied successfully in social media environments. Since online ethnography is an approach that has become increasingly multidisciplinary, the present chapter will provide a broad account that is useful in different research and study contexts. Illustrating this breadth, notable contributions to online ethnography range theoretically from sociology (Hine, 2000) and anthropology, to media and communication studies, cultural studies (Pink et al., 2016), and marketing (Kozinets, 2010, 2015). In short, online ethnography is about creating knowledge about contemporary cultural phenomena by taking account of relations, perspectives, and communication in particular online settings, often in direct contact with insiders who know the studied setting very well. Of particular interest is how insiders make sense of their activities (Hine, 2000) and by which means they get by in the studied situations. The better an ethnography is, with its account of views and behaviors in the culture, the more useful it is compared to other accounts for someone visiting the culture (Humphreys and Watson, 2009). In practical terms, this means carving out an area or issue online to study, entering the environment and getting acquainted with it, and staying there for a time, perhaps weeks or even months or years to gather information and gradually create greater understanding. In this online ethnographic pursuit, Kozinets (2010) explains that mainly three tools are used: gathering archived data, participatory observation which includes taking fieldnotes, as well as interviewing.

What characterizes online ethnography is that it is also about achieving a certain naturalism in the fieldwork, meaning that you create an understanding of the environment and its crowd without affecting them too much, without experimental design that changes the conditions of their behavior and imposes predetermined issues akin to hypothesis testing. In this regard, one can also distinguish different directions within, or extensions of, online ethnography (Bertilsson, 2014: 4). One direction of online ethnography, netnography, especially includes far-reaching ideals of naturalism, and its proponents have therefore preferred to draw on data that already exists, without interference of the research projects, and avoid so-called obtrusive methods such as interviews (Kozinets, 2010). Later, however, many netnographic studies have been seen to go too far in a direction of distanced analysis of archive data, so to the extent that borders to content and text analyses blur, and whereupon a new commitment to increased, active, and personal involvement in studied environments is noted in netnography (Costello et al., 2017; Kozinets, 2015). Thus, the subfield of netnography may be approaching the mainstay of online ethnography again, where active, participatory observation has always been a main method and questions for informants a way to get insiders to share cultural knowledge (Boellstorff et al., 2012). Getting to know enough about the culture and writing without judgment requires, as Christine Hine explains, that ethnographers inhabit "a kind of in-between world, simultaneously native and

DOI: 10.4324/9780429319334-7

stranger. They must become close enough to the culture being studied to understand how it works, and yet be able to detach from it sufficiently to be able to report on it" (Hine, 2000: 5). Thus, there are reasons to have a direct dialogue with insiders of the studied culture.

Consequently, from this perspective of learning from the informants, it is logical that online ethnography is usually an inductive research endeavor. Research questions can take shape while fieldwork is in progress. Moreover, unlike other research, online ethnography as well as traditional ethnography often presents its end product with a strong sense of narrative. The entry to the milieu, acclimatization, the learning experience, observations, illuminating interview extracts, and conclusions are ideally woven together into a highly readable story (see, e.g., Boellstorff, 2008; Nardi, 2010). This ethnographic genre is not always the end result, however, and particularly less so in scientific articles outside ethnographic specialist journals. Yet the narrative and rather personal form of presentation is still part of what is characteristic of ethnographic research, whether online or offline. Through this approach, the ethnographic tradition presents an alternative to mainstream research, which is often presented in a decontextualized, fragmented, and intentionally impersonal way.

Given this brief outline of what online ethnography is, what can be studied with the help of this research approach? Indeed, there is the opportunity to embark on relevant ethnographical inquiries for most social science and humanities disciplines and regarding numerous online environments. Some of the more famous work in online ethnography have been about the life and culture of gaming communities, which especially populate social media such as Discord. Studies that come to mind are the now-classic online ethnographies of Nardi (2010) and Boellstorff (2008) on *World of Warcraft* and *Second Life*, respectively. To extract lessons for the area of marketing, researchers and students can engage in consumer communities on forums and in other social media. In health sciences such as nursing or psychiatry, students and researchers may enter online environments where issues of health, illness, or at-risk behavior are topical. A third area for ethnographic inquiries online is political mobilization and communication. There are many issues to inquire regarding communication and meaning making in democratic settings, but also where democracy is circumvented or where extremist groups are gaining footing.

Given that many disciplines employ online ethnography, this chapter will cover research that can serve as inspiration for studies in various areas. It will also attempt to demonstrate general principles that can serve as a guide in the design and conduct of online ethnographic research focusing on social media environments. In the following two sections, we provide a historical background to online ethnography as well as insight into recent years' research. Thereafter, research design and analytical tools are covered, and lastly how the results of an online ethnography may be written and presented.

A brief history of online ethnography

Decades before the Internet, ethnography was about the researcher going to a different place and culture, taking part in everyday life, and going back home to report about it (Geertz, 1973). Just as traditional ethnography was about visiting and reporting about a setting perceived as different, the first conceptualizations of online ethnography focused on this place – *cyberspace* – as something quite different, and what it entailed and could bring. The Internet milieu was referred to as a *virtual* environment (see, e.g., Gray and Driscoll, 1992; Lindlof and Shatzer, 1998). An entire research program in the UK, early on, focused on "*Virtual* cities, *virtual* universities, *virtual* community care, *virtual* organizations, *virtual* decision making environments" (Wittel, 2000: 3, our italicization). This emphasis on a virtual arena different than the 'real' is not so strange given that researchers indeed observed something that was new. Still, occasional research observed the interplay between offline and online activities, such as an in-depth study of a bulletin board café where members also met offline (Correll, 1995). Later, it has become more common to see various online activities and spaces as products of our culture in general rather than as something that exists alongside it.

After somewhat scattered studies and theoretical papers on online ethnography in the 1990s, Hine (2000) was probably the first to summarize the research and present a more comprehensive methodology for online ethnography. Her account of online ethnography begins by suggesting that rather than technology alone being an agent of change, uses and understandings of the technology are central too. She wrote: "Beliefs about the Internet may have important consequences for the ways in which we relate to the technology and one another through it" (p. 8). Testifying to this, entrepreneurs saw at the time of the publication of her book great opportunities in online shopping and would draw on technological innovations, which would soon fundamentally change how commerce is conducted. The same applies to online music distribution, which would transform the music industry whose core business had been the sale of physical records, and which would soon leave the business model of record companies behind. The existence of technology did not mean that sectors changed overnight, but change was also contingent on people's beliefs and therefore their willingness to invest.

Other interesting points in *Virtual Ethnography* concern the dichotomy between online and offline, the virtual and the 'real', which Hine along with others questioned. First, whereas some early literature had presumed that cyberspace transcended time and space, Hine rather saw an interplay between online and offline activities and varying and interconnected aspects of space and time. A second point concerns authenticity and the presumption that cyberspace was characterized by people appearing behind made-up identities, thus again emphasizing the online world differing from the authentic, real world. Again, Hine put forth a more nuanced argument, stating on the one hand that statements online are indeed traceable to actual identities offline, and that empirical studies do not show particularly frequent or striking differences between identity expression online and offline. In the 2020s, we can see the validity of Hine's points, that although it is possible to appear online behind false identities, individuals can usually be tracked and revealed (De Simone, 2021) and, similarly, encrypted social media can eventually be decrypted with extensive consequences, like in the case of Encrochat (United Kingdom National Crime Agency, 2021). Furthermore, with the growth of networking sites and the proportionally lesser popularity of bulletin boards where made-up avatars are used, identity expression online has not become so much about taking on an imagined identity, as perhaps striving to be and appear as flawless and likeable as possible. While a majority of people nowadays use at least one social media platform to connect with friends and family (Auxier and Anderson, 2021), some ambitiously emphasize different aspects of their person on multiple platforms, which may be a professional identity on LinkedIn, political opinions on Twitter, and fashion or fitness on Instagram.

At the same time, we cannot write off partially non-authentic identities and avatars online, because they still dominate discussion forums. Even more imagined identities thrive in the world of online gaming, where the imaginary is an end of itself, and appearing inauthentic is neither immoral nor contrary to shared objectives. Research on online gaming is also a field that has contributed to the development of online ethnography, not least with prolonged participatory observation that has enabled greater understanding of these online environments. For example, Tom Boellstorff participated in and observed for an entire two years the game *Second Life*, which resulted in the ethnography *Coming of Age in Second Life*. The study focuses on several sociological issues that are usually studied in the offline world, such as gender, conflicts, resources, race, and the relationship between individual and group, emphasizing that *Second Life* is a cultural creation like many other human, cultural phenomena (Boellstorff, 2008). Another online ethnography, Pearce (2009) studied how a fan culture around the game *Uru: Ages Beyond Myst* developed in unexpected ways both through the affordances of design and the creative, collective action of a group of breakaway gamers. Finally, Bonnie Nardi's book, *My Life as a Night Elf Priest: An Anthropological Account of World of Warcraft*, must also be mentioned in this context. Compiling more than three years of participatory research regarding the culture of the game *World of Warcraft*, Nardi (2010) provided an understanding of the seemingly more extreme aspects – the game's characteristics or culture involving issues of violence, sexism, and gambling addiction – while also describing in such detail the less attention-grabbing and routine practices of the gamers of *World of Warcraft* that their lives become quite fascinating.

Around this time when extensive ethnographies were published on multiplayer games, what we commonly regard as social networks developed and grew exponentially. At this point, Gershon (2010) presented one of the earliest and most comprehensive studies on Facebook – a platform she situates in a multifaceted media environment that offers users many alternatives and sometimes difficult trade-offs and social dilemmas. She focuses on how people reason about and handle breakups and uses of Facebook, at a point where the platform lacked some of the norms that already had matured in more established means of communication. During Gershon's fieldwork in the years 2006–2007, the team behind Facebook introduced a new function, so that status updates became visible in other people's newsfeeds. Suddenly, information about relationship statuses and gossip about relationships reached wider circles of friends and involved an audience in the blink of an eye. To make sense of these social phenomena, Gershon uses some key concepts. She believes that so-called *media ideologies* – perceptions of the characteristics and status of different technologies and means of communication – affect how the particular media is handled. Furthermore, she uses the term *remediation* to describe that these different means of communication are also perceived in relation to each other along different variables, from informal to formal communication, from fast to slow, from personal to impersonal, and so on. Thus, different technologies as well as modes of communication, such as written and oral communication, complement each other. What media is used when is not always a given, but is something that is regulated in relationships, through friendly advice and through rules of thumb, what Gershon calls *media idioms*. Using these concepts for analysis of Facebook and the social relations around breakups, Gershon demonstrates that more social dilemmas are added when more ways to communicate present themselves. This is especially true when the socially regulated *media idioms* are not fully established, and at the same time personal privacy is at stake, which means that users have ethical issues to deal with which, Gershon says, justifies some caution.

Current research areas and case studies

In the 2010s until now, numerous ethnographic studies exploring social media environments have been published. Quite a few of these are found in the areas of marketing and consumer culture. In this field, Robert Kozinets has been influential with his take on online ethnography, with the methodological and ethical principles of *netnography* (Kozinets, 2010). Several case studies draw on the method. For example, Colliander and Haughe Wien (2013) study online forums and demonstrate how consumer communities come to the defense of their favorite companies or brands, employing six different 'defense styles': advocating, justifying, trivializing, stalling, vouching, and doubting. The study also examines the reasons for choosing either defense strategy. The authors conclude that fan interventions of this type are effective in stopping or mitigating negative word-of-mouth. Also studying consumer culture, Cristofari and Guitton (2017) propose an operative framework for situations where researchers are also fans in the context studied, the so-called *aca-fan* (academic and fan). They pinpoint some benefits of being familiar with both the languages of fan communities and academia, and therefore that the role of an aca-fan is to integrate knowledge and suggest practical advice. Moreover, Obiegbu et al. (2019) investigate what constitutes and underlies loyalty to music artists. While research in a positivist tradition has seen consumer loyalty as a bias, this online ethnography shows what type of social community, meaning, and retention that fandom can entail, and how loyalty is realized through discursive tokens of preference, emotional attachment, and indeed commitment and vis-á-vis opinions about other acts. To read more about research in marketing that uses online ethnography, or netnography as many in this field prefer, one resource is Heinonen and Medberg (2018), who cover no less than 321 studies published in marketing journals between 1997 and 2017.

Another area where we have seen several ethnographic studies online is political communication. A number of studies focus on online forums and groups for citizen interaction. Fernández Villanueva and Bayarri Toscano (2021) show in a study of the use of memes in WhatsApp that irony and humor are used in new ways to counteract and arouse public opinion against political opponents, in this case in Brazil. The approach included observing the activities of a WhatsApp group with a few hundred members and collecting and analyzing a sample of 132 memes that were shared. Furthermore, reporting from five years of online ethnography from Chinese forums, Han (2015) describes how a seemingly voluntary group uses online communication to establish political identity and counterattack political critique. The case study exemplifies group activities online that are neither to be regarded as state-initiated censorship nor as siding with political opposition, which are regarded as more common online practices in this context. Thus, this online ethnography adds knowledge about new communicative aspects of the political landscape. Similarly focusing on forums, some of the work of Jakob Svensson focuses on political discussions in a Nordic online community, Qruiser. The research points in different ways to how polarized political positions are enacted and attempts at persuading others remain rejected (Svensson, 2014, 2015, 2018). Taking a somewhat different approach, Laaksonen et al. (2017)

combine both big data analysis and the qualitative tradition of online ethnography to examine candidate-to-candidate interactions. They observe that when candidates who are competitors within the same party interact on Facebook, they are fairly neutral to each other. The more heated exchange of words arises between rivals from different parties, in what the authors call "an extreme form of negative campaigning," but they also notice a certain fairness in the fact that the politician who is attacked can respond immediately (p. 121). One last example we want to address concerns more extreme ideological online expressions. Khosravinik and Amer (2020) demonstrate with their analysis of YouTube material how the terror sect ISIS utilizes social media strategically to win over supporters of their jihadist ideology. The authors break down how ISIS discursively divides the world into, on the one hand, a virtuous religious ingroup and, on the other hand, an evil outgroup backed by alleged hegemonic media and military power. This discursively constructed division utilizing idealization and deprecation forms the rhetorical basis for justifying the group's use of violence.

A third area that we would like to highlight comprises online ethnographies in health-related research. To better understand the role and risk of social media content on the topic of self-harm, Lavis and Winter (2020) presents an online ethnography that drew on observations and content from Twitter, Reddit, and Instagram, together with semi-structured interviews. The results show a much more complex role of social media in the context of self-harming behavior, beyond previous ideas that content featuring self-harm makes the behavior contagious. The authors show that people who already engage in self-harming behavior or are at great risk of doing so take part in this type of material online. The causes of self-harming behavior are thus not online-related in nature, but rather have to do with experiences of stigma, mental illness, and long waiting times or a high threshold for getting help from healthcare services. The material also shows that platform users are supportive of each other in different ways, by giving each other advice and aid in seeking help, which again refutes the simplified picture of the social media content as something causing contagion. Similarly, Nimrod et al. (2012) examine the role of leisure and social support for people struggling with depression. The results demonstrate the positive role of social contacts, including communication in the 25 online forums studied, for people's well-being. The study also points to the need for ways to break those patterns when participants end up in periods of loneliness leading to more ill health, followed by more isolation, in a negative spiral. Yet another group that both provides and seeks support through online communication are military veterans. Schuman et al. (2019) studies 17 so-called milvlogs on YouTube, yielding seven prominent themes in the material: "motivation, loss, managing symptoms, help-seeking, guilt and shame, suicide, and connecting to other veterans" (p. 357). The authors conclude that the online communication helps the veterans to connect to others socially, relate to each other's experiences, raise awareness and support for alleviating problems facing members of the group, and finally share information on mental health prevention and support.

Also relating to health, but criminality as well in large parts of the world, Underwood (2016) examines a subculture's attitudes toward the use of image and performance-enhancing drugs (IPEDs). He conducts an online ethnography of Facebook fan pages dedicated to Zyzz, a fitness persona and alleged IPED user who passed away at a young age but still managed to build a respectable social media following. The study demonstrates that IPED use, previously associated with bodybuilding at higher levels, is now accepted in some circles of recreational strength athletes. Substances that are commonly considered immoral and unhealthy are instead represented by forum participants as beneficial, as related to self-realization, and as one's own individual right to use. In addition, they consider criminalization unsuccessful and entailing increased risks, thus adding to a discussion of alternative strategies such as risk mitigation instead of prohibition. In a similar online ethnography, Demant et al. (2019) show that widely used social networking sites such as Facebook, Instagram, Snapchat, and Facebook Messenger are used intensively to sell drugs. Open social networks thus complement darknet sites and cryptomarkets for drug dealers and users, and although the use varied as to which social medium was used more for drug purchasing and why, open social networks were generally used frequently for drug trafficking in the Nordic countries.

Finally, the formation of identity through online communication is a theme that runs through several studies, regarding various themes such as the situation of migrants (Schrooten, 2012), the practice of self-naming (Gatson, 2011), controlling the level of publicness of one's photos (Skageby, 2008), and multilingual groups (Kulavuz-Onal and Vásquez, 2018). The theme of identity also runs through a series of studies by Mirza Georgalou about issues of privacy online (Georgalou, 2016), self-presentation and age (Georgalou, 2015a), and the Greek debt crisis (Georgalou, 2015b). Certainly, identity will continue to be studied through online ethnography in the future as well.

As the overview of existing research has shown, online ethnography is a thoroughly multidisciplinary research approach. Even if the brief review is far from complete, it may be used to orientate oneself on issues that are possible to explore further. Set against this background with examples of studies and issues that have been studied, the next section deals with crafting a research problem, the research questions, and overall research design.

Planning an online ethnography

In the following section, we will describe how an online ethnography can be planned and implemented step by step. Although the structure may look neat and tidy, the reader should be aware that the ethnographer at various stages can return to sections, rewrite, and improve them. The process is iterative, and the work thus shifts focus back and forth between different steps and sections to ensure the highest relevance and degree of coherence (Hammersley and Atkinson, 2007).

A first step in the planning of an online ethnography is to start developing a research problem. A research problem can be described as the very motives for a certain study to be carried out. We usually consider two types of motives, those that stem from understanding the specific field of research and those that stem from our own observations of online behavior and public debate. Both types are important. Developing research-related motives assures that we build on what others have done and do not waste time reinventing the wheel. Since online ethnography is about creating in-depth knowledge of cultural phenomena, we may seek to contribute with a certain study in an area where this is lacking. Such was the case with the online ethnography of Demant et al. (2019) on how the most commonly used social networking sites are used for drug sales, as well as Schuman et al. (2019) on war veterans' YouTube videos. The researchers indeed entered somewhat uncharted territory. Having read and understood existing research is a prerequisite for navigating towards a study object that adds something a little different. Furthermore, developing motives for a particular study based on observations of online behavior and public debate is also important because it adds societal relevance. Observations and reflections from everyday life and media consumption can lead to highly motivated and creative ideas. However, such research endeavors must always be anchored and shaped in relation to existing knowledge. We cannot develop new studies sitting by ourselves on a stump in the forest, at least not without a pile of literature by our side or with a laptop connected to a research database.

The research problem should logically lead to the study's purpose and research questions. In online ethnography as well as traditional ethnography, the purpose of the research is usually exploratory. This means that we do not look at a particular situation to test hypotheses from the onset, but the most relevant questions may emerge as one's knowledge of the studied setting increases. Ideas for more specific research questions can take shape as the researcher becomes more familiar with the studied community.

An exploratory, descriptive research aim can be exemplified through research by Skageby (2008: 290) on photo sharing, whose purpose was "to examine end-user concerns and intentions regarding contributions in between the pure private and the pure public." Set against such a purpose, research questions focus on eliciting careful description of various aspects of the material under study, as exemplified by the types of questions listed by Skageby (2008) in Table 7.1. Already at this stage, it is useful to consider that each aspect highlighted through research questions should result in 'thick description' (Geertz, 1973), that is, summaries, accounts, and examples of the way insiders' speak on a particular matter, perspectives that they voice, and practices that they draw upon in conversation or that are observed. Thick description is thus about detailing the means – discursive and practical – by which insiders manage the topics that are studied.

The exploratory, descriptive purpose of online ethnography thus carries over to the research questions as, exemplified here, they focus on demonstrating (1) users' motives, (2) what the content consists of, (3) to whom the content is directed, and (4) the practical-technical issues involved in media use. Interestingly, one dilemma discovered in this particular study by Skageby (2008) was that photos are often intended for a closer circuit of friends, although photo posts usually reach all one's followers. Overall, however, the areas covered by these research questions are likely relevant for many online ethnographies. Indeed, it is usually highly relevant to elicit knowledge about insiders' narratives of practices, motives, and explanations as well as the characteristics of social media content.

In parallel with or after research questions have been developed, it is appropriate to locate the field from which content is to be drawn and notes are to be taken. Certain criteria can be established to carve out an online environment to study (Hine,

Table 7.1 Skageby (2008: 290) posed research questions regarding four distinct areas in an online ethnography of photo sharing

Why?	*What?*	*To whom?*	*How?*
Motivations for semipublic contributions	Types and (perceived) characteristics of digital content	Receiving relationships and social structures	Sociotechnical means of directing content

2015). As Tunçalp and Lê (2014) explain, projects can opt for conducting single-site, multi-site, and flow studies. The first of these options, the *single-site study*, delimits fieldwork to one forum or platform. The studied online site is thus technically limited to the users and the area that is available on a domain name and through login. For example, Schuman et al. (2019) narrowed their study of war veterans' vlogs to YouTube, whereas Mariza Georgalou's studies on identity management (Georgalou, 2015a, 2016) and stories of the Greek economic crisis (Georgalou, 2015b) all focus on Facebook. Yet another delimitation could then be to focus on one discussion group or the communication around a certain organization or other actor. *Multi-site studies* are carried out in projects that seek to conduct comparative online ethnography, or alternatively when the project simply assesses that spreading the fieldwork can provide more valid results. For example, Johansson and Andreasson (2017) research various blogs in order to better understand loneliness. If focusing on a single blog, it would not be possible to expose as many varied dimensions of loneliness as they were able to do with a multi-site study. The third option is not to delimit the fieldwork so rigidly, but to implement a *flow study*. At the center is a theme rather than a specific platform or discussion group. When conversations about the topic draw on links and leads elsewhere online, this motivates the researcher to follow the 'flow' of information and consider new material. This seems to be the approach that is the most adapted to how information is structured and used online. However, as pointed out by Tunçalp and Lê (2014) and exemplified by Pentina and Amos (2011), this type of study often takes a particular site or platform as the basis for further exploration.

Combining research materials and methods

Online ethnography is known as a *research approach* rather than a specific method. Researchers implementing online ethnography can utilize a family of methods (O'Reilly, 2012; Willis and Trondman, 2000). To combine methods is something that characterizes ethnography offline as well as online. It is not uncommon that the practice of taking field notes is combined with analysis of archival data as well as qualitative interviewing, for instance. Combining methods can provide a more complete and varied account of the culture under study, and thus more valid research results. Laaksonen et al. (2017) and Pohjonen (2020) justify their combination of methods with the claim that it likely leads to more valid results, as they took advantage of the strengths of two methods while these simultaneously compensated for each other's weaknesses. In his study of Facebook group members' communication about bodybuilding, Underwood (2016) took field notes, analyzed archived discussion threads, and conducted interviews. Adding individual interviews made it possible for sensitive issues (such as IPED use) to be discussed with forum members, which otherwise may have been difficult to do openly in a forum. Moreover, with this combination of methods, used to follow the same group of people, it became possible to evaluate how they conducted themselves in forum discussions and then, during interviews, what they said they did in forum discussions (Underwood, 2016: 80). If only one method is used, participatory observation is perhaps the most characteristic method of ethnography in general and online ethnography specifically (Boellstorff et al., 2012). If other single methods are used, such as interviews or archival data, lengthy empirical engagement and utilization of thick description in the analysis can still make the study reflect the character of online ethnography.

Archival, elicited, and field note data

To sort and review various relevant methods, Kozinets (2010) describes that three types of data are usually elicited or collected when online ethnography is used. The first type is archival data, which is content that already exists without the intervention of the researcher. For studies looking into social media, archival data consists most commonly of social media posts that have already been published and that the researcher can access. For Underwood (2016), mentioned earlier, archival data is forum discussions that exist without the researcher's participation.

Second, there is elicited data that the researcher contributes to creating through, for instance, conducting and recording individual or focus group interviews. Elicited data can also feature notes from more casual conversations from when researchers interact with insiders, talk to forum members, ask questions, comment on posts, or make their own posts that lead to reactions. For example, Ilana Gershon's study of communication on Facebook related to love relationships elicited data that is absolutely central because the study is based on interviews to such a large extent (Gershon, 2010).

The third category consists of field note data. When the researcher explores the field being investigated, and conducts participatory observation, notes are kept regarding such questions as how insiders communicate, who communicates more specifically, what is communicated, and why. Field note data also provides an opportunity for self-reflection regarding the researcher's own experience and role in the community being studied. For example, by creating an online form where researchers noted impressions and thoughts, Lundstrom and Lundstrom (2021) arranged for collective field notes in a project that studied a right-wing political podcast. The form was created with three fields for episode number, publishing date, and time code, as well as fields for more analytical observations such as the protagonists and antagonists that the podcast conveyed. Furthermore, the authors conclude that field notes are selective and transformative in that they treat theoretically or personally experienced noteworthy parts of events, and they convert passages of volatile events into accounts that can be viewed and analyzed again later (Lundstrom and Lundstrom, 2021: 293). This method for organizing field notes can be usefully emulated in further studies of social media.

Different degrees of researcher participation

As for the researcher's involvement when conducting fieldwork, online ethnography most often implies an active, participatory role on the part of the researcher (Boellstorff et al., 2012; Hine, 2015). It can be conducted with varying degrees of participation though. In the specialty area of netnography, leading researchers have occasionally vouched for a passive observer role, where projects mainly utilize archived data, for its time efficiency and unobtrusiveness (Kozinets, 2010), although this approach has later been criticized (Costello et al., 2017; Kozinets, 2015). An active, participatory role is advocated more often in the literature on online ethnography.

A high degree of participation means that the researcher announces to insiders at the place being studied that research will be conducted, and possibly also asking for feedback. Once the field period is underway, the person participates with questions and comments over a longer period of time and takes some of the participants' time through interviews and more casual conversations. Participation enables insiders to explain their choices and ways of thinking, whereby the researcher through accounts of these can convey these insiders' perspectives, which has always been one of the main points of ethnography both offline and online.

A passive, observational approach instead means that the communication that takes place is observed without interference. Typically, this research relies heavily on archival data, as mentioned in the previous section, and thus retrieving existing social media content for analysis. It can also mean longer periods of passive observation, or so-called lurking. A passive role means that interviews or other conversations are not conducted with insiders. As mentioned, it is an approach that has been advocated by proponents of netnography (Kozinets, 2010), but it also marks a difference vis-á-vis traditional ethnography and online ethnography that continues along the same traditional ethnographic principles. When the research relies on passive observation and archival data, it may not be clear how netnography differs from other methods that analyze archived content, such as content analysis (Krippendorff, 2013), thematic analysis (Braun and Clarke, 2006), or text analysis (Carter and Goddard, 2016). Indeed, the latter methods are also applied to online material. In addition, the longer history of these other methods implies certain advantages. They have amassed more methodological literature that points concretely to how analysis of archived content should be done.

Arguments in favor of a passive approach claims that the approach affords the collection of naturalistic data, that it is unobtrusive and time efficient (Costello et al., 2017; Kozinets, 2010). However, it can be argued that it is likely impossible or at least very difficult to represent insiders' perspectives without communicating with them. In addition, the spirit in which an ethnographer works is that of the novice who is seeking to learn about the nuts and bolts of insiders' practices and perspectives (Spradley, 1979). So, during the field period, the researcher does not challenge insiders with alternative truth claims. Insiders are the experts. This reduces the risk of research practices affecting the environment too much during fieldwork.

Moreover, although interviews and other conversations with insiders may interfere to an extent, there may be a greater risk with a passive approach if the power asymmetry during fieldwork – with insiders being observed but no conversations take place with them – carries over to the results with lacking representation of insiders' perspectives. Overall, if participatory observation and interviewing are perceived by insiders as obtrusive, the research practices may deviate from sound ethnographic ethics, which usually advocates that the researcher takes on the role of a novice needing guidance. If attempting to avoid obtrusiveness by completely avoiding participation, any possible presumptuousness on the part of the research may only be delayed to the point when the results of the research are published.

Writing up and presenting ethnographic findings

Writing up an online ethnographic study is a central part of the work. The word *ethnography* is a combination of words of Greek etymology, *ethnos* and *graphia*, meaning people living together – a culture – described in writing. This etymology is also picked up and conveyed in the title of the now-classic investigation into ethnography and anthropology, *Writing Culture* (Clifford and Marcus, 1986). Before we go into the writing in some detail, visual representation of ethnographic findings is not to be forgotten. The ethnographic approach often uses more than one method and provides a sense of a setting and circumstance; hence, it is useful to draw on different modes of communication when creating the narrative that presents the overall results. For example, a study in the field of consumer and fan studies could show in a results chapter actual conversations from the online groups being studied. A few screenshots from the project's selection of data can exemplify a theme in the empirical material and the kind of jargon that is developed. Such a theme could be money and purchasing power, as it is not free to be a fan of commercial actors or products, whether it is an artist, fashion house, or musical instrument. Figure 7.1 exemplifies the interaction in a Facebook fan group of a guitar brand. It shows a series of screenshots that illustrate a certain category of posts – something of interest to the group is for sale – and then a number of comments about the prize unravels, simultaneously creating humor and male-coded camaraderie. In the full-scale implementation of such a project, it would be both ethically correct and beneficial for the presentation of the online environment to ask for consent, and hopefully get it, so that users do not remain anonymized as in this example.

In addition to visually demonstrating the online environment being studied, writing is central to the ethnographic work regarding the results. The writing of ethnographic monographs has traditionally differed from social science writing, and even more so from that of physical sciences, in that it features a more personal, detailed narrative, not so different from fiction storytelling in terms of technique and presentation. It has made ethnographic studies a genre that is worth reading for a wider audience than academics in the field. It includes, for example, the narrative description of scenes and characters, writing dialogue in a similar way as a novelist, and shaping a story of real events that best describes key behaviors and attitudes in the studied culture (Humphreys and Watson, 2009). Moreover, guiding the writing is a pragmatic epistemology rather than an epistemology of exact correspondence. A test of the validity of an ethnographic study is captured in the following quote:

> How well would any individual, regardless of what their personal projects are, cope in the situations covered by ethnography if they were informed in their actions by their reading of this account, rather than another?
> (Humphreys and Watson, 2009: 42)

Central to ethnographic writing, thus, is to capture discourse and behavior that uphold the culture, that may be considered successful, or that lead to complications, and that is revealing of norms, approaches, and attitudes that inform insiders' choices. The ethnographic writing described by Humphreys and Watson (2009) varies, though, from study to study on a scale from minimum manipulation and fictionalization, what they call 'plain ethnography' – which is entirely similar to other social sciences in presentation and style – to maximum manipulation for broad readability and protection of insiders' identities, what they call 'fictionalized ethnography'. Although a highly informative and useful typology, we find some of the terminology a bit problematic. First, the manipulation of data may not be at a 'minimum' or even much less significant in other social science areas, but rather a different form of manipulation in the sense that it can be argued that it depersonalizes the research process, whereas empirical observations undergo fragmentation. Second, we believe that certain characteristics of ethnographic writing can be expected to be incorporated into

Figure 7.1 An example of a post and thread of comments from a Facebook fan group

writing labeled 'plain ethnography', and when they are not the writing represents mainstreaming rather than ethnography. Third, it may be problematic to employ a continuum of fictionalization, and making connotations to fictional stories, since ethnographic writing is based on actual observations and experiences, although less significant changes can be made to, for instance, protect insiders' identity. In Table 7.2, we therefore prefer to bring up degrees of narrativization instead of degrees of fictionalization.

The writing and presentational style of many recent studies show a tendency towards mainstreaming in that they adopt the impersonal reporting and structuring of results of general social science (Costello et al., 2017). On the far-left side of the continuum, writing therefore does not differ from the reporting of other strands of social science, such as the results of an interview study or text analysis in an article in a research journal. Impersonal language dominates (absence of I, we, mine, ours) and results, as analytical themes, are presented straight to the point without thick description of the setting. The development of presenting results in this rather depersonalized and time-efficient way is not surprising given the way the method was described, at a point, as centering on archival data rather than dialogue with insiders, and as a naturalistic, time-efficient approach rather than a personal one requiring lengthy fieldwork (Kozinets, 2010).

More typical ethnographic writing may be described as moderately narrativized. Unlike traditional social science, it is common to include a detailed description of the studied environment together with its main characters. The description of a scene, like an episode from early on during the fieldwork, may be used to capture the reader. The researcher's active participation in the studied culture also motivates a more personal language, making oneself visible through pronominal choices (I, we) and through descriptions of one's own and others' actions, reactions, and reflections. As explained by Humphreys and Watson (2009: 43), the ethnographer draws on "the presentational techniques of the novelist," although the content is based on observation and one's own and others' experience from the studied culture.

Further out on the continuum to the right, a third way of writing ethnographically is to draw even more from the novelist's toolbox in terms of writing technique and

Table 7.2 Three ways that online ethnographers write up and present results on a continuum from minimum to maximum narrativization

Minimum narrativization ◄─────────────► *Maximum narrativization*		
The writing implicates mainstreaming of online ethnography in that it is so similar to the structure and style of other qualitative social science writing, with effective presentation and exemplification of, e.g., analytical themes, after introductory sections on previous research and methods have been presented.	A middle ground choice, moderate narrativization involves the use of in-depth, so-called thick description of situations and characters, more personal presence in the text to reproduce participatory observation, and more of the novelist's structuring of dialogue from conversations and interviews, whether individual or in group.	At maximum narrativization, the novelist's narration of events, dialogue, and reflection is fully utilized to create a story worth reading for many but also a degree of adjustment, to protect the insider's identity in sensitive situations, as long as key episodes, behaviors, and attitudes observed in the culture are well-preserved.

presentation skills. Since this approach stands apart even more from traditional science, it may not be something to recommend to novice researchers or students. Truth claims are based on the previously mentioned pragmatic epistemology, that the ethnographer's descriptions of key behaviors and mindsets in the culture should prepare someone who is to enter the culture better than other accounts would. Thus, these behaviors and ways of thinking and their consequences are what should be represented as well as possible. If there is a need to hide an insider's identity, details can be altered such as exactly who has been involved and when. The narrative can reverse the sequence of events and merge characters, if necessary, as long as the important behaviors and ways of thinking are preserved. This narrativization, or fictionalization, carried out through writing and presentation techniques, is especially suitable in sensitive situations when the insider's identity and perhaps organizations need to be protected (Humphreys and Watson, 2009). Thus, the ethnographic strategy for sensitive situations does not have to be to take a step back and carry out the research as a passive observer with mainly archival material under study, but fully participate as an ethnographer using a degree of narrativization and adjustment of details to protect insiders.

Chapter 8 FOCUS GROUP INTERVIEWS

Introduction

This chapter will provide an overview of the use of focus group interviews, emphasizing in particular the study of social media. To begin with, the focus group interview is a planned conversation with a moderator and a small group of participants on a topic that all participants can weigh in on. Usually, the interviews are quite well structured with background material to be read or viewed and several questions from the moderator prepared in an interview guide. But there are also exceptions where the focus group interaction proceeds more like a naturally occurring group conversation, and the moderator's intervention is limited to an introductory explanation and opening question. If done face-to-face or using video conferencing, sessions are recorded, and the handling of data thus continues with transcription before the main analysis is performed. Alternative online methods have informants responding in writing and utilize chats and online forums for the focus groups, thus avoiding the extra step of transcription.

Because focus group interviews encourage participants to speak their minds, they are used to provide insight into people's experiences, perceptions, interpretations, or discourse on various phenomena. A well-conducted focus group interview provides time and space for conversation, exchange, and reflection, and can therefore generate useful research material on selected themes. The focus group interview's long-form conversation is suitable for investigating various questions regarding social media: What do consumers think about the presence of a particular brand in social media? How do relationships with loved ones and friends seem to be affected by social media? How can social media be used by groups that have different types of health problems, and does using social media help them in any way? What risks are different groups of regular users exposed to due to criminal behavior on social media? These types of questions have been studied by means of focus group interviewing.

Exceptions when focus groups may be less suitable than individual interviews include studies of particularly personal and sensitive topics (Kruger et al., 2019) or life trajectories, whereby the one-on-one format affords (a) more confidentiality compared to speaking in the presence of a group as well as (b) longer first-person narratives without competition for speaking opportunities. On such occasions, however, focus groups that use written feedback and offer anonymity may be an option, which will be addressed later.

Undoubtedly, the digital development has brought new opportunities for the focus group method. In addition to the fact that focus groups are used in research on social media use, social media can also be used when recruiting informants. Furthermore, if focus groups are conducted online, it is possible to recruit informants who may live in completely different geographical locations but who have some experience or interest in common that is relevant to the research. Doing interviews at a distance implies new opportunities that did not exist when you, for practical reasons, were tied to a

DOI: 10.4324/9780429319334-8

physical place for selection of informants and implementation of the method. When using online focus group interviews, there is a growing stream of research to draw lessons from (Abrams and Gaiser, 2017; Lobe, 2017; Parmentier and Rolland, 2013; Thrul et al., 2017). Both the recruitment of informants through social media and the conduct of focus group interviews online are topics that are explained in this chapter. Thus, this chapter addresses some of these developments and opportunities online.

Although some aspects of conducting focus groups are new in the digital era, if social media or other online tools are utilized, the basis of the craft of planning and implementing focus groups is still about more timeless things such as proper construction and organization of interview questions. Knowing how to interview – without directing the conversation too much or too little – is a great advantage and indeed is needed when conducting focus groups. Thus, any overview of focus groups needs to address some of the knowledge required to formulate a breadth of questions that cover the topic and arranging them in a suitable succession, with regard to common human reactions, and being sensitive to the informants' statements so that important follow-up questions do not go amiss. This is also an area that is addressed in the chapter.

In the following, a section is provided on the historical background of focus group interviews as well as a brief literature review of recent studies researching social media using focus groups. Subsequently, the chapter addresses the planning and implementation of focus group interviews. Social media is brought to the fore partly in that the examples provided comprise studies of social media, partly through explanations of how projects can utilize social media for recruitment of informants and also conduct focus groups online. Finally, the chapter provides tips on how to work with analysis and the presentation of results.

History and current research

The so-called focused interview, later known as a focus group interview, was developed and made known in the 1940s by public opinion and media effects researchers Paul Lazarsfeld and Robert Merton. Some features that characterized these pioneers' approach to the method are the following: Focus group analysis was assumed to provide information on not only opinions but also motives for and contextual, influencing factors on opinions. The researcher should thus aim to record particularly information-rich descriptions that give ideas about the context and interconnected, explanatory factors surrounding a particular issue. Focus group interviews were therefore also assumed to produce qualitatively different knowledge than opinion polls. Such qualitative content includes, for example, the difference between perceived genuine and non-genuine intentions and how either evaluation occurs. Furthermore, focus groups were seen as a generic method, applicable to any field that seeks to add knowledge about people's attitudes, mindsets, and their framing of issues. Hence, Merton (1987: 566) defined focus group interviews as "a set of procedures for the collection and analysis of qualitative data that may help us gain an enlarged sociological and psychological understanding in whatsoever sphere of human experience."

This broad definition foreshadowed the spread of the method to virtually all social science and humanities disciplines. A final observation to take with us from the early development of focus group research is that the method was not seen as a panacea for solving any research question, but as a method among other complementary methods.

For instance, although focus groups can be used to explore approaches to an issue, we cannot, using focus groups alone, comment on the distribution of the perspectives that have been found (Merton, 1987). So, numbers matter less when samples are too low to have any statistical strength. There is thus reason to approach and present the results of a focus group study in a very different way than if you would have done a survey.

After focus group interviews were established in various types of citizen and audience research, the method was also taken up in the 1950s and 1960s outside of academia by marketing departments and the commercial sector. Focus groups were established to such an extent in this sector that if consumers' views were explored using a qualitative approach, it was done with the help of focus groups (Calder, 1977). It took until the 1980s for the method to become popular in academia again. In this era, quite a few of the studies using focus groups drew attention to social injustices, providing grassroots perspectives on societal issues in media audience research (Morley, 1980), health psychology (Joseph et al., 1984), and critical pedagogy (Kozol, 1985). Since then, the method has been established in a wide range of disciplines.

In the current era, we see continued use of the method and a plethora of studies on social media. In media studies, the research spans studies on how traditional media and social media are integrated (Padmakumar and Rani, 2018), on motivations and preferences for using social media to follow sports (Spinda and Puckette, 2018), or to connect with magazines and magazine genres (Jain et al., 2017), and many other areas. Studies of the effects of persuasion – an area that occupied media studies around World War II – are now much more common in marketing research. Focus groups have been used to demonstrate that brands can use social media (in this case, Snapchat) to provide customers and customers-to-be with a welcoming, happy experience. By appearing as a relatable acquaintance (Sashittal et al., 2016) and by employing "aesthetic, affective and alternating stimuli" in the communication (Tropp and Baetzgen, 2019:130), brands enrich the customer experience.

Another stream of research that uses focus groups examines how social media use affects relationships in private life. The research has demonstrated a range of motivations for and effects of social media use. To begin with, social networking sites can contribute to enhance the efficiency of communication among family and friends and contribute to more symbiotic relationships through the affordances of swift, multimodal, and regular messaging. But carrying a smartphone with social media apps can also involve constant digital presence, and some people increase their control while others experience a loss of independence. There is furthermore evidence of how social media users co-create idealization and normalization of self and others (Throuvala et al., 2019). More specific theories have also been tested in focus group research. Testing assumptions about increased individualization, Mayer et al. (2020) have shown how a younger generation, whose life is more immersed with social media, experiences higher degrees of stress due to self-tracking devices and the comparisons with others that social media use invites. We are also gaining more and more knowledge about individual platforms, as a study by Vaterlaus et al. (2016) is an example of, demonstrating how either advantages or disadvantages of uses of Snapchat can prevail in various situations. On the negative end of the scale, it may contribute to the development of everything from mild jealousy to infidelity. On the positive end of the scale, it contributes to closer and more enjoyable relationships among peers despite physical distances through more multimodal communication, affording that emotions are shown. However, the parent generation is not perceived to understand these affordances and their socio-technical components.

Part of the focus group research on social media use and interpersonal relationships focuses specifically on issues of risk. Focus groups have been used to understand young women's perceptions of serious risks surrounding social media use. The resulting insights are assumed to fit preventive information to young college women (Virden et al., 2014), thus putting great responsibility for prevention on women and not on men. Another more specific theme that is being researched is sexting, which shows that girls and women are sometimes exposed to pressure to send sexual content. In the case of abuse, perpetrators may threaten or actually continue to forward the material for the purpose of devaluing the person, exercising blackmail, or boasting (Van Ouytsel et al., 2017). Focus groups with young men in Australia show that men engaging in texting are above all dealing with the norm of being careful and not behaving like a 'creep'. The risks that women face are individualized, however, in that further distribution of content from men to other men is excused on the basis that there is demand, something that women are required to be aware of. The woman who is exposed is thus seen as someone who is not precautious enough and does not take care of herself (Ravn et al., 2021).

In research concerning health and risk, we have seen a number of studies using focus groups to study the significance of social media use or interventions for groups with health problems such as obesity (Allman-Farinelli and Nour, 2021), diabetes (Malik et al., 2019), arthritis (Muir et al., 2020), substance abuse and smoking (Thrul et al., 2017), low physical activity (Van Dyck et al., 2019), and Snapchat use while driving (Truelove et al., 2019).

Hopefully, the overview shows that there is a very broad use of focus groups regarding issues of social media, and thus several streams of research that are interesting to pursue for new projects.

The purpose of focus group research

The starting point for any study must always be a two-fold research problem, describing (1) an issue of some significance and urgency to individuals, groups, organizations, or even society in a broader perspective and (2) purporting some arguments as to why more knowledge is needed about this area given the research that already exists. When focus groups are relevant, the issue at stake benefits from, and has not been sufficiently researched regarding, people's experiences, perspectives, or discourse (depending on qualitative approach). The problem should furthermore call for knowledge of a breadth of experiences and perspectives, not the distribution of them at group level.

Social media presents numerous topics and research fields where focus group interviews are useful, since all the networked practices involve people co-creating and interpreting the world surrounding them through both content creation and reception, with potential effects on themselves, other people, and organizations. Focus groups are moreover useful when the purpose of a study is to investigate an event that has already occurred, when the events can no longer be observed.

When a purpose for a study is to be formulated and there are plans to use focus groups, it is important to consider what kind of knowledge the focus groups can provide. Considering this question involves evaluating *epistemology*, how knowledge is reached. On the one hand, there are periods and schools of thought in the social sciences where great skepticism has been expressed about the kind of knowledge that interviews, individually or in groups, contribute. As demonstrated by a number of methodological texts (Alvesson and Deetz, 2000; Potter, 1996; Silverman, 2001, 2004), seeing reality as communicatively constructed implies that interview material can be understood as valid regarding questions about impression management, representations, norms, or a culture realized through discourse, but less so regarding questions about the veracity of external events or internal psychological states. A study of ours may serve as an example of research that approaches language as social action, approaching interview statements as co-constructions of positions and worldviews rather than as reflections of inner or outer states.

> **Example study:** Focusing on the emergency services sector's use of humor in social media, Rasmussen (2017) aimed to study how communications professionals working in the sector positioned themselves and others as regards the use of humor in social media. Thus, since social media content was not a source of empirical material in this case, the study's knowledge claims did not rope in social media content per se but rather interviewees' pro and con arguments on the matter.

On the other hand, many other fields, such as studies in the health and nursing sciences, rather treat language as mediation and interview statements as descriptions of inner or outer realities, without perhaps so much clarification of the epistemological assumptions of the research (Vaismoradi et al., 2013). One example is a focus group study by Muir et al. (2020) on the effects of social media use on arthritis patients' illness experience and on the patient-practitioner relationship. It is thus very clear that the study uses the focus group method with a claim to comment on conditions, both internal and external.

> **Example study:** A study by Muir et al. (2020:503) aimed to "(a) explore how the illness experience of people with arthritis-related fatigue is impacted by OHI [online health information] and social media and (b) investigate whether use of OHI and social media has an influence on patient – practitioner relationships in people with arthritis-related fatigue and whether this impacts on their illness experience."

These differences between and within disciplines make it important to reflect on what knowledge a focus group study can reasonably attain and what a particular subfield or journal may accept. What has not been emphasized enough, however, is that one or the other approach is not wrong. Too little attention has been paid to the fact that the differences in knowledge claims across different disciplines using focus groups may have to do with different objects and contexts of study and different resulting ethical considerations. The sociologically oriented organizational and social research that has been skeptical about the kind of knowledge that interviews produce has often been interested in how power relations are reproduced in society, where subjectivities and discourses articulated in interviews may contribute to reproducing regimes of power and inhibit productive change (see, e.g., Alvesson and Deetz, 2000). In research in health and nursing science, however, a statement by an individual is likely situated in a different context and power dynamic. Talking about one's medical symptoms may be the last resort of self-determination and resistance in relation to an ever-more-powerful healthcare system. Furthermore, a statement about one's own state of health rarely has any effect on anyone other than oneself. In addition, the person arguably has some unique access to physical data. So, arguably, the purpose and knowledge claims of a focus group study may differ depending on the study object and its context. There are hardly any good reasons to approach a woman's personal story about childbirth injuries as if we had to do with an instance of social construction that justifies deciphering and critique. Stronger reasons to apply such a framework exist if participants in the research occupy positions of power. Reasonably, critical approaches to interview statements may be used when the context calls for it. What every project should do, however, is to clarify their epistemological assumptions, and in analogy with these align their research method and the knowledge claims expressed through the purpose or aim of the research.

Developing themes and research questions

Once a research problem and purpose have been designed, it is important to find aspects to both focus more deeply on and that delimit the main area of interest. This is often done with the help of research questions, which from the beginning may only be postulated as a few themes to cover. Going over these different parts – the problem, purpose, and research questions – and adjusting here and there to improve coherence is common and often necessary. In the creative process of creating themes, which can later be developed into research questions, it is common to start from theory and previous empirical studies.

A good starting point can be to try to identify a contradiction or dilemma of some kind. Some of our research (Rasmussen, 2017, 2020) has taken interest in the fact that public authorities tend to adopt management practices from the corporate world, although their own organizations are not regulated in the same way and do not share all those same goals. One example is when branding, which encourages organizations to highlight their unique offering, is to be embraced by state-funded hospitals whose mission is to provide the same high-quality care throughout a country. Their mission is *not* to be unique. Unreserved implementation of branding is thus likely to create inconsistencies and identity issues (Sataøen and Wæraas, 2013). Considering such a trend, this research turned to the question of how bureaucracies that historically have communicated quite formally in the public domain now manage their social media presence on platforms that contain a lot of informal and personalized content. Indeed, things that go viral often incorporate humor or a personal touch, yet there are still demands on public authorities that they uphold a standard of objectivity, impartiality, handling equal cases equally, and so on (du Gay, 2008). There seemed to be an interesting dilemma in all of this. Emerging dilemmas and issues regarding identity would be especially evident in interviews with those who work with this type of communication. It was also an unexplored area, which gave further reason to focus on it. A few themes to explore in particular were the following:

- To what extent are statements about social media use, the self, one's organization, and citizens encompassing a marketing logic?
- How far can you go using humor in social media and remain 'in character' as a public authority?
- Does any dilemma arise from social media use and, if so, what conflicting practices and norms does it involve?

Although the project would cover these themes, it is important to clarify that they were not questions for interviewees to answer. The difference between questions that the researcher has to answer and questions that the interviewees have to answer becomes greater the greater the level of abstraction that the research applies. Abstraction, it should be added, refers to conceptualization. When applied well, the chosen concepts denote patterns identified in observed practices, but the concepts and observed practices are not the same. The concepts that the research apply are related to but distinct from observed practices (Wallis, 2014). It can also be said that the more general, explanatory claims the concepts imply, the higher the level of abstraction. Figuratively speaking, the level of abstraction is higher if the distance between concepts and observed reality is greater. Higher level of abstraction furthermore implies that a greater number of social practices can be summarized and understood based on a limited number of theoretical concepts.

For example, informants could talk in a focus group about their own and others' physical appearance on social media, while the researcher who initiated the interview thinks about the statements based on the sociological concept of individualization, which could also be a theme in the study. Applying a similar level of abstraction, Rasmussen (2017, 2020) observes statements about public authorities' desire to create entertaining content that attract attention from a public that chooses whether to follow and like the content, and sees this pattern as derived from a marketing logic which asserts that what is demanded be offered and that the public primarily chooses between consuming or not, rather than having a multitude of choices as citizen. In that case and others, chosen concepts match observed practice through pattern recognition. Other studies apply a lower degree of abstraction, and systematize observed, empirical material more descriptively, using concepts not far removed from informants' own. Exemplifying this, Muir et al. (2020:501) present a focus group study concerning social media use and health, which mainly deals with the following three themes:

- How online social support changes illness experiences
- Communicating fatigue to health professionals using OHI [online health information]
- Health care experiences online

The concepts that the research applies primarily serve to describe and summarize what interviewees have said, which implies a lower degree of abstraction. The theorizing ambition with the concepts applied is thus relatively low. Still, concepts are indeed used to systematize and create understanding of the material. All research applies some degree of abstraction. Which path is best to choose – lower or higher level

… FOCUS GROUP INTERVIEWS

	Low level of abstraction ← → High level of abstraction	
Language as action	Interview statements are treated as 'small d' discourse, contributing to shaping identity and group relations in various situations, but hardly claiming to comment on the bigger picture of history and society ('Big D' discourse) as either cause or effect. Example: Social psychological studies' take on interview statements as shaping and re-shaping identities in a work group or classroom.	The discourse that interviewees draw upon organizes and constructs the world they know – with names and categories – everything from nation states and organizations to identity, values, and experiences. Example: Studies based on poststructuralists, such as Foucault, that approach language use as both conditioned by and reproducing history, institutions, and various human relations.
Language as mediation	Interviews are treated as reports about an inner or outer reality but limited in scope and knowledge claims to a practical situation. Example: Interviews about communication regarding experience and solutions on matters of health, or optimal communication paths in emergency management. Developing best practices is often a priority.	Interviews are treated as reports about an inner or outer reality, as indications of group experience and societal conditions. Example: The approach of classical Marxist or feminist studies to statements in interviews as reports of a reality, but also as symptoms of problems on a systemic level.

Figure 8.1 Epistemological approaches and knowledge outcomes from interview research

of abstraction – depends on the purpose and the field of the research (see Figure 8.1). However, when themes are designed to provide focus and delimitation to a focus group study on social media, it is wise to make conscious choices regarding the level of abstraction, whether the study should summarize and describe – or to a greater extent theorize about – observed empirical data.

Selecting and reaching informants

Focus groups aim to create knowledge about a population of interest. However, as in other studies, it is not practically feasible or meaningful to include the entire population of interest in a sample. Research projects thus need a selection strategy. With a qualitative focus, it is not the distribution of positions that is of interest, but rather the in-depth understanding and variety of positions on an issue. In-depth knowledge of a variety of positions can be achieved with a relatively limited number of focus groups. With a limited number of focus groups, it is also not very effective to use probability sampling, because the groups are too few for probability sampling to lead to the representativeness you want, and the resulting sample still does not have statistical power, which would be the whole point of choosing probability sampling. So, with a relatively small sample, it is better to make a non-probability-based, strategic selection and ensure that the population that the study seeks to create knowledge about is represented. In this process, one's research problem and purpose provide direction and guidance – what kind of issue is pressing and what kind of knowledge is needed – indicating which population is of interest.

If the research is about issues where broad reach and representativeness are important – such as an election or public service news – then it is wise to create focus groups that mimic the variation of the general population as far as possible, with as many women as men, and so further. However, if the research is about a subject such as art and social media, and art that is created with artistic expression at the center rather than for public education or broad reach, then it may be entirely reasonable to select interviewees who are attracted to the art and want to be part of such a study. For the research, it may not matter how the art is understood by a cross-section of the population. The logic of representativeness can rather run counter to the essence of art and its role in a democracy, as it centers on self-expression and does not have a self-imposed or mandated purpose to reach everyone.

How many focus group interviews should be conducted then? Most research concerning focus groups claims that the selection is sufficient when saturation is achieved, i.e., when another focus group only adds more of the same themes and categories as previous groups instead of new findings. However, it is difficult to know exactly how many focus groups are required for saturation to be achieved. Exact recommendations can vary greatly, from two to 40 focus groups, a literature review showed. Guest et al. (2016) found that 90% of themes can be identified after three to six focus groups. At the same time, one must keep in mind that qualitative analysis is not a numbers game. Indeed, saturation means that nothing new and important emerges, and the remaining 10% could indeed be very important. A more micro-oriented level of analysis will also find more that is new in additional interviews than if the focus is only on themes at a more general level of analysis. This range of three to six groups can, depending on the issue and context under study, therefore, be considered low. Depending on the type of study, a sufficient number of focus groups may rather be around 6 to 20. The relevance of a lower, average, or higher number of groups depends on how heterogeneous the population of interest is and how complex the subject of the interview is (see Figure 8.2).

Thus, how large and heterogeneous the population is that the project wants to create knowledge about affects how many focus group interviews need to be conducted. If focus groups are implemented to create knowledge of the range of attitudes on an issue among the general public, there is a need for a larger number of focus groups. Then there are potentially many different approaches to an issue just given the size of the population and variables such as gender, age, class, ethnicity, political views, and urban-rural dynamics. If the problem and purpose of the research concerns a smaller group, then fewer groups are needed to reach saturation. Another reason why you should aim for gathering a larger number of focus groups is if the issue being studied is comprehensive and complex. Complex issues imply more aspects to go over and have views on, rendering a larger variation of possible interpretations and positions. Furthermore, it is possible that few participants per group, e.g., three to four instead of five to six, may require more focus groups to achieve saturation, and thus a slightly longer or more intensive data collection process with more rounds of interviews.

Another viable strategy may be to make an extreme selection, which means choosing focus group members who are likely to deviate from the average population in some relevant way. For example, if you are interested in risk and worry regarding social media use, there may be reasons to select participants based on demographic factors that covariate with high concern. When identifying various expressions of worry in this group, whether significant or not, one can assume that the experience is

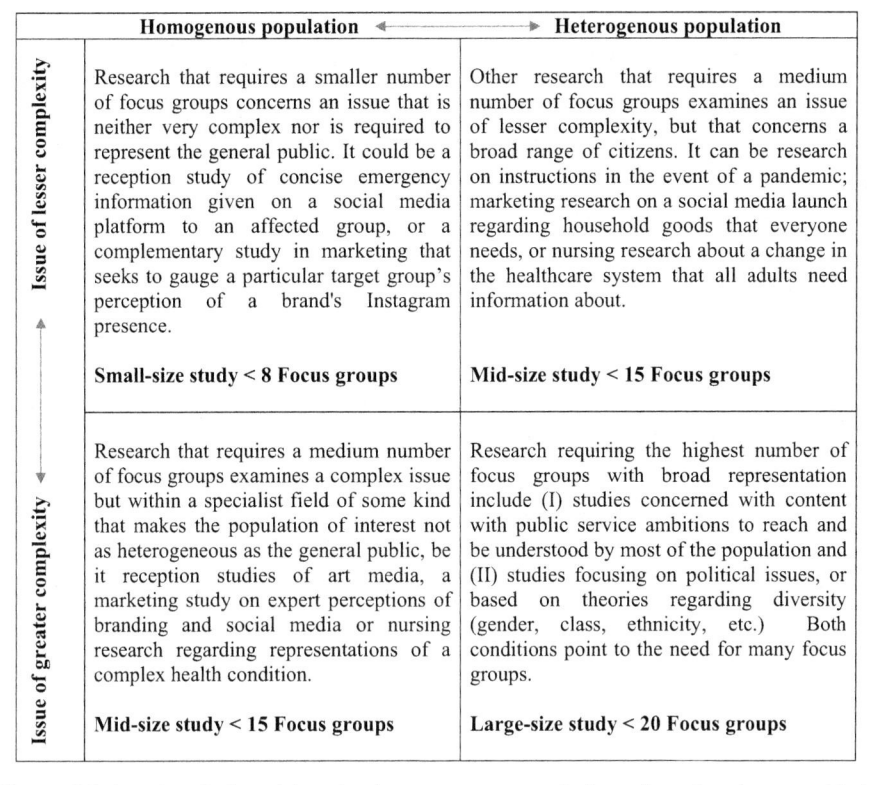

	Homogenous population ←——————→ Heterogenous population	
Issue of lesser complexity	Research that requires a smaller number of focus groups concerns an issue that is neither very complex nor is required to represent the general public. It could be a reception study of concise emergency information given on a social media platform to an affected group, or a complementary study in marketing that seeks to gauge a particular target group's perception of a brand's Instagram presence. **Small-size study < 8 Focus groups**	Other research that requires a medium number of focus groups examines an issue of lesser complexity, but that concerns a broad range of citizens. It can be research on instructions in the event of a pandemic; marketing research on a social media launch regarding household goods that everyone needs, or nursing research about a change in the healthcare system that all adults need information about. **Mid-size study < 15 Focus groups**
Issue of greater complexity	Research that requires a medium number of focus groups examines a complex issue but within a specialist field of some kind that makes the population of interest not as heterogeneous as the general public, be it reception studies of art media, a marketing study on expert perceptions of branding and social media or nursing research regarding representations of a complex health condition. **Mid-size study < 15 Focus groups**	Research requiring the highest number of focus groups with broad representation include (I) studies concerned with content with public service ambitions to reach and be understood by most of the population and (II) studies focusing on political issues, or based on theories regarding diversity (gender, class, ethnicity, etc.) Both conditions point to the need for many focus groups. **Large-size study < 20 Focus groups**

Figure 8.2 A rationale for sizing the focus group sample based on the degree of heterogeneity of the population of interest combined with the complexity of the issue under study

not worse for other groups. Another option would be to select focus group members with demographic factors that covariate with low worry. If this group still expresses concern, then one can assume that the experience is worse among others. Extreme selection thus provides an opportunity to generalize on the basis of previous research and theory, although with some caution of course. Social science takes advantage of such research design too rarely (Flyvbjerg, 2001). Another type of extreme selection may be to turn to groups with special interests. In the field of health, a project may sample focus group members from a group on a social networking site devoted to a disease or health condition. Or if one is researching marketing and is interested in users' identification with brands, the basis for sampling may be brand support groups on a social networking site such as Facebook. An extreme selection strategy can thus be well-suited for different projects in various disciplines.

There is also the question of how many participants each focus group should consist of and whether they should know each other beforehand. If one considers large groups, upwards of seven to ten people, the main criticism concerns peer pressure that arises in sessions with many participants. The dynamics can almost be more like in a large group than in a small one, which runs counter to the purpose of focus groups to achieve open, exhaustive conversations. For this reason, it is good to plan for the groups to be quite small, as in three to six people; it benefits the dialogue and openness of the conversation. Larger groups can possibly be considered if the topic to be discussed is not personal at all.

Another critical point of view is that the discussion is hampered when the interviewees are strangers to one another. Consequently, to avoid peer pressure and a stiff mood as far as possible, projects may also benefit from organizing same-gender groups consisting of friends and acquaintances. In order to avoid an overly unusual social situation, groups are put together with people who already know each other to an extent. When the groups are constructed in this way, the social pressure and interpersonal cautiousness appear to decrease. According to Lunt and Livingstone (1996), it decreases more even than in an individual interview when two people who are unknown to each other meet. In the first focus group study I conducted myself, the informants gave positive feedback on the fact that the group members were familiar with each other: "it was good to know each other in the group. . . . Then you can more easily stand by your opinions. . . . So that you really dare to say 'no, I do not think so.' It gets easier as well." Thus, there may be advantages in maintaining small group dynamics and as familiar an atmosphere as possible. An exception when sampling people who already know each other may not be possible is when looking for knowledge of a special area of some kind, but then the fact that the group has the topic in common can give a sense of community.

These recommendations run counter to some of the research that has emerged that samples large groups of people who do not know each other. Arguably, even if they reach higher numbers with large groups of strangers gathering, the numbers are still not so large that they make any sense in statistical terms. What they miss, however, is the small group of acquaintances, with their dynamism and familiarity, that makes it possible to study group culture.

How is the recruitment done then? If an opinion or marketing institute is hired, they of course handle the recruitment based on instructions on the target group's demographics, but at a fairly large cost. For projects that handle the recruitment of informants themselves, it may be a good idea to turn to associations of various kinds, such as cultural associations, pensioners' associations, or sports associations, with the request to gather a focus group or two from each. When you get information about the informants' level of education and the like, if broad representativeness is important for the topic at hand, you can supplement with groups that are still missing. Studies in health and nursing science may turn to patient organizations and other groups that have relevant issues in common. Similarly, each research area can reach informants.

It is good to get in touch by both letter and telephone. A half-page letter explains in general terms the purpose of the study, why interviews are conducted, how many focus groups and participants you wish to gather, time required for the interview, and approximate time for the interview. If you have the opportunity to nudge with some reward – for example, movie tickets or a small amount of money – that is also mentioned. Once the letter or email has been sent, it is important to follow up with a phone call after a few days. Furthermore, the type of text presented in the proposed letter can sometimes, even better, be presented in an ad where the target audience is located. It can be a paper ad that is posted in places where physical ads are posted, or digitally in groups on social media, or as a paid ad on a social media platform, or even relevant news outlets. Surprising results can be achieved if taking advantage of creativity. One should expect to work hard to recruit informants. It is harder now than it was decades ago, when perhaps the pace of society was slower and the pressure from advertising and telemarketers was less than it is these days.

Creating an interview guide

An interview guide gives the moderator a structure for the interview, questions to ask, and practical reminders that are also needed. A suggested structure is provided in Figure 8.3. Even if very structured interviews are not intended for a project, but rather a lot of dialogue between the informants, it is still good to have an informative interview guide with a battery of questions in case the informants would have difficulty getting involved spontaneously. However, the vast majority of studies are semi-structured. They serve their purpose by including a fairly large number of questions in an interview guide.

Although the majority of the interview guide contains questions, a small part still needs to consist of practical cues and reminders. These pointers can be good to have for any moderator, regardless of experience level, as it is easy to forget something. For example, the interview guide may first of all contain a reminder that the purpose of the interview and the moderator should be presented briefly. This can be followed by a reminder that the informants should be introduced to each other, at least with given names, if they do not already know each other. Then, it is appropriate to ask if it is okay for the interview to be recorded, and in connection with this, the issue of handling personal data is mentioned. This should have been handled earlier, for example, in written information when recruiting, but it is good to repeat it and seek mutual understanding. It is common, for example, to anonymize interviews, but also that exact recorded statements may then be used by the researchers. Finally, a pointer is needed on starting to record. Recording is something no one wants to forget. Then, if the project studies public reception of any material, it is time to present the material and show it to the informants – video, pictures, texts – whatever it is. If viewing materials is not the specified procedure, the moderator goes directly to the questions.

It is important to spend time on the questions to be asked as they constitute an operationalization and the concrete extension of the study's purpose and research questions. They also facilitate a smoothly conducted interview for everyone involved. A first step is therefore to take the research questions that have been formulated and the themes that are found relevant and ensure that the different areas are covered with interview questions. However, it is important to point out that the higher the degree of abstraction a study applies (see Figure 8.1), the greater the difference between research questions and interview questions. In that case, the research questions are more abstract and perhaps critical, while the questions asked of the interviewees intend to stimulate as honest and open responses as possible without any evaluation on the moderator's part. In a study on authorities' use of social media and possible adoption of marketing logics (Rasmussen, 2020), informants' were not asked directly if processes of marketization took place. Doing so could have put the informants in a defensive position or lead them to answer in a certain way. Rather, open questions were used to probe informants to tell about their everyday working life using social media and what motivated them. This ensured that the interview material would constitute a valid basis for interpretation and conclusions.

Furthermore, some knowledge is needed to ask relevant questions. The more a researcher knows about the informants and their context, the more relevant questions can be asked. For instance, if a researcher does not know what social media a certain age group spends time on, s/he cannot begin by asking specific questions about when and for what reason they use a certain platform. It is therefore a good idea to find out as much as one can before creating an interview guide. Maybe there is previous research or statistics that can provide guidance. Another way to prepare for meaningful interviews is to do a very basic pilot interview. Then one can ask, as Black and Metzger (1965) have suggested, which questions the relevant group consider to be important regarding the chosen topic. A project on communication specialists' use of social media could ask a small group of specialists, "what would be relevant questions regarding your sectors' social media use?" Nursing research concerning social media use could ask a small group of hospital staff, "what are some important questions to investigate further regarding health care and social media?" Such a session can provide many valuable clues for the design of the rest of the interviews.

Following Spradley (1979), one can generally also say that short questions often give short answers, whereas longer questions indicate interest. So, in any area, for instance, if someone would like to investigate how younger people use social media, it would be wise to ask longer questions to indicate curiosity and interest. If the interview had touched on a platform such as TikTok, a question could look like this: "I'm not 20 and have never been to TikTok, so can you take me through what it is you and others do on TikTok, what is shared, and how you interact with each other?" This question is likely to elicit a longer description. In addition to taking time with questions, one should not be afraid that the room gets a little quiet from time to time. It gives the informants the opportunity to pick up the thread and share their thoughts on the subject. It also gives room for reflection, instead of questions and answers being delivered quickly and with little thought. At the same time, there is a balance to be kept so that the interview does not get boring.

The bulk of the interview guide consists of the questions. It is appropriate to start with a question that everyone can easily answer at some length, such as how much experience the informants' have in a profession or how long they have been interested in an issue. Then, because the themes covered by different interviews are case specific, what can be recommended in general is the type of questions that can be asked rather than what they are about. Spradley (1979) recommended a number of different questions, including so-called grand tour questions, mini tour questions, example questions, experience questions, language-related questions, and hypothetical interaction questions. These categories of questions were made for use in ethnography, but they are useful in many contexts. The interview guide should include a mix of such questions and reminders to use them as follow-up questions. Finally, after a number of different questions have been mentioned in the guide, it is appropriate to conclude by asking the informants if they think there is something more to bring up, something that the interview so far has missed or they wish to expand on. People often have something more they have thought of to share.

Different types of interview questions

In the following, a number of questions will be described that can be combined in an interview guide. Indeed, it is advisable that each of the study's themes is covered with

FOCUS GROUP INTERVIEWS 163

Pointers
- Introduce the project and moderator
- Short round of presentations if needed
- Ask if recording is agreed
- Start recording

Reception material (if needed)
If material is to be shown for reception/interpretation – introduce and show it

Questions
Introductory questions – easy-to-answer, background questions

Thematic questions:
Theme I ⎫
Theme II ⎪ Grand tour questions, mini tour questions, language-use
Theme III ⎬ questions, example questions, experience questions and
Theme IV ⎭ hypothetical questions (Spradley, 1979)

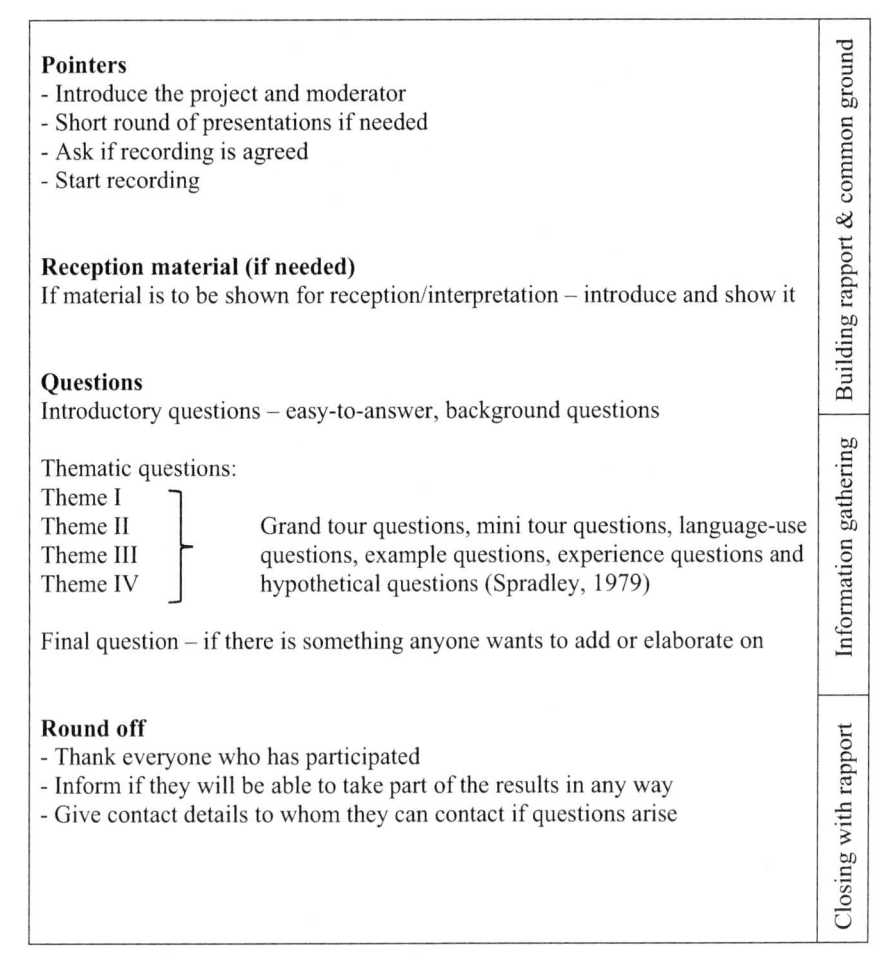

Final question – if there is something anyone wants to add or elaborate on

Round off
- Thank everyone who has participated
- Inform if they will be able to take part of the results in any way
- Give contact details to whom they can contact if questions arise

Side labels: Building rapport & common ground | Information gathering | Closing with rapport

Figure 8.3 Example of a structure for an interview guide

different types of questions. First, the name *grand tour question* refers to the ethnographic situation where a researcher becomes acquainted with the environment being studied by an informant who shows him or her around. Adapted to interview situations, the meaning is similar in that the researcher is taken through different aspects of a topic as the informants see it. A grand tour question should preferably elicit a longer description, and with small follow-up questions from the interviewer the answers and discussion in a focus group can be quite lengthy and detailed. Here are some examples of social media–related grand tour questions:

❏ Assuming that I have made a time travel from the year 2000 and do not know what social media is, can you take me through each social platform you know and tell me, who spends time there and what are they up to on the platform?
❏ Can you tell me about your friends and how you think each of them uses social media?
❏ Can you tell me which social media platforms different age groups use and what they are used for?

Good grand tour questions help the informants to create a narrative with different elements, similar to stopping by and talking about different rooms on a guided tour on a venue. In the previous examples, such cues represent different social media platforms, each of one's friends, and different age groups.

A *mini-tour question* is similar to the grand tour question in that it also encourages stories that cover several aspects of a phenomenon, albeit a more limited one. For example, an answer to a grand tour question about Instagram might mention selfies. Two mini-tour questions can then be asked in the following way: Can you tell me what types of selfies your circle of acquaintances publish? Can you also tell me what steps are included, and what you would think about, if each of you would take a selfie?

Other questions are more specific and are often asked throughout interviews and as follow-up questions. To get informants to talk about concrete practices, it is good to ask *example questions*. When they talk about something on a general level, one can ask them to tell you about an example. In case an organization's social media use is studied, the moderator may ask, "can you give an example of one of your latest social media posts that you think went well?" In a similar project, the moderator can also elicit information about social media practices by asking so-called *experience questions*, for example: "You have all worked in communications for some time, can you tell me about any recent experience of communicating externally on social media about an incident or risk?"

There are also useful *language-use questions*. To understand informants' views and practices, it is good to ask questions about the terms and phrases they use. For example, if an informant talks about Twitter as a push channel, one explores their management in more depth by asking what the phrase *push channel* means in their teams. Alternatively, if someone mentions a post that has gone viral, the moderator may ask, "what does it mean more concretely that something is going viral in your sector?" Another variant of a language-related question may be to ask how the informants would name a certain communicative practice using categories or phrases. The moderator may ask, "what are some technical terms or phrases that would be mentioned in your discussions in the office while you work with a social media campaign?"

The last type of questions to address is the *hypothetical question*. Here the moderator draws a scenario and asks informants to tell how they view it or would act. For example, the moderator may ask a group of communications specialists, "if you want to create a post from your organization that reaches as wide an audience as possible, what are some choices you would make?" Or, "if a major crisis of confidence afflicts the organization, let's say someone in management has committed an immoral act, what do you do then?" Hypothetical questions can often lead to long descriptions and conversations.

Online spaces for conducting interviews

There are many ways to implement focus groups these days. On the one hand, the traditional method of gathering largely homogeneous groups that are familiar with each other face-to-face is still optimal for studying many issues. The similarity with a normal social situation increases the chances of an engaging and open discussion. To be able to give attention to each other as a physically present person calls for, and to fully read body language and so on, should not be underestimated. On the other hand, it is also possible to conduct focus groups online, as a rapidly growing strand of research shows (Abrams and Gaiser, 2017; Gordon, 2021; Lijadi and van Schalkwyk, 2015; Lobe, 2017; Morgan and Lobe, 2011; Stancanelli, 2014), and which may be beneficial not least when studying social media. While focus groups have traditionally been used to create a planned yet as natural an environment as possible – a conversation as similar as possible to a conversation that would occur in social life – one could argue that studies of social media may reach a higher degree of naturalistic participation through focus groups online than if done face-to-face, due to the imminence of the online environments. However, the methods online are also different, where the so-called asynchronous focus group mainly uses writing for informants' responses, while the so-called synchronous focus group, which may utilize videoconferencing, can have great similarities with traditional focus groups when it comes to interaction and the number of issues addressed in one go.

Common to all variants of focus groups is that the moderator should establish some ground rules about communication at the beginning of a session with a new group (Lobe, 2017). This may need to be emphasized even more where exchanges take place in writing, because in oral conversation in groups there is a habit of taking turns. Writing in groups is for many a more unusual situation with more unclear social rules. The moderator also needs to make sure that everyone is involved. Regardless of the medium of the interview, the moderator may need to encourage individuals to contribute their perspective or sometimes let a question go around the table. Moreover, common for the text-based groups online, they should be small, a maximum of five people. With too many people and posts, the conversation can move too fast for the moderator and for the participants to keep up and write their own questions or responses (Lobe, 2017).

Finally, all online interview methods require a degree of computer literacy. This limits to some extent who can participate. Exchanges in writing require good handling of a keyboard, not least in a synchronously executed group. One solution is to take into account how fast the individuals write when creating groups, placing the fast and slow typists into different groups.

Asynchronous online focus groups

When arranging an asynchronous online focus group, certain information about how the interview is to be conducted should be shared during the recruitment of informants. Ensuring that people are familiar with the system, or at least that it is easy to use, certainly benefits participant involvement. Another issue to consider is how confidentiality is handled and how secure the material is if it is shared on a platform with visibility for a group of users. A related question then is if informants should participate with their full name or if their privacy should be protected somehow. These issues all need to be addressed and handled in time and appropriately. The more sensitive and personal the subject, the less appropriate it would be to demand full disclosure.

Since an asynchronous focus group means that participants' statements are sent independently of other participants' corresponding communication, one can expect less collectively created discourse. The method is therefore better suited if the research is more interested in individuals than group culture. If group culture is less in focus, then one can also ask the basic question what the benefit is of an asynchronous group over, for example, a survey with open-ended questions. Perhaps the asynchronous focus group still entails advantages of establishing a certain group community, as well as longer and more thoughtful answers because the participants are expected to answer on several occasions and at times that suit themselves (Parmentier and Rolland, 2013).

The issue of anonymity may be treated differently by different projects. Researching cultural identity issues, Lijadi and van Schalkwyk (2015) did not find strong enough reasons to maintain participant anonymity. They gathered focus group members who befriended each other on Facebook and could subsequently enter a group chat together. In another case, a study on body image issues among transgender and gender-diverse (TGD) young adults, the authors found that it could facilitate the participants' sense of security that they were allowed to register an anonymous username on the platform used for an asynchronous focus group (Gordon, 2021). Different projects thus come to different conclusions on the matter of respondent anonymity depending on the field of study.

When it comes to information needed for the respondents and the questions asked, it is largely possible to follow recommendations regarding traditional focus group interviews (see Figure 8.3 and the section on interview questions), with the exception that not everything is done at once. The big difference is that the questions are portioned out over, usually, a few days (Zwaanswijk and van Dulmen, 2014). Day one may deal with the introductory questions of the interview guide, days two and three more informative material regarding the different themes, and day four a final theme as well as any concluding questions. If necessary, however, the period may be longer.

Some advantages of using an asynchronous data collection method online are that a project can actually reach hard-to-reach audiences, i.e., groups who may live far away, in different time zones, or who have difficulty participating for a longer continuous time. It is also suitable for sensitive research topics, as participants can achieve a higher degree of privacy in answering the study's questions. Given a more flexible time frame, two other advantages mentioned by Lobe (2017) are that the participants do not have to be so fast and precise at the keyboard and also that the answers can be more in-depth as the interview situation is not limited by the turn-taking constraints in a real-time conversation.

Synchronous online focus groups

The synchronous focus group online can be quite similar to a traditional focus group. However, in previous years, much focus was placed on text-based synchronous focus groups online (Lobe, 2017). Then the method is quite different, still, with typing and reading as the modes of communication rather than oral conversation. In recent times and in line with the spread of video conferencing technology, it is increasingly practical to conduct interviews via audio and video applications (Lobe et al., 2020), with quite a similarity to traditional focus groups.

Researchers using text-based, synchronous online focus groups have a choice between online messaging applications (e.g., Messenger, WhatsApp, WeChat, with over a billion users each) or a bulletin board environment (e.g., phpBB, MyBB, or Simple Machines Forum). Similar alternatives may well be found in the universities' own software offerings. What is used the most and the easiest by users may, however, differ between countries and generations, WeChat being a first choice in China as of now but less known in other parts of the world. In research on social media, one can also benefit from group messaging features on the platforms being studied. For example, online research on young people and Snapchat could benefit from the group messaging feature on the platform for focus groups. Similarly, research on Instagram or Facebook could benefit from the associated messaging applications. However, these platforms where many already have accounts can be difficult to handle in case you want to maintain anonymity. Cases when users should be offered to create new accounts apply to sensitive research where respondents should have the option of being anonymous. Then it is advisable to use a platform where it is possible to create an account where the username is not authentic and that provides sufficient security.

Moreover, with a text-based interview, researchers have the advantage that the material the participants help produce is what is used in the analysis. No transcription is required, but it is important to remember to log the chat somehow. Such functions can often be found in the software used. Otherwise, text may be copied to a word processing program now and then.

The last variant to address is the synchronous focus group interview that uses online audio and video equipment of some kind. The method has grown through the technological development in the last decade but also through the social distancing required by the pandemic that broke out all over the world in 2020 (Lobe et al., 2020). This form of synchronous online interview is handled to a large extent as the literature indicates for traditional focus groups, but with the help of tools such as Zoom, Skype, Teams, Facetime, or any other audio-video application that allows group calls. Figure 8.4 displays an online focus group interview conducted during the pandemic.

As the project in question, that we show snapshots from (Figure 8.4), applied demographically homogeneous groups, where some participants already knew each other, it was fairly easy to create a participatory environment despite the online format. Otherwise, one difference that can be noted when participants are in separate locations, seeing each other only on the screen, compared to traditional focus groups, is that the participants' attention can wander to a slightly greater degree. This may require more occasions where questions go around the group or that the moderator particularly encourages some individuals so that they give their views on the issue that is discussed.

Transcription

Before the analysis begins, face-to-face interviews and video-conferencing interviews need to be transcribed. This process takes quite a long time, somewhere around a day's work per one-hour interview. Projects often hire someone to complete transcription, but as a researcher or student transcribing one also processes the material to some extent, which is good preparation for the analysis. The transcription can be performed at different levels of detail. Most research does not have a specific interest in language use, like a linguist does. Then it is enough to use written language principles with periods and commas in the transcription and trim somewhat what is actually said, omitting small doubts, pause length, language melody, and confirming small words from others who do not have the floor at the moment. However, whole words used by the speaker must be transcribed. If something is difficult to hear from the recording, it is advisable to write a note within the brackets. Occasionally you can also write the time, so that passages become easier to find if you want to return to part of the original recording. Moreover, depending on the purpose of the study, the transcription can put emphasis on certain aspects. For example, if the study is interested in

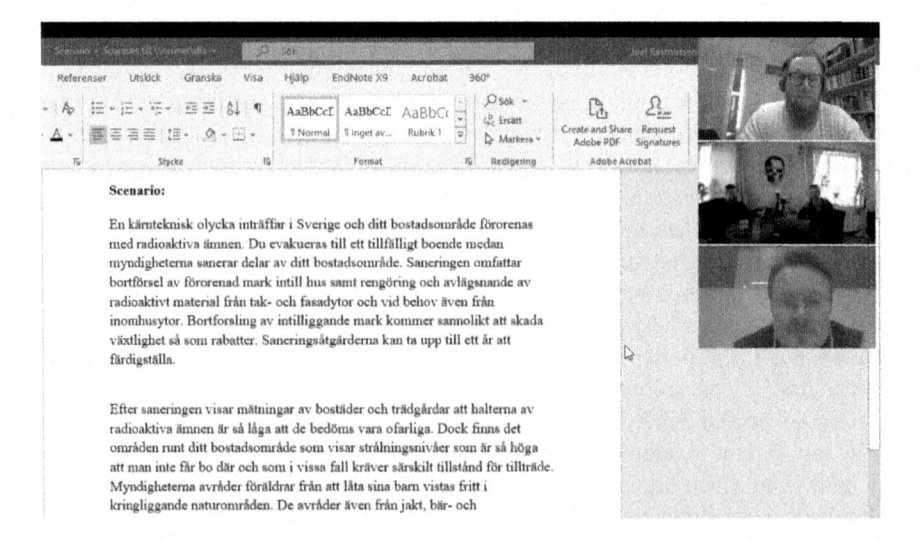

Figure 8.4 An online focus group interview conducted through Zoom, displaying the use of a background scenario to set the theme of the interview (upper image) and then on how the interactants were displayed on the screen (lower image), two participants capturing audio and video in the same room, and two doing so separately (everyone, moreover, consenting to be in the picture)

affect, it is advisable that the transcription includes expressions of affect by italicizing expressions that are emphasized. With greater interest in studying group culture, the researchers may consider making transcripts that make the collective construction of meaning visible, with the notation of smaller supportive words even from those who do not have the word at a certain moment. Depending on the purpose of the study, the translation into text can be made as meaningful as possible. A certain aspect that is important can be highlighted throughout the transcription using select conventions for transcription from conversation analysis (see Jefferson, 2004).

Analyzing focus groups

With often hundreds of pages transcribed, it is easy to plunge into analysis with too little planning. It can also be argued that quite a few studies that use focus groups do spend too little time designing a good approach to the analysis and presenting it, a bit as if the method consists of data collection. It is thus important that a plan is established for how the analysis should be carried out. Common to almost all analysis using some form of focus group method is that it, at least initially, consists of reading the transcripts carefully and thematizing or coding the material. Throughout this part of the analytical process, one focuses on pattern recognition and pattern distinction, based on the research questions and ideas from existing research. A basic rule is that data included in a theme or category should be related in a meaningful way, while at the same time there should be clear differences between themes or categories.

Two approaches to analysis that are relevant to the majority of projects across the social sciences and health sciences that conduct focus groups are thematic analysis and qualitative content analysis (QCA, see Chapter 2). As a guide to whether a study should proceed with either one of these approaches, there are some differences to consider. In general, thematic analysis focuses more on implicit meanings of manifest content than QCA does. QCA thus tends to take a more descriptive stance, adopting a lower degree of abstraction (see Figure 8.1). Moreover, thematic analysis is often more inductively oriented, continuing its legacy from grounded theory – with building theory from the ground up – while QCA tends to be used more for testing hypotheses (Cho and Lee, 2014; Vaismoradi et al., 2013). Both approaches, however, are in the more descriptive phalanx of social research. If one is interested in the underlying causes and aspects of power and language in relation to observed phenomena, other analytical approaches arising from the discourse analytical field may be preferable (see Marková et al., 2007).

Furthermore, one way to distinguish between themes and categories is to think of themes as more abstract designations for patterns in the material, whereas categories represent manifest patterns. Themes are furthermore constructed to a greater degree from the material, in a bottom-up process, whereas categories to a greater extent derive from existing knowledge. The concept of themes thus tends to suit inductive analysis, whereas categories tend to better suit more deductive analysis (Cho and Lee, 2014; Vaismoradi et al., 2013). Depending on the focus of the study, one can choose either concept or combine both. A more discourse-analytically oriented study may similarly identify overarching patterns, but likely with other terms such as framings, positions, social representations, or discourses (Marková et al., 2007), in line with its theory of choice.

The analytical approach may look somewhat different depending on whether the study is strongly theory-driven and deductively oriented or whether it is exploratory and inductively oriented, or something in between. In a strongly theory-driven approach, the study's analytical topics may to a large extent have been influenced by the design of the interview guide, and the analysis is thus not so much about identifying the most overarching patterns but rather about the subthemes or subcategories, how informants position themselves *within* the questions under study. It can thus be quite clear what is relevant and less relevant material, and the researcher may move from one proposed idea to another in evaluating select material. As described in Chapter 2, the inductive approach involves observing and interpreting patterns that emerge and either finding keywords from the text or theoretical concepts that correspond to somewhat longer passages. Part by part, interview material is analyzed that way, with themes and conceptualizations emerging continuously.

How can one begin analyzing then? Using a word processing program, one alternative is to decide that different colors represent different themes or categories, and simply color the patterned text that is identified. This is continued until all relevant material has been managed. When the analyst is done, each color-coded text is moved to separate, soon-to-be chapters for further analysis and inclusion in a narrative. Another alternative is to take transcripts and place them on a horizontal layout on the left, and on the right side create columns for different themes or categories. When reading the transcripts, the analyst takes notes on the right side in the relevant column. A third way would be to mark patterns in the text with words that represent categories or themes. Also, according to these two latter ways, text that has been marked as belonging to the same theme or category is moved to the same section so that they can be further analyzed together. Further analysis is difficult to describe in general terms because it will be based on the approach of the particular project. The focus is often on understanding each theme or category, including its internal variations – informants' different positions or attitudes – using concepts from the theory that the research adopts. The overall patterns described, however, can form the basis for further analysis and thematically divided chapters.

Presenting results

As the analysis has been described hitherto, it consists at the most general level of pattern identification and distinction. These overarching patterns, with categories and subcategories or themes and subthemes, can be used in a good way to structure the results chapter. Considering the structure of an article or master's thesis, each section of the results chapter then consists of a theme or category, perhaps with subheadings that represent subthemes or subcategories. Furthermore, interesting findings should be included in headings and subheadings. Thereby, the author conveys not only the theme but also a major result that belongs to it. This calls for attention and makes reading more fun. For example, a headline from the results chapter of a study on marketing logic and social media in the public sector reads as follows: *The justificatory discourse element – quantitative success*. And another one: *The continuity-creating discourse element – storytelling* (Rasmussen, 2020). The headlines show and emphasize results. Thereby, a meaningful structure and a certain appeal is created for the results chapter through the use of both analytical themes and the active management of headlines.

Furthermore, it is important that each theme or category is handled in both a concrete and analytical way, giving insight into what informants have actually said and how this discourse is interpreted. Some of the excerpts belonging to themes and categories and their inherent variations must therefore be selected for inclusion in the results. A first principle in this selection process is typicality. One should include excerpts that are typical of its category. A second principle is comprehensiveness. One should include excerpts in all the sections and subsections of the results chapter. One last principle is novelty. You should choose excerpts that provide opportunities for new insights. Thereby, the data is used in a comprehensive and meaningful way.

Lastly, this practice of demonstrating what informants have actually said adds to the validity and reliability of the study. The 'coding' becomes partially visible, as extracts assigned to different subparts of the analysis are displayed. The reader can thus evaluate whether this overall analysis seems to be logical and consistent.

Moreover, the extracts included in the analysis should be interpreted by the author. This is sometimes done to an insufficient extent among published studies. They then include examples from transcripts as if the extracts speak for themselves. This is a peculiar inclination in some qualitative analysis. Indeed, what respondents say is not the result of the research. The researcher's *interpretation* of what the respondents say is the result of the research. A good rule of thumb is therefore that every quote from informants should be interpreted, either before it is presented or perhaps, even better, after. Here, there are great opportunities to take advantage of the analytical tools that a chosen theory offers. What the informants say may contain dilemmas that need to be highlighted, they may say things that imply identities that clash, or they may convey norms that should be noted. This is thus an important analytical step. Without the interpretation of excerpts, it is less likely that the study presents something that the informants do not already know in their working community or cultural community.

Furthermore, if performed well, these analytical maneuvers of interpreting excerpts also contribute to the validity and reliability of the study. Anyone who reads the study can see both excerpt and interpretation and evaluate whether the interpretation, again, is logical and consistent. Perhaps the author puts in a higher gear in the analysis with claims that there is not really enough justification in what the informants actually say? The reader can evaluate this, but something that is reassuring is that the researcher or student, and with a circle of acquaintances who also read the manuscript, also can evaluate the work in progress before publication. Here is the opportunity for several rounds of reading and evaluation. Looking at interpretations placed alongside excerpts, one considers whether the interpretations are sustainable and entirely credible. A lot of work should be put into this process of writing, reading, evaluating, and improving. This affordance of transparency and direct evaluation can ultimately lead to results with a high degree of validity and reliability. Arguably, such a procedure is also more transparent and thereby possible to examine than studies whose validity and reliability are based solely on the description of appropriate processes, where the data is in effect hidden.

Chapter 9 CONCLUSION

Situating the book: social media data in media and communication studies

It is no easy task to present different ways of embarking upon qualitative analysis of social media in an entirely meaningful way, as any separation of offline and online activities is becoming increasingly arbitrary. As noted early in online ethnographic research, cultural practices involve an interchange between online and offline environments (Correll, 1995), sometimes within moments. Increasingly, shared and individual life in our societies is the result of an interplay of activities online and offline, in new configurations of space and time relationships that the digital media landscape has brought about. Even more than a decade before writing this book, some were suggesting that we now live our lives in the media rather than with the media (Deuze, 2011). Since this time, we have seen increasing integration of smartphones into all aspects of everyday life, up to the point where the degree of integration seen by one author during their professional life in China had become that nothing could be done without your smartphone. Social media that have been perceived as something distinct and separate, and just one thing among other tools in life, may have to be seen in a different light. They are not just part of communications, but have shaped, as we have seen in the chapters of this book, what we think communicating is, what we accept as knowledge, and our sense of shared experience and community. In practical terms, social media are found in all sorts of areas that we have referred to in this book, from nursing to marketing and psychology, but they are also involved in shifting what we even think these things are and how we can best share knowledge about them.

Moreover, social media also seem to have been a part of a shift in how we feel about things. It has been observed that the neoliberal ideology that now shapes our societies, which sees the individual as a kind of entrepreneurial self-project, self-governing and self-responsible, comes with a discourse that makes this deeply moral. To work on ourselves, our lives, and our beliefs has become moralized. We see this view in the kinds of charged moral certainties that take place in regard to identity politics as well as the moral campaigns of communities, usually done or fostered on social media, from different parts of the political spectrum. Debate can be substituted by affect, which can quickly lead to outrage.

In what is increasingly seen as post-truth society views (Shelton, 2020), it is now increasingly understood or assumed that all things presented as 'facts' are mere opinions. This has become easy for social media to do, as our user habits tend to orbit around worldviews and forms of identity expression that we find familiar and comfortable. Algorithms, too, play a role in this by steering us deeper into those worlds where set perspectives are normalized and legitimized. This presents one of the huge challenges for scholars who seek to understand social media communication. In this case, going back to the ethnographic recommendation that we see media use in context, what else lies behind these things?

DOI: 10.4324/9780429319334-9

Our point here is twofold. On the one hand, social media is shaping what we do, is changing how we approach knowledge, and seems interwoven with other social shifts, but on the other hand, these patterns of 'post-truth' and the rise of the 'regime of opinion' do not exist in isolation, as we discussed in the introduction to this book. In a sense, researching social media is not about social media per se, but is about our societies, our ways of thinking about ourselves, our priorities, and our moral judgments.

As life and media overlap, one may wonder what the reasons may be for even developing methods that are tailored specifically for social media. What we hope to have shown in these chapters is that there is good reason, providing we are asking the right kinds of clearly formulated questions. What makes a good, relevant, and workable research topic or question in this context is answerable in part, we would suggest, by carefully reading the chapters in this book. In all chapters, we show not only how to research, but in each case why we are doing so and what is at stake.

Qualitative methodology in an evolving world

If we now have a mix of discursive, social practices across online and offline environments, it is still the case that a predominant part of all methodological literature is written as if these changes have not taken place, as if we are acting within time, space, and expression constraints of traditional means of communication. Indeed, studies of social media require other data-gathering techniques than newspaper or television analysis, and an updated understanding of partially self-produced, multimodal communication that simultaneously shapes the self. In a more self-speaking society (Chouliaraki, 2010), we have emphasized throughout the book how different actors shape and reshape identity through communication, as individuals or as professionals in organizations. In this book, we have therefore adapted qualitative methods to the conditions that apply in a landscape that includes social media, where a much larger share of people produce meaningful content for others to see than previously in history, and where this content may take some of the forms laid out in the introduction, which includes things such as echo chambers and the retreat into opinion. Social media allows us to look for wider ideas about the worldviews that people hold, even through the most mundane uses and posts, such as a discussion about fitness programs, a girl dancing on TikTok, or a complaint about local policing.

Furthermore, we have valued summarizing previous qualitative research on social media throughout the chapters because an existing body of work can form a basis for further studies, as well as exemplifying study topics and ways of planning and conducting research. Choosing a subject to study and a method are parts of the same holistic process, which we hope to have shown. During this endeavor, and given our background of having applied qualitative research methods before social media was a thing, we certainly did not want to throw the baby out with the bathwater either. Everything that is still useful with research methods as they were described 20-plus years ago, we try to maintain and emphasize in the context of social media.

The book in relation to big data and quantification

Adaptation of qualitative methods to research communication in social media could draw more on developments in the utilization and analysis of so-called big data.

In part, we cover some of this development in the chapters on qualitative content analysis, which contain a component of quantification. However, we perceive a more comprehensive inclusion of big data (gathering as well as analysis) as a more suitable project for those who want to combine qualitative and quantitative analysis (see Charles and Gherman, 2018; Laaksonen et al., 2017). It is a project large enough for a separate book. We have also not wanted to analyze large amounts of discrete properties of social media use or participants, but in line with qualitative analysis in general, we have taken an interest in representations that people draw upon and the sensemaking they produce. To this, the critic may object that without big data we do not contribute to the methodological development of statistically valid studies, and thus support research that will never arrive at generalizable results. To such possible critique, we want to emphasize that quantifiable data is something quite different than holistic, human sensemaking that is considered in its context. These are different strands of empirical data for different purposes, and both are highly useful. Still, we would like to emphasize the value of the case study, an often-misunderstood approach that is very useful for knowledge production and in the context of qualitative research.

The value of case study research

Most examples of studies in the book are to be understood as case studies. In contrast to research that reviews big data, which contributes to useful, broad understanding of online practices, the case study achieves something else in that it constitutes a more detailed investigation regarding a very select realm of social media. Such a research approach has some strengths that should be mentioned. Overall, by contributing many observations of a selection of units, case studies contribute detailed knowledge and knowledge that involves experience-feedback. Such features of human activity have been typical and crucial for the development of both expertise and the advancement of ideas, practices, and organizations. In addition, Flyvbjerg (2006) emphasizes falsification as something that case study research is particularly suitable for. In connection to this, selection and careful observation of critical cases – extremes on a scale – may enable generalization. Critical cases and falsification are thus two strategies in case study research we hope will be carried into social media research even more. The focus of a case study on making many observations of a few units makes it possible to find the not-so-obvious signs that a hypothesis or theory does not measure up, as a single deviation is enough for falsification. Such falsification can also carry over to theoretical generalization. One of the authors (Joel) has applied this type of research design when conducting online focus groups in risk communication research. By sampling extreme groups – both the demographic group that previous research shows expresses the most risk-taking attitudes and the one that can be assumed to be most risk aversive – falsification can become a significant tool. If those who can be assumed to be most risk-taking nevertheless turn out to express concerns, then we can falsify far-reaching generalizations about the group. Furthermore, because the group is also at the far end of the scale of risk-taking, we can rightly assume that everyone else is expressing at least as much concern regarding the risk in question. In addition to the fact that study design can enable generalization, it is also worth considering that online interviews, synchronous or non-synchronous, can involve people across continents who have something in common regarding social media. It really enables studies of subcultures and experiences that are unique at the local level but that can gather a crowd internationally.

Apart from the case study design, another common feature of the methods for social media analysis that have been presented is that the analytical procedures are highly transparent. By that we mean that the end product of the research, the actual text, must (1) present empirical data and (2) display interpretations of the material. Although the extracts or examples may not be completely exhaustive or representative, with a good selection of typical categories of data, key elements of the analytical process – from data to interpretation and conclusion – can be shown quite openly. This transparency is a key to a work process that leads to improvements. Colleagues and peers can read and evaluate: is the data valued fairly and do the interpretations hold up when critically read? This can then be followed by a round of revisions and improvements. In addition to such formative evaluation, transparency implies that the research can be assessed summatively as well. Criteria for whether this type of qualitative research on social media is of high quality can focus on these questions about the viability of interpretations in the light of the presented data. In line with Potter and Wetherell (1987), one can also evaluate more broadly whether the research actually deals with the complexity presented by the social situation and context, whether the analysis is consistent without leaving loose ends, whether the research actually presents new problems and questions, and ultimately whether it generates novel understanding and explanations.

Coda

The authors are two academics who teach research methods, carry out research using social media data, and publish in top international journals. This book is the product of their experiences, as well as extensive literature reviews. Featuring introductory knowledge with practical applications and further research implications, the book also draws on real-life experiences from a wide variety of social media platforms to show how methods translate into practice, and offers a rigorous set of examples to make sure the reader understands what the methods entail. The authors have made every effort to write this book in a straightforward, easy-to-follow manner, using simple language to introduce students and researchers to the use of qualitative methods applied to social media data. Each chapter of this volume has offered background literature, step-by-step guidance, easy-to-follow examples, and relevant studies to create a comprehensive overview of each method.

BIBLIOGRAPHY

Abramovitz, M., and G. Zelnick. 2010. "Double Jeopardy: The Impact of Neoliberalism on Care Workers in the United State and South Africa." *International Journal of Health Service* 40, (1): 97–117.

Abrams, K., and T. Gaiser. 2017. "Online Focus Groups." In *The SAGE Handbook of Online Research Methods*, edited by Nigel Fielding, Raymond M. Lee, and Grant Blank, 435–450. London: Sage.

Adamic, L., and N. Glance. 2005. "The Political Blogosphere and the 2004 U.S. Election: Divided They Blog." In *Proceedings of the 3rd International Workshop on Link Discovery, Chicago Illinois, August 21–25*, 36–43. New York: Association for Computing Machinery.

Alvesson, M. 2013. *The Triumph of Emptiness: Consumption, Higher Education, and Work*. Oxford: Oxford University Press.

Allman-Farinelli, M., and M. Nour. 2021. "Exploring the Role of Social Support and Social Media for Lifestyle Interventions to Prevent Weight Gain with Young Adults: Focus Group Findings." *Journal of Human Nutrition and Dietetics* 34, (1): 178–187.

Al-Tahmazi, T. H. 2015. "The Pursuit of Power in Iraqi Political Discourse: Unpacking the Construction of Sociopolitical Communities on Facbeook." *Journal of Multicultural Discourses* 10, (2): 163–179.

Alves, H., C. Fernandes, and M. Raposo. 2016. "Social Media Marketing: A Literature Review and Implications." *Psychology & Marketing* 33, (12): 1029–1038.

Alvesson, M., and S. Deetz. 2000. *Doing Critical Management Studies*. London: Sage.

Anagnost, A. 2008. "From 'Class' to 'Social Strata': Grasping the Social Totality in Reform-Era China." *Third World Quarterly* 29: 497–519.

Araujo, T., I. Lock, and B. Van de Velde. 2020. "Automated Visual Content Analysis (AVCA) in Communication Research: A Protocol for Large Scale Image Classification with Pre-Trained Computer Vision Models." *Communication Methods & Measures* 14, (4): 239–265.

Ashley, C., and T. Tuten. 2015. "Creative Strategies in Social Media Marketing: An Exploratory Study of Branded Social Content and Consumer Engagement." *Psychology & Marketing* 32, (1): 15–27.

Auxier, B., and M. Anderson. 2021. "Social Networking Usage in 2021." *Pew Research Center*. www.pewresearch.org/internet/2021/04/07/social-media-use-in-2021/.

Bakardjieva, M. 2009. "Subactivism: Lifeworld and Politics in the Age of the Internet." *The Information Society* 25, (2): 91–104.

Bakardjieva, M. 2010. "The Internet and Subactivism: Cultivating Young Citizenship in Everyday Life." In *Young People, ICTs and Democracy*, edited by Tobias Olsson, and Peter Dahlgren, 129–146. Gothenburg: Nordicom.

Bakhshi, S., D. A. Shamma, and E. Gilbert. 2014. "Faces Engage Us: Photos with Faces Attract More Likes and Comments on Instagram." In *Proceedings of the SIGCHI Conference on Human Factors in Computing Systems, Toronto, 26 April–1 May*, 965–974. New York: Association for Computing Machinery

Banks, M. 2009. *Using Visual Data in Qualitative Research*. Thousand Oaks, CA: Sage.

Barocas, S., and H. Nissenbaum. 2014. "Big Data's End Run around Procedural Privacy Protections." *Communications of the ACM* 57, (11): 3–33.

Barthes, R. 1977. "Rhetoric of the Image." In *Image, Music, Text*, translated by Stephen Heath, 32–51. London: Fontana Press.

Barthes, R., and L. Duisit. 1975. "An Introduction to the Structural Analysis of Narrative." *New Literary History* 6, (2): 237–272.

Baumgaertner, B. O., R. C. Tyson, and S. M. Krone. 2016. "Opinion Strength Influences the Spatial Dynamics of Opinion Formation." *The Journal of Mathematical Sociology* 40, (4): 207–218.

BBC Trending. 2016. "#TwoWomenTravel - Live-Tweeting the Journey for an Abortion." *BBC*, August 8. http://www.bbc.com/news/blogs-trending-37156673.

Bell, P. 2004. "Content Analysis of Visual Images." In *The Handbook of Visual Analysis*, edited by T. Van Leeuwen, and C. Jewitt, 10–34. London: Sage.

Berelson, B. 1952. *Content Analysis in Communication Research*. New York: Free Press.

Bergström, A., and M. J. Belfrage. 2018. "News in Social Media: Incidental Consumption and the Role of Opinion Leaders." *Digital Journalism* 6, (5): 583–598.

Bertilsson, J. 2014. "Critical Netnography: Conducting Critical Research Online." In *Critical Management Research: Reflections from the Field*, edited by Emma Jeanes, and Tony Huzzard, 135. London: Sage.

Bettelheim, B. 1976. *The Uses of Enchantment: The Meaning and Importance of Fairytales*. New York: Knopf.

Bevir, M. 1999. *The Logic of the History of Ideas*. Cambridge: Cambridge University Press.

Black, M., and D. Metzger. 1965. "Ethnographic Description and the Study of Law." *American Anthropologist* 67, (6): 141–165.

Boellstorff, T, eds. 2008. *Coming of Age in Second Life: An Anthropologist Explores the Virtually Human*. New Jersey: Princeton University Press.

Boellstorff, T., B. Nardi, C. Pearce, and T. Taylor. 2012. *Ethnography and Virtual Worlds: A Handbook of Method*. Princeton: Princeton University Press.

Bosch, T. 2017. "Twitter Activism and Youth in South Africa: The Case of #RhodesMustFall." *Information, Communication & Society* 20, (2): 221–232.

Bouvier, G. 2014. "British Press Photographs and the Misrepresentation of the 2011 'Uprising' in Libya: A Content Analysis." In *Visual Communication*, edited by D. Machin, 281–299. Berlin: De Gruyter Mouton.

Bouvier, G. 2019. "How Journalists Source Trending Social Media Feeds: A Critical Discourse Perspective on Twitter." *Journalism Studies* 20, (2): 212–231.

Bouvier, G. 2020a. "From 'Echo Chambers' to 'Chaos Chambers': Discursive Coherence and Contradiction in the #MeToo Twitter Feed." *Critical Discourse Studies*. www.tandfonline.com/doi/abs/10.1080/17405904.2020.1822898.

Bouvier, G. 2020b. "Is Social Media Activism Really Activism?" *Participations* 17, (1): 217–221. www.participations.org/Volume%2017/Issue%201/13.pdf.

Bouvier, G., and L. Cheng, 2019. "Understanding the Potential of Twitter for Political Activism." In *Activism, Campaigning and Political Discourse on Twitter*, edited by I. Chiluwa, and G. Bouvier, 1–16. Nova: New York.

Bouvier, G. and D. Machin. 2021. "What Gets Lost in Twitter 'Cancel Culture': Hashtags? Calling Out Racists Reveals Some Limitations of Social Justice Campaigns." *Discourse & Society* 32, (3): 307–327.

Bouvier, G., and J. E. Rosenbaum, eds. 2020. *Twitter, the Public Sphere, and the Chaos of Online Deliberation*. London: Palgrave Macmillan.

Bouvier, G., and L. C. Way. 2021. "Revealing the Politics in 'Soft', Everyday Uses of Social Media: The Challenge for Critical Discourse Studies." *Social Semiotics* 31, (3): 345–364.

boyd, d. 2010. "Social Network Sites as Networked Publics: Affordances, Dynamics, and Implications." In *A Networked Self: Identity, Community, and Culture on Social Network Sites*, edited by Zizi Papacharissi, 39–58. New York: Routledge.

boyd, d. 2014. *It's Complicated: Social Lives of Networked Teens*. New Haven: Yale University Press.

boyd, d., and K. Crawford. 2012. "Critical Questions for Big Data: Provocations for a Cultural, Technological, and Scholarly Phenomenon." *Information, Communication & Society* 15, (5): 662–679.

Bratslavsky, L., N. Carpenter, and J. Zompetti. 2019. "Twitter, Incivility, and Presidential Communication: A Theoretical Incursion into Spectacle and Power." *Cultural Studies* 34, (4): 593–642.

Braun, V., and V. Clarke. 2006. "Using Thematic Analysis in Psychology." *Qualitative Research in Psychology* 3, (2): 77–101.

Breazu, P., and D. Machin. 2019. "Racism toward the Roma through the Affordances of Facebook: Bonding, Laughter and Spite." *Discourse & Society* 30, (4): 376–394.

Breazu, P., and D. Machin. 2020. "How Television News Disguises its Racist Representations: The Case of Romanian Antena 1 Reporting on the Roma." *Ethnicities* 20, (5): 823–843.

Breazu, P., and D. Machin. 2021. "Racism Is Not Just Hate-Speech: Ethno-Nationalist Victimhood in YouTube Comments about the Roma during Covid-19." *Language in Society* (forthcoming).

Brossard, D., and D. A. Scheufele. 2013. "Science, New Media, and the Public." *Science* 339, (6115): 40–41.

Bruckman, A. 2002. "Studying the Amateur Artist: A Perspective on Disguising Data Collected in Human Subjects Research on the Internet." *Ethics and Information Technology* 4: 217–231.

Bruckman, A. 2014. "Research Ethics and HCI." In *Ways of knowing in HCI*, edited by W. A. Kellogg, and J. S. Olson, 449–468. New York: Springer.

Bruner, J. 1990. *Acts of Meaning*. Cambridge, MA: Harvard University Press.

Brunner, E. 2019. "Chinese Urban Elites Return to Nature: Translating and Commodifying Rural Voices, Places, and Practices." *China Media Research* 15, (2): 29–38.

Bruno, N. 2011. "Tweet First, Verify Later: How Real-Time Information Is Changing the Coverage of Worldwide Crisis Events." *Reuters Institute for the Study of Journalism*. Oxford: University of Oxford. http://reutersinstitute.politics.ox.ac.uk/publication/tweet-first-verify-later.

Bruns, A., T. Highfield, and J. Burgess. 2013. "The Arab Spring and Social Media Audiences: English and Arabic Twitter users and Their Networks. *American Behavioral Scientist* 57, (7): 871–898.

Burgess, J., J. Green, and H. Jenkins. 2009. *YouTube*. Cambridge: Polity.

Burke, M., R. Kraut, and C. Marlow. 2011. "Social Capital on Facebook: Differentiating Uses and Users. In *Proceedings of the SIGCHI Conference on Human Factors in Computing Systems, Vancouver, May 7–12*, 571–580. New York: Association for Computing Machinery.

Burke, M., C. Marlow, and T. Lento. 2010. "Social Network Activity and Social Well-Being." In *Proceedings of the SIGCHI Conference on Human Factors in Computing Systems, Atlanta, April 10–15*, 1909–1912. New York: Association for Computing Machinery.

Caldas-Coulthard, C. R., and M. Coulthard. 1996. "Preface." In *Texts and Practices: Readings in Critical Discourse Analysis*, edited by Carmen R. Caldas-Coulthard, and Malcolm Coulthard, xi–xii. London: Routledge.

Calder, B. J. 1977. "Focus Groups and the Nature of Qualitative Marketing Research." *Journal of Marketing Research* 14, (3): 353–364.

Campbell, D. T. 1986. "Relabeling Internal and External Validity for Applied Social Scientists." *New Directions for Program Evaluation* 1986, (31): 67–77.

Carlson, M., and S. Lewis. 2015. *Boundaries of Journalism: Professionalism, Practices and Participation*. London: Routledge.

Carter, R., and A. Goddard. 2016. *How to Analyse Texts: A Toolkit for Students of English*. London: Routledge.

Castells, M. 2015. *Networks of Outrage and Hope: Social Movements in the Internet Age*. London: Polity.

Chaffee, S., and D. Lieberman. 2001. "The Challenge of Writing the Literature Review: Synthesizing Research for Theory and Practice." In *How to Publish Your Communication Research*, edited by A. Alexander, and W. Potter, 23–46. Thousand Oaks, CA: Sage.

Charmarkeh, H. 2013. "Social Media Usage, Tahriib (Migration), and Settlement among Somali Refugees in France." *Refugee* 29, (1). http://pi.library.yorku.ca/ojs/index.php/refuge/article/view/37505.

Chen, A., and D. Machin. 2014. "The Local and the Global in the Visual Design of a Chinese Women's Lifestyle Magazine: A Multimodal Critical Discourse Approach." *Visual Communication* 13, (3): 287–301.

Cheung, C. M. K., and M. K. O. Lee. 2012. "What Drives Consumers to Spread Electronic Word of Mouth in Online Consumer-Opinion Platforms." *Decision Support Systems* 53, (1): 218–225.

Child, J., and M. Warner. 2003. "Culture and Management in China." In *Culture and Management in Asia*, edited by M. Warner, 24–47. London: Routledge.

Charles, V., and T. Gherman. 2018. "Big Data Analytics and Ethnography: Together for the Greater Good." In *Big Data for the Greater Good: Studies in Big Data*, edited by A. Emrouznejadm, and V. Charles, 19–33.

Cho, J. Y., and E.-H. Lee. 2014. "Reducing Confusion about Grounded Theory and Qualitative Content Analysis: Similarities and Differences." *The Qualitative Report* 19: 1–20.

Chouliaraki, L. 2010. "Self-Mediation: New Media and Citizenship." *Critical Discourse Studies* 7, (4): 227–232.

Clifford, J., and G. E. Marcus, eds. 1986. *Writing Culture: The Poetics and Politics of Ethnography*. Berkely: University of California Press.

Colliander, J., and A. Haughe Wien. 2013. "Trash Talk Rebuffed: Consumers' Defense of Companies Criticized in Online Communities." *European Journal of Marketing* 47, (10): 1733–1757.

Collini, S. 2012. *What Are Universities For?* London: Penguin.

Collmann, J., K. T. Fitzgerald, S. Wu, J. Kupersmith, and S. A. Matei. 2016. "Data Management Plans, Institutional Review Boards, and the Ethical Management of Big Data about Human Subjects." In *Ethical Reasoning in Big Data*, edited by J. Collmann, and S. A. Matei, 141–184. Cham: Springer.

Conover, M. D., J. Ratkiewicz, B. Gonçales, A. Flammmini, and F. Menczer. 2011. "Political Polarization on Twitter." In *Fifth International AAAI Conference on Weblogs and Social Media, Barcelona, July 17–21*, 89–96. California: Association for the Advancement of Artificial Intelligence.

Conversi, D. 2012. "Irresponsible Radicalisation: 'Diasporas, Globalisation and Long-Distance Nationalism in the Digital Age'." *Journal of Ethnic and Migration Studies* 38, (9): 1357–1379.

Correll, S. 1995. "The Ethnography of an Electronic Bar: The Lesbian Cafe. *Journal of Contemporary Ethnography* 24, (3): 270–298.

Costello, L., M.-L. McDermott, and R. Wallace. 2017. "Netnography: Range of Practices, Misperceptions, and Missed Opportunities." *International Journal of Qualitative Methods* 16, (1).

Crawford, K., and M. Finn. 2015. "The Limits of Crisis Data: Analytical and Ethical Challenges of Using Social and Mobile Data to Understand Disasters." *GeoJournal* 80: 491–502.

Crawford, R. 2006. "Health as a Meaningful Social Practice." *Health: An Interdisciplinary Journal for the Social Study of Health, Illness Medicine* 10, (4): 401–420.

Creemers, R. 2017. "Cyber China: Upgrading Propaganda, Public Opinion Work and Social Management For the Twenty-First Century." *Journal of Contemporary China* 26, (103): 85–100.

Cristofari, C., and M. J. Guitton. 2017. "Aca-Fans and Fan Communities: An Operative Framework." *Journal of Consumer Culture* 17, (3): 713–731.

Curran, J., and J. Seaton. 2018. *Power without Responsibility: Press, Broadcasting and the Internet in Britain*. London: Routledge.

Datareportal. 2021. "Global Social Media Stats: Social Media Overview January 2021." *Datareportal*. https://datareportal.com/social-media-users#:~:text=Our%20latest%20data%20show%20that,of%20the%20total%20global%20population.&text=Social%20media%20user%20numbers%20have,the%20year%20to%20January%202021.

Davies, A. 2013. "'Slacktivism' vs. Thick, Impactful Civic Participation." *The Young Foundation*. https://youngfoundation.org/ research/slacktivism-vs-thick-and-impactful-civic-participation/.

de Saussure, F. 1983. *Course in General Linguistics*. Edited by C. Bally, A. Sechehaye, and A. Riedlinger; translated by R. Harris. London: Duckworth.

De Simone, D. 2021. "Andrew Dymock: The Neo-Nazi Exposed by the BBC." *BBC News*, June 11. www.bbc.com/news/uk-57406673.

De Zuniga, H., and S. Valenzuela. 2010. "The Mediating Path to a Stronger Citizenship: Online and Offline Networks, Weak Ties, and Civic Engagement." *Communication Research* 38, (3): 397–421.

Dean, J. 2010. *Blog Theory*. London: Polity.

Deighton-Smith, N., and B. Bell. 2016. "Objectifying Fitness: A Content and Thematic Analysis of #Fitspiration Images on Social Media." *Psychology of Popular Media Culture* 6.

Demant, J., S. A. Bakken, A. Oksanen, and H. Gunnlaugsson. 2019. "Drug Dealing on Facebook, Snapchat and Instagram: A Qualitative Analysis of Novel Drug Markets in The Nordic Countries." *Drug and Alcohol Review* 38, (4): 377–385.

Deuze, M. 2011. "Media Life." *Media, Culture & Society* 33, (1): 137–148.

Doctor, K. 2010. *Newsonomics: Twelve New Trends That Will Shape the News You Get*. London: St Martin's Press.

du Gay, P. 2008. "'Without Affection or Enthusiasm': Problems of Involvement and Attachment in 'Responsive' Public Management." *Organization* 15, (3): 335–353.

du Plessis, C. 2017. "The Role of Content Marketing in Social Media Content Communities." *South African Journal of Information Management* 19: 1–7.

Duggan, L. 2002. "The New Homonormativity: The Sexual Politics of Neoliberalism." In *Materialising Democracy: Toward a Revitalised Cultural Politics*, edited by R. Castronovo, and D. D. Nelson, 175–194. Durham, NC: Duke University Press.

Duriau, V., R. Reger, and M. Pfarrer. 2007. "A Content Analysis of the Content Analysis Literature in Organization Studies: Research Themes, Data Sources, and Methodological Refinements." *Organizational Research Methods* 10, (5): 5–34.

Eatwell, R., and M. Goodwin. 2018. *National Populism: The Revolt against Liberal Democracy*. London: Pelican.

Eide, M. 2020. "Religion in Children's Visual Media: A Qualitative Content Analysis of Preschool Holiday Specials." *Journal of Media & Religion* 19, (3): 108–126.

Ellison, N. B., C. Steinfield, and C. Lampe. 2007. "The Benefits of Facebook 'Friends': Social Capital and College Students' Use of Online Social Network Sites." *Journal of Computer-Mediated Communication* 12, (4): 1143–1168.

Elo, S., and H. Kyngäs. 2008. "The Qualitative Content Analysis Process." *Journal of Advanced Nursing* 62, (1): 107–115.

Engesser, S., N. Ernst, F. Esser, and F. Büchel. 2016. "Populism and Social Media; How Politicians Spread a Fragmented Ideology." *Information, Communication & Society* 20, (8): 1109–1126.

Enli, G. 2015. *Mediated Authenticity: How the Media Constructs Reality*. New York, NY: Peter Lang.

Enli, G. 2017. "Twitter as Arena for the Authentic Outsider: Exploring the Social Media Campaigns of Trump and Clinton in the 2016 Presidential Election." *European Journal of Communication* 32, (1): 50–61.

Enli, G., and C. A. Simonsen. 2017. "'Social Media Logic' Meets Professional Norms: Twitter Hashtags Usage by Journalists and Politicians." *Information, Communication & Society* 21, (8): 1081–1096.

Eriksson, G. 2015. "Ridicule As a Strategy for the Recontextualization of the Working Class." *Critical Discourse Studies* 12, (1): 20–38.

Eriksson, M. 2018. "Lessons for Crisis Communication on Social Media: A Systematic Review of What Research Tells the Practice." *International Journal of Strategic Communication* 12, (5): 526–551.

Esomar. 2011. "Esomar Guidelines on Social Media Research." *World Research Codes and Guidelines*. www.esomar.org/uploads/public/knowledge-and-standards/codes-and-guidelines/ESOMAR-Guideline-on-Social-Media-Research.pdf.

Ess, C., and AOIR Ethics Working Committee. 2002. "Ethical Decision-Making and Internet Research (Version 1)." *AoIR*, November. http://aoir.org/reports/ethics.pdf.

Fairclough, N. 1989. *Language and Power*. London: Longman.

Fairclough, N. 1992. *Discourse and Social Change*. Oxford: Polity Press.

Fairclough, N. 2000. *New language, New Labour*. London: Routledge.

Feng, Y., and K. Karan. 2011. "The Global and Local Influences in the Portrayal of Women's Roles: Content Analysis of Women's Magazines in China." *Journal of Media and Communication Studies* 3, (2): 33–44.

Fernández Villanueva, C., and G. Bayarri Toscano. 2021. "Legitimation of Hate and Political Violence through Memetic Images: The Bolsonaro Campaign." *Communication & Society* 34, (2): 449–468.

Ferrari, S. 2015. "Marketing Strategies in the Age of Web 3.0." In *Artificial Intelligence Technologies and the Evolution of the Web 3.0*, edited by T. Issa, and P. Isaías, 307–324. Hersey: IGI Publishing.

Fields, E. E. 1988. "Qualitative Content Analysis of Television News: Systematic Techniques." *Qualitative Sociology* 11, (3): 183–193.

Fiesler, C., C. Lampe, and A. S. Bruckman. 2016. "Reality and Perception of Copyright Terms of Service for Online Content Creation." In *Proceedings of the ACM Conference on Computer-Supported Cooperative Work & Social Computing (CSCW), San Francisco, February 27–March 2, 2016*, 1450–1461. New York: Association for Computing Machinery.

Fiesler, C., and N. Proferes. 2018. "'Participant' Perceptions of Twitter Research Ethics." *Social Media + Society* 4, (1): 1–14.

Florini, S., 2014. "Tweets, Tweeps and Signifyin: Communication and Cultural Performance on 'Black Twitter'." *Television New Media* 15, (3): 223–237.

Flyvbjerg, B. 2001. *Making Social Science Matter: Why Social Inquiry Fails and How It Can Succeed Again*. Cambridge: Cambridge University Press.

Flyvbjerg, B. 2006. "Five Misunderstandings about Case-Study Research." *Qualitative Inquiry* 12: 219–245.

Fossheim, H., and H. Ingierd. 2015. "Introductory Remarks." In *Internet research Ethics*, edited by H. Fossheim, and H. Ingierd, 9–13. Oslo: Cappelen Damm Akademisk.

Foucault, M. 1972. *The Archaeology of Knowledge and the Discourse on Language*. New York: Pantheon Books.

Foucault, M. 1978. *The History of Sexuality: An Introduction*. Hammonsworth: Penguin.

Fox, J., K. M. Warber, and D. C. Makstaller. 2013. "The Role of Facebook in Romantic Relationship Development: An Exploration of Knappвђ™s Relational Stage Model." *Journal of Social and Personal Relationships* 30, (6): 771–794.

Foxman, A. H., and C. Wolf. 2013. *Viral Hate: Containing Its Spread on the Internet*. New York: Palgrave Macmillan.

Fu, Q., and Q. Ren. 2010. "Educational Inequality Under China's Rural-Urban Divide: The Hukou System and Return to Education." *Environment and Planning A: Economy and Space* 42, (3): 592–610.

Fuchs, C. 2011. "The Contemporary World Wide Web: Social Medium or New Space of Accumulation?" In *The Political Economies of Media: The Transformation of the Global Media Industries*, edited by D. Winseck, and D. Y. Jin, 201–220. London: Bloomsbury.

Gaden, G, and D. Dumitrica. 2014. "The 'Real Deal': Strategic Authenticity, Politics and Social Media." *First Monday* 20, (1).

García-Rapp, F. 2016. "The Digital Media Phenomenon of YouTube Beauty Gurus: The Case of 'Bubzbeauty'." *International Journal of Web Based Communities* 12, (4): 360–375.

Gatson, S. N. 2011. "Self-Naming Practices on the Internet: Identity, Authenticity, and Community." *Cultural Studies, Critical Methodologies* 11, (3): 224–235.

Geertz, C. 1973. *The Interpretation of Cultures: Selected Essays*. New York: Basic Books.

Gentleman, A. 2011. "London Riots: Social Media Helped Gangs Orchestrate the Looting, Says MP." *The Guardian*. www.theguardian.com/uk/2011/aug/11/riots-social-media-gang-culture.

Georgakopoulou, A. 2014. "Small Stories Transposition and Social Media: A Micro-Perspective on The 'Greek Crisis'." *Discourse Society* 25, (4): 519–539.

Georgalou, M. 2015a. "Beyond the Timeline: Constructing Time and Age Identities on Facebook." *Discourse, Context & Media* 9: 24–33.

Georgalou, M. 2015b. "Small Stories of the Greek Crisis on Facebook." *Social Media + Society* 1, (2):1–12.

Georgalou, M. 2016. "'I Make the Rules on My Wall': Privacy and Identity Management Practices on Facebook." *Discourse & Communication* 10, (1): 40–64.

Gershon, I. 2010. *The Breakup 2.0: Disconnecting over New Media*. Ithaca, NY: Cornell University Press.

Gilroy, P. 2012. "'My Britain Is Fuck All' Zombie Multiculturalism and the Race Politics of Citizenship." *Identities: Global Studies in Culture and Power* 19, (4): 380–397.

Glaser, B., and A. Strauss. 1998. *Grounded Theory*. Bern: Huber.

Gleason, B. 2013. "#Occupy Wall Street: Exploring Informal Learning about a Social Movement on Twitter." *American Behavioral Scientist* 57, (7): 966–982.

Goffman, E. 1976. *Gender Advertisements*. New York: Harper and Row.

Goldberg, D. T. 2009. *The Threat of Race: Reflections on Racial Neoliberalism*. Oxford, UK: Wiley-Blackwell.

Golder, S., S. Ahmed, G. Norman, and A. Booth. 2017. "Attitudes toward the Ethics of Research Using Social Media: A Systematic Review." *Journal of Medical Internet Research* 19, (6): 1–19.

Goodrich, K. 2011. "Anarchy of Effects? Exploring Attention to Online Advertising and Multiple Outcomes." *Psychology & Marketing* 28, (4): 417–440.

Gordon, A. R., J. P. Calzo, R. Eiduson, K. Sharp, S. Silverstein, E. Lopez, K. Thomson, and S. L. Reisner. 2021. "Asynchronous Online Focus Groups for Health Research: Case Study and Lessons Learned." *International Journal of Qualitative Methods* 20, (1), January: 1609406921990489.

Graneheim, U. H., B.-M. Lindgren, and B. Lundman. 2017. "Methodological Challenges in Qualitative Content Analysis: A Discussion Paper." *Nurse Education Today* 56: 29–34.

Gray, C. H., and M. Driscoll. 1992. "What's Real about Virtual Reality?: Anthropology of, and in, Cyberspace." *Visual Anthropology Review* 8, (2): 39–49.

Groshek, J., and C. Cutino. 2016. "Meaner on Mobile: Incivility and Impoliteness in Communication Contentious Politics on Sociotechnical Networks." *Social Media + Society* 2, (4): 1–10.

Guest, G., E. Namey, and K. McKenna. 2016. "How Many Focus Groups are Enough? Building an Evidence Base for Nonprobability Sample Sizes." *Field Methods* 29, (1): 3–22.

Habermas, J. 2006. "Political Communication in Media Society: Does Democracy Still Enjoy an Epistemic Dimension? The Impact of Normative Theory on Empirical Research." *Communication Theory* 16: 411–426.

Hall Jamieson, K., and J. N. Capella. 2010. *Echo Chamber*. Oxford: OUP.

Halliday, M. A. K. 1978. *Language as social Semiotic*. London: Arnold.

Halliday, M. A. K., and R. Hasan. 1976. *Cohesion in English*. London: Longman.

Hammersley, M., and P. Atkinson. 2007. *Ethnography: Principles in Practice*. 3rd ed. London: Routledge.

Han, R. 2015. "Defending the Authoritarian Regime Online: China's 'Voluntary Fifty-Cent Army'." *The China Quarterly* 224: 1006–1025.

Heikkilä, N. 2017. "Online Antagonism of the Alt-Right in the 2016 Election." *European Journal of American Studies* 12, (2): 1–22.

Heinonen, K., and G. Medberg. 2018. "Netnography as a Tool for Understanding Customers: Implications for Service Research and Practice." *The Journal of Services Marketing* 32, (6): 657–679.

Hemsley-Brown, J. 2011. "Market Heal Thyself: The Challenges of a Free Marketing in Higher Education." *Journal of Marketing for Higher Education* 21: 115–132.

Henningsen, L. 2012. "Individualism for the Masses? Coffee Consumption and the Chinese Middle Class' Search for Authenticity." *Inter-Asia Cultural Studies* 13, (3): 408–427.

Hermida, A. 2012. "Tweets and Truth: Journalism as a Discipline of Collaborative Verification." *Journalism Practice* 6, (5–6): 659–668.

Hermida, A., S. C. Lewis, and R. Zamith. 2014. "Sourcing the Arab Spring: A Case Study of Andy Carvin's Sources on Twitter during the Tunisian and Egyptian Revolutions." *Journal of Computer-Mediated Communication* 19, (3): 479–499.

Hertz, N. 2002. *The Silent Takeover: Global Capitalism and the Death of Democracy*. London: Arrow Books.

Hibbin, R. A., G. Samule, and G. E. Derrick. 2018. "From 'a Fair Game' to 'a Form of Covert Research': Research Ethics Committee Members' Differing Notions of Consent and Potential Risk to Participants within Social Media Research." *Journal of Empirical Research on Human Research Ethics* 13, (2): 149–159.

Highfield, T., and T. Leaver. 2016. "Instagrammatics and Digital Methods: Studying Visual Social Media, from Selfies and GIFs to Memes and Emoji." *Communication Research and Practice* 2, (1): 47–62.

Hine, C. 2000. *Virtual Ethnography*. London: Sage.

Hine, C. 2015. *Ethnography for the Internet: Embedded, Embodied and Everyday*. London: Bloomsbury Academic.

Hodge, B., and G. Kress. 1988. *Social Semiotics*. Cambridge: Polity.

Hoffmann, A. L., and A. Jones. 2016. "Recasting Justice For Internet and Online Industry Research Ethics." In *Internet Research Ethics for the Social Age: New Cases and Challenges*, edited by M. Zimmer, and K. E. Kinder-Kurlanda, 3–18. Bern: Peter Lang.

Hong, F. 1997. *Footbinding, Feminism and Freedom: The Liberation of Women's Bodies in Modern China*. London: Frank Cass & Co.

Horowitz, L. S. 2013. "Toward Empathic Agonism: Conflicting Vulnerabilities in Urban Wetland Governance." *Environment and Planning* 45: 2344–2361.

Housley, W., H. Webb, M. Williams, R. Procter, A. Edwards, M. Jirotka, P. Burnap, B. C. Stahl, and W. Matthew. 2018. "Interaction and Transformation on Social Media: The Case of Twitter Campaigns." *Social Media + Society* 4, (1): 1–10.

Howard, P. N., and S. Jones. 2000. *Society Online*. London, Sage.

Hsieh, H.-F., and S. E. Shannon. 2005. "Three Approaches to Qualitative Content Analysis." *Qualitative Health Research* 15, (9): 1277–1288.

Hudson, J. M., and A. Bruckman. 2004. "'Go Away': Participant Objections to Being Studied and the Ethics of Chatroom Research." *The Information Society* 20: 127–139.

Huey, L., 2015. "This Is Not Your Mother's Terrorism: Social Media, Online Radicalization, and the Practice of Political Jamming." *Journal of Terrorism Research* 6, (2): 1–16.

Humphreys, M. L., and T. Watson. 2009. "Ethnographic Practices: From 'Writing-Up Ethnographic Research' To 'Writing Ethnography'." In *Organizational Ethnography: Studying the Complexities of Everyday Life*, edited by S. Ybema, D. Yanow, H. Wels, and F. Kamsteeg, 40–55. London: Sage.

Hunt, E. 2016. "Irish Woman Live-Tweets Journey for Abortion in Great Britain." *The Guardian*, August 20. www.theguardian.com/world/2016/aug/20/irish-woman-live-tweets-journey-for-abortion-in-britain.

Inglehart, R. F., and P. Norris. 2019. *Cultural Backlash: Trump, Brexit and Authoritarian Populism*. Cambridge: Cambridge University Press.

Jackler, R. K., and D. Ramamurthi. 2017. "Unicorns Cartoons: Marketing Sweet and Creamy E-Juice to Youth." *Tobacco Control* 26, (4): 471–475.

Jackson, S. J., M. Bailey, and B. Foucault Welles. 2020. *#HashtagActivism: Networks of Race and Gender Justice*. Cambridge, MA: MIT Press.

Jacobson, S., E. Myung, and L. J. Steven. 2016. "Open Media or Echo Chamber: The Use of Links in Audience Discussions on the Facebook Pages of Partisan News Organizations." *Information, Communication & Society* 19, (7): 875–891.

Jain, P., Z. Zaher, and E. Roy. 2017. "Magazines and Social Media Platforms: Strategies for Enhancing User Engagement and Implications for Publishers." *Journal of Magazine & New Media Research* 17, (2): 1–23.

Jansen, F. 2010. "Digital Activism in the Middle East: Mapping Issues Networks in Egypt, Iran, Syria and Tunisia." *Knowledge Manage: Development Journal* 6, (1): 37–52.

Jefferson, G. 2004. "Glossary of Transcript Symbols with an Introduction. In *Conversation Analysis: Studies from the First Generation*, edited by G. Lerner, 13–31. Amsterdam: John Benjamins.

Ji, Y. 2015. "Between Tradition and Modernity: 'Leftover' Women in Shanghai." *Journal of Marriage and Family* 77: 1057–1073.

Johansson, T., and J. Andreasson. 2017. "The Web of Loneliness: A Netnographic Study of Narratives of Being Alone in an Online Context." *Social Sciences* 6, (3): 101. www.mdpi.com/2076-0760/6/3/101.

Joinson, A. N. 1998. "Causes and Effects of Disinhibition on the Internet." In *The Psychology of the Internet*, edited by J. Gackenbach, 43–60. New York: Academic Press.

Jones, C. 2011. "Ethical Issues in Online Research." *British Educational Research Association On-Line Resource*. www.bera.ac.uk/publication/ethical-issues-in-online-research.

Jong, W., M. L. A. Dückers, and P. G. Velden. 2016. "Crisis Leadership by Mayors: A Qualitative Content Analysis of Newspapers and Social Media on the MH17 Disaster." *Journal of Contingencies & Crisis Management* 24, (4): 286–295.

Joseph, J. G., C.-A. Emmons, R. C. Kessler, C. B. Wortman, K. O'Brien, W. T. Hocker, and C. Schaefer. 1984. "Coping with the Threat of AIDS: An Approach to Psychosocial Assessment." *American Psychologist* 39, (11): 1297–1302.

Kaczkowski, W. 2019. "Qualitative Content Analysis of Images of Children in Islamic State's Dabiq and Rumiyah Magazines." *Contemporary Voices: St Andrews Journal of International Relations* 1, (1): 26–38.

Kádeková, Z., and M. Holienčinová. 2018. "Influencer Marketing as a Modern Phenomenon Creating a New Frontier of Virtual Opportunities." *Communication Today* 9, (2): 90–105.

Keats, P. A. 2009. "Multiple Text Analysis in Narrative Research: Visual, Written, and Spoken Stories of Experience." *Qualitative Research* 9, (2): 181–195.

Keller, J. 2011. "Photojournalism in the New Media Economy." *The Atlantic*. www.theatlantic.com/technology/archive/2011/04/photojournalism-in-the-age-of-new-media/73083/.

Khamis, S., L. Ang, and R. Welling. 2016. "Self- Branding, 'Micro-Celebrity' and the Rise of Social Media Influencers." *Celebrity Studies* 8, (2): 191–208.

KhosraviNik, M. 2017. "Social Media Critical Discourse Studies (SM-CDS)." In *Handbook of Critical Discourse Analysis*, edited by J Flowerdew, and J. Richardson, 582–596. London: Routledge.

Khosravinik, M., and M. Amer. 2020. "Social Media and Terrorism Discourse: The Islamic State's (IS) Social Media Discursive Content and Practices." *Critical Discourse Studies*, 1–20.

KhosraviNik, M., and J. Unger. 2015. "Critical Discourse Studies and Social Media: Power, Resistance and Critique in Changing Media Ecologies." In *Methods of Critical Discourse Studies*, edited by R. Wodak, and M. Meyer, 205–233. London: Sage.

KhosraviNik, M., and M. Zia. 2014. "Persian Nationalism, Identity and Anti-Arab Sentiments in Iranian Facebook Discourses: Critical Discourse Analysis and Social Media Communication." *Journal of Language and Politics* 13, (4): 755–780.

Kim, H., S. M. Jang, S.-H. Kim, and A. Wan. 2018. "Evaluating Sampling Methods for Content Analysis of Twitter Data." *Social Media + Society* 4, (2): 1–8.

Kozinets, R. 2010. *Netnography: Doing Ethnographic Research Online*. London: Sage.

Kozinets, R. 2015. *Netnography: Redefined*. London: Sage.

Kozol, J. 1985. *Illiterate America*. New York: Doubleday.

Kracauer, S. 1952. "The Challenge of Qualitative Content Analysis." *Public Opinion Quarterly* 16, (4): 631–642.

Kreiss, D. 2016. "Seizing the Moment: The Presidential Campaigns' Use of Twitter during the 2012 Electoral Cycle." *New Media & Society* 18: 1473–1490.

Kress, G. 1989. *Linguistic Processes in Sociocultural Practice*. Oxford: Oxford University Press.

Kress, G., and T. Van Leeuwen. 1996. *Reading Images: The Grammar of Visual Design*. 1st ed. Abingdon: Routledge.

Kress, G., and T. Van Leeuwen. 2001. *Multimodal Discourse: The Modes and Media of Contemporary Communication*. London: Arnold Publishers.

Krippendorff, K. 2013. *Content Analysis: An Introduction to Its Methodology*. 3rd ed. Thousand Oaks, CA, London: Sage.

Kruger, L. J., R. F. Rodgers, S. J. Long, and A. S. Lowy. 2019. "Individual Interviews or Focus Groups? Interview Format and Women's Self-Disclosure." *International Journal of Social Research Methodology* 22, (3): 245–255.

Krzyzanowski, M., and P. Ledin. 2017. "Uncivility on the Web: Populism in/and the Borderline Discourses of Exclusion." *Journal of Language and Politics* 16, (4): 566–581.

Kulavuz-Onal, D., and C. Vásquez. 2018. "'Thanks, Shokran, Gracias': Translingual Practices in a Facebook Group." *Language Learning & Technology* 22, (1): 240–256.

Laaksonen, S.-M., M. Nelimarkka, M. Tuokko, M. Marttila, A. Kekkonen, and M. Villi. 2017. "Working the Fields of Big Data: Using Big-Data-Augmented Online Ethnography to Study Candidate-Candidate Interaction at Election Time." *Journal of Information Technology & Politics* 14, (2): 110–131.

Labov, W. 1972. "The Transformation of Experience in Narrative Syntax." In *Language in the Inner City: Studies in the Black English Vernacular*, edited by W. Labov, 354–396. Philadelphia: University of Pennsylvania Press.

Labov, W., and J. Waletzky. 1967. "Narrative Analysis." In *Essays on the Verbal and Visual Arts*, edited by J. Helm, 12–44. Seattle: U. of Washington Press.

Laestadius, L. I., M. M. Wahl, P. Pokhrel, and Y. I. Cho. 2019. "From Apple to Werewolf: A Content Analysis of Marketing for E-Liquids on Instagram." *Addictive Behaviors* 91: 119–127.

Lash, S. 2001. "Technological Forms of Life." *Theory, Culture & Society* 18, (1): 105–120.

Lasorsa, D. L., S. C. Lewis, and A. E. Holton. 2012. "Normalizing Twitter: Journalism Practice in an Emerging Communication Space." *Journalism Studies* 13, (1): 19–36.

Lavis, A., and R. Winter. 2020. "Online Harms or Benefits? An Ethnographic Analysis of the Positives and Negatives of Peer-Support around Self-Harm on Social Media." *Journal of Child Psychology and Psychiatry* 61, (8): 842–854.

Lazar, M. 2005. *Feminist Critical Discourse Analysis: Gender, Power and Ideology in Discourse*. London: Palgrave.

LeBeau, K., C. Carr, and M. Hart. 2020. "Examination of Gender Stereotypes and Norms in Health-Related Content Posted to Snapchat Discover Channels: Qualitative Content Analysis." *Journal of Medical Internet Research* 22, (3): e15330.

Ledin, P., and D. Machin. 2018. *Doing Visual Analysis*. London: Sage.

Ledin, P., and D. Machin. 2020. *Introduction to Multimodal Analysis*. London: Bloomsbury.

Ledin, P., and D. Machin. 2021. *Introduction to Multimodal Analysis*. 2rd ed. London: Bloomsbury.

Lee, J. L., M. DeCamp, M. Dredze, M. S. Chisolm, and Z. D. Berger. 2014. "What Are Health-Related Users Tweeting? A Qualitative Content Analysis of Health-Related Users and Their Messages on Twitter." *Journal of Medical Internet Research* 16, (10): e237.

Leggett, A. 2020. "Bringing Green Food to the Chinese Table: How Civil Society Actors Are Changing Consumer Culture in China." *Journal of Consumer Culture* 20, (1): 83–101.

Lentin, A. 2014. "Post-Race, Post Politics: The Paradoxical Rise of Culture after Multiculturalism." *Ethnic and Racial Studies* 37, (8): 1268–1285.

Lentin, A. 2016. "Racism in Public or Public Racism: Doing Anti-Racism in 'Post-Racial' Times." *Ethnic and Racial Studies* 39, (1): 33–48.

Leung, S. M. 1998. "Metamorphosis, Stasis and Retro-Metamorphosis: Professional Women's Struggle for Trans-Formation in Post-Mao China." Unpublished Ph.D. Dissertation, University of Lancaster, UK.

Lévi-Strauss, C. 1963. *Structural Anthropology*. Translated by Claire Jacobson, and Brooke Grundfest Schoepf. New York: Basic Books.

Lijadi, A. A., and G. J. van Schalkwyk. 2015. "Online Facebook Focus Group Research of Hard-to-Reach Participants." *International Journal of Qualitative Methods* 14, (5).

Lindgren, S. 2010. "YouTube Gunmen? Mapping Participatory Media Discourse on School Shooting Videos." *Media, Culture & Society* 33, (1): 123–136.

Lindlof, T. R., and M. J. Shatzer. 1998. "Media Ethnography in Virtual Space: Strategies, Limits, and Possibilities." *Journal of Broadcasting & Electronic Media* 42, (2): 170–189.

Lobe, B. 2017. "Best Practices for Synchronous Online Focus Groups." In *A New Era in Focus Group Research*, edited by R. Barbour, and D. Morgan, 227–250. London: Palgrave Macmillan.

Lobe, B., D. Morgan, and K. Hoffman. 2020. "Qualitative Data Collection in an Era of Social Distancing." *The International Journal of Qualitative Methods* 19.

Lotman, J. 1977. *The Structure of the Artistic Text*. Ann Arbor, Michigan: Michigan University Press.

Low, K. C. P. 2012. "Leadership Lessons from Confucius, the 9Ps and Confucian Pillars of Self-Discipline." *Business Journal for Entrepreneurs* 2012, (1): 1–15.

Luger, E., S. Moran, and T. Rodden. 2013. "Consent for All: Revealing the Hidden Complexity of Terms and Conditions." In *Proceedings of the SIGCHI Conference on Human Factors in Computing Systems, Paris, 27 April–2 May*, 2687–2696. New York: Association for Computing Machinery.

Lundstrom, M., and T. P. Lundstrom. 2021. "Podcast Ethnography." *International Journal of Social Research Methodology* 24, (3): 289–299.

Lunt, P., and S. Livingstone. 1996. "Rethinking the Focus Group in Media and Communications Research." *Journal of Communication* 46, (2): 79–98.

Lutz, C., and J. Collins. 1993. *Reading National Geographic*. Chicago: University of Chicago Press.

MacDonald, R., T. Shildrick, C. Webster, and D. Simpson. 2005. "Growing Up in Poor Neighbourhoods: The Significance of Class and Place in the Extended Transitions of 'Socially Excluded' Young Adults." *Sociology* 39, (5): 873–891.

Machin, D. 2004. "Building the World's Visual Language: The Increasing Global Importance of Image Banks in Corporate Media." *Visual Communication* 3: 316–336.

Machin, D. 2007. *Introduction to Multimodal Analysis*. London: Bloomsbury.

Machin, D., and T. Van Leeuwen. 2007. *Global Media Discourse*. London: Routledge.

Machin, D., and A. Mayr. 2012. *How to Do Critical Discourse Analysis: A Multimodal Introduction*. London: Sage.

MacKinnon, R. 2011. "Liberation Technology: China's 'Networked Authoritarianism'." *Journal of Democracy* 22, (2): 32–46.

Macnamara, J., and G. Kenning. 2011. "E-Electioneering 2010: Trends in Social Media Use in Australian Political Communication." *Media International Australia* 139, (1): 7–22.

Malik, F. S., N. Panlasigui, J. Gritton, H. Gill, J. P. Yi-Frazier, and M. A. Moreno. 2019. "Adolescent Perspectives on the Use of Social Media to Support Type 1 Diabetes Management: Focus Group Study." *Journal of Medical Internet Research* 21, (6). e12149.

Mann, C., and F. Stewart. 2000. *Internet Communication and Qualitative Research: A Handbook for Researching Online*. London: Sage.

Mann, D. 2019. "'I Am Spartacus': Individualising Visual Media and Warfare." *Media, Culture & Society* 41, (1): 38–53.

Markham, A., and Buchanan, E. 2012. "AoIR – Ethical Decision-Marking and Internet Research." *Association of Internet Researchers*. www.aoir.org/reports/ethics2.pdf.

Markham, A., E. Buchanan, and AOIR Ethics Working Committee. 2012. "Ethical Decision-Making and Internet Research (Version 2)." *Association of Internet Researchers On-Line Resource*. https://pure.au.dk/portal/files/55543125/UN%20Declaration%20of%20Human%20Rights.

Marková, I., P. Linell., M. Grossen, and A. Salazar-Orvig. 2007. *Dialogue in Focus Groups: Exploring in Socially Shared Knowledge*. London: Equinox Publishing.

Markula, P. 1995. "Firm but Shapely, Fit but Sexy, Strong but Thin: The Postmodern Aerobicising Female Bodies." *Sociology of Sport Journal* 12: 424–453.

Marwick, A. E. 2013. *Status Update:Celebrity, Publicity, and Branding in the Social Media Age*. New Haven: Yale University Press.

Marwick, A. E., and d. boyd. 2010. "I Tweet Honestly, I Tweet Passionately: Twitter Users, Context Collapse, and the Imagined Audience." *New media & society* 13, (1): 114–133.

Matamoros-Fernández, A. 2017. "Platformed Racism: the Mediation and Circulation of an Australian Race-Based Controversy on Twitter, Facebook and YouTube." *Information, Communication & Society* 20, (6): 930–946.

Mayer, G., S. Alvarez, N. Gronewold, and J.-H. Schultz. 2020. "Expressions of Individualization on the Internet and Social Media: Multigenerational Focus Group Study." *Journal of Medical Internet Research* 22, (11).

McCosker, A., P. Kamstra, T. De Cotta, J. Farmer, F. Shaw, Z. Teh, and P. A. Soltani. 2020. "Social Media for Social Good? A Thematic, Spatial and Visual Analysis of Humanitarian Action on Instagram." *Information, Communication & Society*, 1–21.

McNeal, G. 2014. "Facebook Manipulated User News Feeds to Create Emotional Responses." *Forbes*, June 28. www.forbes.com/sites/gregorymcneal/2014/06/28/facebook-manipulated-user-news-feeds-to-create-emotional-contagion/#184494f539dc.

Medaglia, R., and L. Zheng. 2017. "Mapping Government Social Media Research and Moving It Forward: A Framework and a Research Agenda." *Government Information Quarterly* 34, (3): 496–510.

Medina, R. Z., and J. C. L. Diaz. 2016. "Social Media Use in Crisis Communication Management: An Opportunity for Local Communities?" In *Social Media and Local Government*, edited by M. Z. Sobaci, 321–335. Cham: Springer.

Merton, R. K. 1987. "The Focussed Interview and Focus Groups: Continuities and Discontinuities." *The Public Opinion Quarterly* 51, (4): 550–566.

Molesworth, M., N. Elizabeth, and S. Richard. 2011. *The Marketisation of Higher Education and the Student as Consumer*. London: Routledge.

Moreno, M. A., N. Gnoiu, P. S. Moreno, and D. Diekema. 2013. "Ethics of Social Media Research: Common Concerns and Practical Considerations." *Cyberpsychology, Behavior, and Social Networking* 16, (9): 108–713.

Morgan, D. 1993. "Qualitative Content Analysis: A Guide to Paths Not Taken." *Qualitative Health Research* 3: 112–121.

Morgan, D., and B. Lobe. 2011. "Online Focus Groups." In *The Handbook of Emergent Technologies in Social Research*, edited by S. Hesse-Biber, 199–230. Oxford: Oxford University Press.

Morley, D. 1980. *The Nationwide Audience*. London: British Film Institute.

Mortimer, N. 2014. "Trinity Mirror Makes 'Major Investment' in Online Video as It Admits Current Offering is a 'Poor Example'." *The Drum*. www.thedrum.com/news/2014/03/04/trinity-mirror-makes-major-investment-online-video-it-admits-current-offering-poor.

Muir, J., R. S. M. Hegarty, S. Stebbings, and G. J. Treharne. 2020. "Exploring the Role of Online Health Information and Social Media in the Illness Experience of Arthritis-Related Fatigue: A Focus Group Study." *Musculoskeletal Care* 18, (4): 501–509.

Mukattash, T. L., A. S. Jarab, I. Mukattash, M. B. Nusair, R. Abu Farha, M. Bisharat, and I. A. Basheti. 2020. "Pharmacists' Perception of Their Role during COVID-19: A Qualitative Content Analysis of Posts on Facebook Pharmacy Groups in Jordan." *Pharmacy Practice* 18, (3): 1900.

Mukherjee, R., and S. Banet-Weiser. 2012. *Commodity Activism: Cultural Resistance in Neoliberal Times*. New York: NYU Press.

Mulvey, L. 1975. "Visual Pleasure and Narrative Cinema." *Screen* 16, (3): 6–18.

Narayanan, A., and V. Shmatikov. 2008. "Robust De-Anonymization of Large Datasets." *2008 IEEE Symposium on Security and Privacy*, 111–125.

Nardi, B. A. 2010. *My Life as a Night Elf Priest: An Anthropological Account of World of Warcraft*. Ann Arbor: University of Michigan Press.

Ng, E. 2020. "No Grand Pronouncements Here . . .: Reflections on Cancel Culture and Digital Media Participation." *Television & New Media* 21, (6): 621–627.

Nimrod, G., D. A. Kleiber, and L. Berdychevsky. 2012. "Leisure in Coping with Depression." *Journal of Leisure Research* 44, (4): 419–449.

Obiegbu, C. J., G. Larsen, N. Ellis, and D. O'Reilly. 2019. "Co-Constructing Loyalty in an Era of Digital Music Fandom: An Experiential-Discursive Perspective." *European Journal of Marketing* 53, (3): 463–482.

O'Reilly, K. 2012. *Ethnographic Methods*. London: Routledge.

Orton-Johnson, K. 2010. "Ethics in Online Research; Evaluating the ESRC Framework for Research Ethics Categorisation of Risk." *Sociological Research Online* 15, (4). www.socresonline.org.uk/15/4/13.html.

Ott, B. L. 2017. "The Age of Twitter: Donald J. Trump and the Politics of Debasement." *Critical Studies in Media Communication* 34, (1): 59–68.

Padmakumar, K., and P. Rani. 2018. "Social Media Content Integrations on Radio and Its Effects on Listeners." *Global Media Journal: Indian Edition* 10, (2): 123–134.

Page, R. 2012. "The Linguistics of Self-Branding and Micro-Celebrity in Twitter: The Role of Hashtags." *Discourse and Communication* 6, (2): 181–201.

Papacharissi, Z. 2016. "Affective Publics and Structure of Storytelling: Sentiment, Events and Mediality." *Information, Communication and Society* 19, (3): 307–324.

Papacharissi, Z., and M. de Fatima Oliveira. 2012. "Affective News and Networked Publics: The Rhythms of News Storytelling on #Egypt." *Journal of Communication* 62, (2): 266–282.

Pariser, E. 2011. *The Filter Bubble: How the New Personalized Web Is Changing What We Read and How We Think*. New York, NY: Penguin Press.

Parker, L. 2011. "University Corporatisation: Driving Redefinition." *Critical Perspectives on Accounting* 22, (4): 434–450.

Parmentier, G., and S. Rolland. 2013. "The Benefit of Social Media: Bulletin Board Focus Groups as a Tool for Co-Creation." *International Journal of Market Research* 55.

Patton, M. 2002. *Qualitative, Research & Evaluation Methods*. Thousand Oaks, CA: Sage.

Pearce, C. 2009. *Communities of Play: Emergent Cultures in Multiplayer Games and Virtual Worlds*. Cambridge, MA: MIT Press.

Pearce, W., S. Ozkula, A. Greene, L. Teeling, J. Bansard, J. Jocelli., and E. Rabello. 2018. "Visual Cross-Platform Analysis: Digital Methods to Research Social Media Images." *Information, Communication and Society* 23, (2): 161–180.

Peng, Y. 2019. "Sharing Food Photographs on Social Media: Performative Xiaozi Lifestyle in Young, Middle-Class Chinese Urbanites' Wechat 'Movements'." *Social Identity* 25, (2): 269–287.

Penney, J., and C. Dadas. 2013. "(Re)Tweeting in the Service of Protest: Digital Composition and Circulation in the Occupy Wall Street Movement." *New Media Society* 16, (1): 74–90.

Pentina, I., and C. Amos. 2011. "The Freegan Phenomenon: Anti-Consumption or Consumer Resistance?" *European Journal of Marketing* 45, (11/12): 1768–1778.

Pereira, S., P. Moura, and J. Fillol. 2018. "The YouTubers Phenomenon: What Makes YouTube Stars So Popular for Young People?" *Fonseca Journal of Communication* 17: 107–123.

Picard, R. G. 2014. "Twilight or New Dawn of Journalism: Evidence from the Changing News Ecosystem." *Digital Journalism* 2, (3): 273–283.

Pieters, R., and M. Wedel. 2004. "Attention Capture and Transfer in Advertising: Brand, Pictorial, and Text-Size Effects." *Journal of Marketing Journal of Marketing* 68: 36–50.

Pink, S., H. A. Horst, J. Postill, L. Hjorth, T. Lewis, and J. Tacchi. 2016. *Digital Ethnography: Principles and Practice*. London: Sage.

Poell, T., and J. Van Dijck. 2015. "Social Media and Activist Communication." In *The Routledge Companion to Alternative and Community Media*, edited by C. Atton, 527–537. London: Routledge.

Pohjonen, M. 2020. "Preliminary Arguments for a Critical Data-Driven Ethnography in the Time of 'Deep Mediatization'." *Communicative Figurations*, (31). www.kommunikative-figurationen.de/fileadmin/user_upload/Arbeitspapiere/CoFi_EWP_No-31_Matti-Pohjonen.pdf.

Potter, J. 1996. *Representing Reality: Discourse, Rhetoric and Social Construction*. London: Sage.

Potter, J., and M. Wetherell. 1987. *Discourse and Social Psychology: Beyond Attitudes and Behaviour*. London: Sage.

Prasad, D. 2019. "Qualitative Content Analysis: Why Is It Still a Path Less Taken?" *Forum: Qualitative Sozialforschung* 20, (36).

Rambukkana, N. 2015. "Hashtags as Technosocial Events." In *Hashtag Publics: The Power and Politics of Discursive Networks*, edited by N. Rambukkana, 1–10. New York: Peter Lang.

Rasmussen, J. 2017. "'Welcome to Twitter, @CIA. Better Late Than Never': Communication Professionals' Views of Social Media Humour and Implications for Organizational Identity." *Discourse & Communication* 11, (1): 89–110.

Rasmussen, J. 2020. "Share a Little of That Human Touch: The Marketable Ordinariness of Security and Emergency Agencies' Social Media Efforts." *Human Relations* 74, (9): 1421–1446.

Rasmussen, J., and Ø. Ihlen. 2017. "Risk, Crisis, and Social Media: A Systematic Review of Seven Years' Research." *Nordicom Review* 38, (2): 1–17.

Ravn, S., J. Coffey, and S. Roberts. 2021. "The Currency of Images: Risk, Value and Gendered Power Dynamics in Young Men's Accounts of Sexting." *Feminist Media Studies* 21, (2): 315–331.

Reidenberg, J. R., T. Breaux, L. F. Cranor, and B. French. 2015. "Disagreeable Privacy Policies: Mismatches between Meaning and Users' Understanding." *Berkeley Technology Law Journal* 30, (1): 39–68.

Riboni, G. 2017. "The YouTube Makeup Tutorial Video: A Preliminary Linguistic Analysis of The Language of 'Makeup Gurus'." *Lingue e Linguaggi* 21: 189–205.

Richardson, J. E., and R. Wodak. 2009. "The Impact of Visual Racism: Visual Arguments in Political Leaflets of Austrian and British Far-Right Parties." *Controversia* 6, (2): 45–77.

Rose, G. 2012. *Visual Methodologies: An Introduction to Researching with Visual Materials*. 3rd ed. London: Sage.

Rosenbaum, J. E. 2018. *Constructing Digital Cultures: Tweets, Trends, Race, and Gender*. Lanham, MD: Lexington.

Rosenberg, B. C. 2011. "The Our House DIY Club: Amateurs, Leisure Knowledge and Lifestyle Media." *International Journal of Cultural Studies* 14, (2): 173–190.

Salisbury, M., and J. Pooley. 2017. "The #Nofilter Self: The Contest for Authenticity among Social Networking Sites, 2002–2016." *Social Media, Internet and Society* 6, (10): 1–24.

Sashittal, H. C., M. DeMar, and A. R. Jassawalla. 2016. "Building Acquaintance Brands via Snapchat for the College Student Market." *Business Horizons* 59, (2): 193–204.

Sataøen, H., and A. Wæraas. 2013. "Branding without Unique Brands: Managing Similarity and Difference in a Public Sector Context." *Public Management Review* 17.

Schreier, M. 2012. *Qualitative Content Analysis in Practice*. London: Sage.

Schreier, M. 2014. "Qualitative Content Analysis." In *The SAGE Handbook of Qualitative Data Analysis*, edited by U. Flick, 171–183. London: Sage.

Schrooten, M. 2012. "Moving Ethnography Online: Researching Brazilian Migrants' Online Togetherness." *Ethnic and Racial Studies* 35, (10): 1794–1809.

Schuman, D. L., K. A. Lawrence, and N. Pope. 2019. "Broadcasting War Trauma: An Exploratory Netnography of Veterans' YouTube Vlogs." *Qualitative Health Research* 29, (3): 357–370.

Scrivens, R., and B. Perry. 2017. "Resisting the Right: Countering Right-Wing Extremism in Canada." *Canadian Journal of Criminology and Criminal Justice* 59, (4): 534–558.

Shafie, L., S. Nayan, and N. Osman. 2012. "Constructing Identity through Facebook Profiles: Online Identity and Visual Impression Management of University Students in Malaysia." *Procedia – Social and Behavioral Sciences* 65: 134–140.

Shanahan, N., C. Brennan, and A. House. 2019. "Self-Harm and Social Media: Thematic Analysis of Images Posted on Three Social Media Sites." *BMJ Open* 9, (2).

Shane, T. 2018. "The Semiotics of Authenticity: Indexicality in Donald Trump's Tweets." *New Media & Society* 4, (3): 1–14.

Shearlaw, M. 2015. "Did the #Bringbackourgirls Campaign Make a Difference in Nigeria?" *The Guardian*, April 14. www.theguardian.com/world/2015/apr/14/nigeria-bringbackourgirlscampaign-one-year-on.

Sheldon, P., and K. Bryant. 2016. "Instagram: Motives for Its Use and Relationship to Narcissism and Contextual Age." *Computers in Human Behavior* 58: 89–97.

Shelton, T. 2020. "A Post-Truth Pandemic?" *Big Data and Society* July–December: 1–6.

Shepherd, A., C. Sanders, M. Doyle, and J. Shaw. 2015. "Using Social Media for Support and Feedback by Mental Health Service Users: Thematic Analysis of a Twitter Conversation." *BMC Psychiatry* 15, (1): 29.

Shifman, L. 2012. "An Anatomy of a YouTube Meme." *New Media & Society* 14, (2): 187–203.

Shirky, C. 2001. "The Political Power of Social Media." *Foreign Affairs*, January/February, 2011. www.foreignaffairs.com/articles/2010-12-20/political-power-social-media.

Shirky, Clay. 2003. "Power Laws, Weblogs, and Inequality." *Clay Shirky's Writings about the Internet*, February 8. www.shirky.com/writings/powerlaw_weblog.html.

Shore, C., and S. Wright. 1999. "Audit Culture and Anthropology: Neo-Liberalism in British Higher Education." *The Journal of the Royal Anthropological Institute* 5, (4): 557–575.

Shumar, W. 2013. *College For Sale: A Critique of the Commodification of Higher Education*. London: Routledge.

Siapera, E., G. Hunt, and T. Lynn. 2015. "#Gazaunderattack: Twitter, Palestine and Diffused War." *Information, Communication & Society* 18, (11):1297–1319.

Silverman, D. 2001. *Interpreting Qualitative Data: Methods for Analysing Talk, Text and Interaction*. London: Sage.

Silverman, D. 2004. "Who Cares about 'Experience'? Missing Issues in Qualitative Research." In *Qualitative Research: Theory, Method and Practice*, edited by David Silverman, 342–367. London: Sage.

Singh, V. K., and R. Jain. 2010. "Structural Analysis of the Emerging Event-Web." In *Proceedings of the 19th International Conference on World Wide Web, Raleigh North Carolina, April 26–30*, 1183–1184. New York: Association for Computing Machinery.

Skageby, J. 2008. "Semi-Public End-User Content Contributions: A Case-Study of Concerns and Intentions in Online Photo-Sharing." *International Journal of Human-Computer Studies* 66, (4): 287–300.

Sleigh, J., J. Amann, M. Schneider, and E. Vayena. 2021. "Qualitative Analysis of Visual Risk Communication on Twitter during the Covid-19 Pandemic." *BMC Public Health* 21, (1): 810.

Snelson, C. L. 2016. "Qualitative and Mixed Methods Social Media Research: A Review of the Literature." *International Journal of Qualitative Methods* 15, (1).

Social Data Science Lab. 2020. "Lab Online Guide to Social Media Research Ethics." http://socialdatalab.net/ethics-resources.

Spinda, J. S. W., and S. Puckette. 2018. "Just a Snap: Fan Uses and Gratifications for Following Sports Snapchat." *Communication and Sport* 6, (5): 627–649.

Spradley, J. 1979. *The Ethnographic Interview*. New York: Holt Rinehart & Winston.

Stancanelli, J. 2014. "Conducting an Online Focus Group." *Qualitative Report*.

Stroud, N. J. 2010. "Polarization and Partisan Selective Exposure." *Journal of Communication* 60, (3): 556–576.

Su, B. 2010. "Rural Tourism in China." *Tourism Management* 32: 1438–1441.

Suler, J. 2004. "The Online Disinhibition Effect." *CyberPsychology & Behavior* 7, (3): 321–325.

Sun, S., and F. Chen. 2015. "Reprivatized Womanhood: Changes in Mainstream Media's Framing of Urban Women's Issues in China, 1995–2012." *Journal of Marriage and Family* 77, (5): 1091–1107.

Sunstein, C. 2001. "The Daily We: Is the Internet Really a Blessing for Democracy?" *The Boston Review*, June 1. http://bostonreview.net/ BR26.3/sunstein.php.

Svensson, J. 2014. "Polarizing Political Participation Frames in a Nordic LGBT Community." *eJournal of eDemocracy & Open Government* 6, (2): 166–181.

Svensson, J. 2015. "Participation as a Pastime: Political Discussion in a Queer Community Online." *Javnost: The Public* 22, (3): 283–297.

Svensson, J. 2018. "Lurkers and the Fantasy of Persuasion in an Online Cultural Public Sphere." In *Managing Democracy in the Digital Age*, edited by Julia Schwanholz, Todd Graham, and Peter-Tobias Stoll, 223–241. Cham: Springer.

Taylor, J., and C. Pagliari. 2018. "Mining Social Media Data: How Are Researcher Sponsors and Researchers Addressing the Ethical Challenges?" *Research Ethics* 14, (2): 1–39.

Thelwall, M. 2010. "Researching the Public Web." *eHumanities*, July 12. http://eresearch-ethics.org/position/researching-the-public-web.

Thomas, D., and I. Hodges. 2010. *Designing and Planning Your Research Project*. Thousand Oaks, CA: Sage.

Throuvala, M. A., M. D. Griffiths, M. Rennoldson, and D. J. Kuss. 2019. "Motivational Processes and Dysfunctional Mechanisms of Social Media Use among Adolescents: A Qualitative Focus Group Study." *Computers in Human Behavior* 93, 164–175.

Thrul, J., A. Belohlavek, D. A. Hambrick, M. Kaur, and D. E. Ramo. 2017. "Conducting Online Focus Groups on Facebook to Inform Health Behavior Change Interventions: Two Case Studies and Lessons Learned." *Internet Interventions* 9: 106–111.

Thurlow, C., L. Lengel, and A. Tomic. 2004. *Computer-Mediated Communication: Social Interaction and the Internet*. London: Sage.

Toffoletti, K 2014. "Iranian Women's Sports Fandom: Gender, Resistance, and Identity in the Football Movie Offside." *Journal of Sport & Social Issues* 38, (1): 75–92.

Tropp, J., and A. Baetzgen. 2019. "Users' Definition of Snapchat Usage: Implications for Marketing on Snapchat." *International Journal on Media Management* 21, (2): 130–156.

Truelove, V., J. Freeman, and J. Davey. 2019. "'I Snapchat and Drive!' A Mixed Methods Approach Examining Snapchat Use While Driving and Deterrent Perceptions among Young Adults." *Accident Analysis and Prevention* 131, 146–156.

Tuchman, G. 1978. *Making News: A Study in the Construction of Reality*. New York: Free Press.

Tufekci, Z. 2017. *Twitter and Tear Gas*. New Haven: Yale University Press.

Tufekci, Z., and C. Wilson. 2012. "Social Media and the Decision to Participate in Political Protest: Observations from Tahrir Square." *Journal of Communication* 62, (2): 363–379.

Tunçalp, D., and P. Lê. 2014. "(Re)Locating Boundaries: A Systematic Review of Online Ethnography." *Journal of Organizational Ethnography* 3, 59–79.

Udupa, S. 2017. "Gaali Cultures: The Politics of Abusive Exchange on Social Media." *New Media & Society* 20, (4): 1506–1522.

Underwood, M. 2016. "Exploring the Social Lives of Image and Performance Enhancing Drugs: An Online Ethnography of the Zyzz Fandom of Recreational Bodybuilders." *The International Journal of Drug Policy* 39, 78–85.

United Kingdom. National Crime Agency. 2021. "£400,000 Cash Seized in EncroChat Drugs Investigation." *NCA News*, www.nationalcrimeagency.gov.uk/news/400-000-cash-seized-in-encrochat-drugs-investigation.

Vaismoradi, M., H. Turunen, and T. Bondas. 2013. "Content Analysis and Thematic Analysis: Implications for Conducting a Qualitative Descriptive Study." *Nursing & Health Sciences* 15, (3): 398–405.

Valenzuela, S., A. Arriagada, and S. Andres. 2012. "The Social Media Basis of Youth Protest Behavior: The Case of Chile." *Journal of Communication* 62, (2): 299–314.

Valenzuela, S., N. Park, and K. F. Kee. 2009. "Is There Social Capital in a Social Network Site? Facebook Use and College Students' Life Satisfaction, Trust and Participation." *Journal of Comuter-Mediated Communication* 14, (4): 875–901.

Van der Pijl, M. S. G., M. H. Hollander, T. van der Linden, R. Verweij, L. Holten, E. Kingma, A. de Jonge, and C. J. M. Verhoeven. 2020. Left Powerless: A Qualitative Social Media Content Analysis of the Dutch #Breakthesilence Campaign on Negative and Traumatic Experiences of Labour and Birth." *PloS One* 15, (5): 1–21.

Van Dijk, T. A. 1995. "Discourse Semantics and Ideology." *Discourse & Society* 6, (2): 243–289.

Van Dijk, T. A. 1998. *Ideology: A Multidisciplinary Approach*. London: Sage.

Van Dijk, T. A. 2009. "Critical Discourse Analysis: A Sociocongnitive Approach." In *Methods of Critical Discourse Analysis*, edited by R. Wodak and M. Meyer, 62–84. London: Sage.

Van Dijck, J. 2013. *The Culture of Connectivity: A Critical History of Social Media*. Oxford: Oxford University Press.

Van Driel, L., and D. Dumetrica. 2020. "Selling Brands While Staying 'Authentic': The Professionalization of Instagram Influences." *Convergence: The International Journal of Research into New Media Technologies* 27, (1): 66–84.

Van Dyck, D., S. D'Haese, J. Plaete, I. De Bourdeaudhuij, B. Deforche, and G. Cardon. 2019. "Opinions towards Physical Activity Interventions Using Facebook or Text Messaging: Focus Group Interviews with Vocational School-Aged Adolescents." *Health & Social Care in the Community* 27, (3): 654–664.

Van Leeuwen, T. 2004. *Introducing Social Semiotics*. London: Routledge

Van Leeuwen, T., and R. Wodak. 1999. "Legitimizing Immigration Control: A Discourse-Historical Analysis." *Discourse Studies* 1, (1): 83–118.

Van Ouytsel, J., E. Van Gool, M. Walrave, K. Ponnet, and E. Peeters. 2017. "Sexting: Adolescents' Perceptions of the Applications Used for, Motives for, and Consequences of Sexting." *Journal of Youth Studies* 20, (4): 446–470.

Vaterlaus, J. M., K. Barnett, C. Roche, and J. A. Young. 2016. "'Snapchat Is More Personal': An Exploratory Study on Snapchat Behaviors and Young Adult Interpersonal Relationships." *Computers in Human Behavior* 62: 594–601.

Virden, A. L., A. Trujillo, and E. Predeger. 2014. "Young Adult Females' Perceptions of High-Risk Social Media Behaviors: A Focus-Group Approach." *Journal of Community Health Nursing* 31, (3): 133–144.

Vitak, J., N. Proferes, K. Shilton, and Z. Ashktorab. 2017. "Ethics Regulation in Social Computing Research: Examining the Role of Institutional Review Boards." *Journal of Empirical Research on Human Research Ethics* 12: 372–382.

Vitak, J., K. Shilton, and Z. Ashktorab. 2016. "Beyond the Belmont Principles: Ethical Challenges, Practices, and Beliefs in the Online Data Research Community." In *Proceedings of the ACM Conference on Computer Supported Cooperative*

Work & Social Computing, San Francisco, 27 February–2 March, 941–953. New York: Association for Computing Machinery.

Wacquant, L. 2009. *Punishing the Poor: The Neoliberal Government of Social Insecurity*. Durham, NC: Duke University Press.

Wagner, P. E. 2017. "Bulking Up (Identities): A Communication Framework for Male Fitness Identity." *Communication Quarterly* 65, (5): 580–602.

Walkerdine, V. 2003. "Reclassifying Upward Mobility: Femininity and the Neo-Liberal Subject." *Gender and Education* 15, (3): 237–248.

Wallis, S. 2014. "Abstraction and Insight: Building Better Conceptual Systems to Support More Effective Social Change." *Foundations of Science* 20, (2): 189–196.

Walseth, K., I. Aartun, and E. Gunn. 2017. "Girls' Bodily Activities in Physical Education: How Current Fitness and Sport Discourses Influence Girls' Identity Construction." *Sport, Education and Society* 22, (4): 442–459.

Wang Le. 2013, *The Road to Privatization of Higher Education in China: A New Cultural Revolution?* Heidelberg: Springer.

Way, C. S. L. 2015. "YouTube as a Site of Debate through Populist Politics: The Case of a Turkish Protest Pop Video." *Journal of Multicultural Discourses* 10, (2): 180–196.

Whiting, J. B., R. D. Olufuwote, J. D. Cravens-Pickens, and A. B. Witting. 2019. "Online Blaming and Intimate Partner Violence: A Content Analysis of Social Media Comments." *Qualitative Report* 24, (1): 78.

Wilkinson, D., and M. Thelwall. 2010. "Researching Personal Information on the Public Web: Methods and Ethics." *Social Science Computer Review* 29, (4): 387–401. http://ssc.sagepub.com/content/early/2010/08/16/0894439310378979.

Williams, M. L. 2006. *Virtually Criminal: Crime, Deviance and Regulation Online*. London: Routledge.

Willis, P., and M. Trondman. 2000. "Manifesto for 'Ethnography'." *Ethnography* 1, (1): 5–16.

Wilson, W. J. 2011. "Being Poor, Black, and American: The Impact of Political, Economic, and Cultural Forces." *American Educator* 35, (1): 10–23.

Wittel, A. 2000. "Ethnography on the Move: From Field to Net to Internet." *Forum Qualitative Social Research* 1, (1).

Wood, M. 2014. "OKCupid Plays with Love in User Experiments." *The New York Times*, July 28. www.nytimes.com/2014/07/29/technology/okcupid-publishes-findings-of-user-experiments.html.

Wright, W. 1975. *Six Guns and Society: A Structural Study of the Western*. Oakland: University of California Press.

Wu, J-X., and L-Y. He. 2018. "Urban–Rural Gap and Poverty Traps in China: A Prefecture Level Analysis." *Applied Economics* 50, (30): 3300–3314.

Xu, J. 2007. "Brand-New Lifestyle: Consumer-Oriented Programmes on Chinese Television." *Media Culture & Society* 29, (3): 363–376.

Yang, G. 2014. "Internet Activism and the Party-State in China." *Daedalus* 143, (2): 110–123.

Zappavigna, M. 2015. "Searchable Talk: The Linguistic Functions of Hashtags." *Social Semiotics* 25, (3): 274–291.

Zarkov, D. 2018. "Ambiguities and Dilemmas around #MeToo: #ForHow Long and #WhereTo?" *European Journal of Women's Studies* 25, (1): 3–9.

Zhang, W. 2020. "Consumption Taste, and the Economic Transition in Modern China." *Consumption Market & Culture* 23, (1): 1–20.

Zhu, S., and Zhu, Q. 2017. "On Shanghai's Middle Class: A Preliminary Survey Report." *Inter-Asia Cultural Studies* 18, (4): 632–642.

Zimmer, M. 2010. "'But the Data Is Already Public': On the Ethics of Research in Facebook." *Ethics and Information Technology* 12: 313–325.

Zimmer, M., and N. J. Proferes. 2014. "A Topology of Twitter Research: Disciplines, Methods, and Ethics." *Aslib Journal of Information Management* 66: 250–261.

Žižek, S. 1997. *The Plague of Fantasies*. London: Verso.

Zwaanswijk, M., and S. van Dulmen. 2014. "Advantages of Asynchronous Online Focus Groups and Face-to-Face Focus Groups as Perceived by Child, Adolescent and Adult Participants: A Survey Study." *BMC Research Notes* 7, (1): 756.

INDEX

#bringbackourgirls 4
#MeToo 2, 81–84, 88–89, 94
#StopFundingHate 3
#StopFundingHate 3, 5
#TwoWomenTravel 8–10, 18–19

actions (of participants) 89, 98, 106
activism 2–3
advertising 39–40, 51, 99, 108, 113
affective communities 10–11, 16–17
affective connectivity 90
algorithms 7–8, 10, 17–18, 172
anonymization 22–23, 89
Application Programming Interfaces (APIs) 49
archived data 135, 144
authenticity 16, 44, 66, 117, 137–138
avatars 138

big data 173–174
branding 14, 62–63, 87, 94, 119, 127–128
buzzwords 10–12, 14, 82, 96, 113

capitalism 86–87
captions 108
case study 130, 174–175
China 68–69
Chinese middle-class 97, 103–104, 106, 117–118, 128
choices (visual communication) 85–86
classification 87
clicktivism 5
codification 87
coding 33, 35–6, 49–50;
    unidimensionality 33, 35–6, 50;
    mutual exclusivity 33, 35–6, 50;
    exhaustiveness 33, 35–36, 50;
    protocol, traditional 36; protocol, minimalist 36–37; protocol, software 37; concept-driven 35; data driven 35
coding, dilemma 35, 38
collectivization 64, 88, 107
color scheme 84, 100
communicative rationality 17
comparative research 47–8
composition 84
confidentiality 22–23
Confucianism 69, 75, 102, 119, 128
connotations 94
consent 21–22
consumer loyalty 139
content analysis – a definition 27;
    debates about 27
Covid-19 42, 46
crime 105
critical discourse analysis 58–61
cultural capitalism 68, 97
cyberspace 136–7

data collection 49; Visual Tagnet Explorer 49; Netvizz 49; The Twitter Capture and Analysis Toolset 49; TumblrTool 49; Google BigQuery 49; DownThemAll 49
data delimitations 47
deductive research 25, 50, 169
discourse 63, 86–87, 102, 104–108, 117–118, 128, 172
discursive scripts 63, 66–67, 86, 88, 96, 98, 134
distinction 117

echo chambers 7, 173
emotion/affect 10–11, 16, 66, 95, 172
Encrochat 137

entrepreneurial self 75
epistemology 154, 155, 157
ethics 20–23
extreme cases 48

Facebook 3, 25, 28, 32, 39, 47, 106, 119, 138, 140–1, 143, 144
Facebook Messenger 141
falsification 175
fieldnotes 135, 144
filter bubble 7
focus group interviews 150; definition 150–1; purpose of 150, 153; online 151, 164–7; online and offline difference 151; history 151–2; current research 152; in media studies 152; in studies on social media 152–3; in health studies 153–5; developing a research problem 153; research questions 155–6; analytical themes 155–6; selecting and reaching informants 157–161; number of interviews 158–9; interview guide 161, 163; asynchronous 165; synchronous 166; transcription 167; analysis 169–70; presenting results 170–1; thematic analysis 169; discourse analysis 169

gaming communities 136
gender 41
gender advertisements 41
generalizability 174
generalization 30, 37, 48
Global North 127
Global South 107, 119, 127
government institutions 28

hashtags 4, 8, 10, 32–3, 82, 98
humor 54, 139, 154

identity 141
ideological square 65
ideology 6, 43, 61–63, 86–87, 97, 104
immigrants 61
imperative mood 75

inauthenticity 65–66
indicative mood 75
individualism 68–70, 97, 113, 119, 129
individualization 39, 64, 88, 106–107, 118, 127, 152, 156
inductive research 25, 136
influencers 13–14, 63–63, 79, 92, 94, 98, 102, 104, 113, 132
Instagram 30, 32, 39, 42, 49, 59, 62–63, 137, 140–141
integrated design 87, 100
interview questions 161–3; grand tour questions 163–4; mini-tour questions 164; example questions 164; experience questions 164; language-use questions 164; hypothetical questions 164
interviews 135, 140, 144–5

lexicon 43
lifestyle consumer capitalism 62
LinkedIn 32, 137

male gaze 41, 45
marketing 23, 84, 87, 131
meaning 27–8, 43; manifest and latent 43; denotative and connotative 43–5; simple and complex 43
meaning making 27–8; definition 27
media ideologies 138
media idioms 138
memes 94
modernization 119
moral capital 82
morality 13, 62, 72, 82, 89, 106, 108, 127, 172–173
multimodality 79, 88
multiplayer games 138

narration 108
National Geographic 42
neoliberalism 69, 70–75, 97, 101, 172
news 17–18, 20, 105–106
Netlytic 32
netnography 135, 139, 145
nodes 6–7, 17

nominalizations 72, 78
NVivo 69, 98

objects 88, 103
online ethnography 135; definition 135; naturalism 135, 145; multi-disciplinary 135–6, 141; research questions 136; narrative 136; history of 136–7; current research 139; in consumer culture research 139; in political communication research 139–40; in health sciences 140; research design 141–143; developing a research problem 141–2; crafting a purpose 142; crafting research questions 142–3; single-site study 143, multi-site study 143; flow study 143; combining methods 143–4; types of data 144; writing up results 145–6; narrativization 148–9
online forums 140, 166
online/offline 172
out of focus setting 95

personal address 92
participants 88, 98, 103, 106, 127, 174
participatory observation 135, 144
physical proximity (distance) 89, 94
political consumerism 112
poses 102
post-truth 172–173
postures 92
poverty 104
power femininity 97
presuppositions 75
private sector 28
processes 92
pronouns 65
protests 2–3

qualitative content analysis 25; definitions of 25, 27; in health sciences 25; in political science 26; in marketing research 25–6; in risk/ crisis communication research 26; methodological literature 26; history 26–7; systematic and flexible 27; context-sensitive interpretation 27; research process 28–9; a schematic overview 29; the research problem 28–30; data selection 30; crafting a purpose 31; designing research questions 31; data selection 32–3; random selection 33; total selection 33; data collection 32–3; coding frame 33–6; categories and subcategories 33–4, 50; presentation of results 37
Qualitative visual content analysis 39; purpose of 40; history 40, 41; data selection 42; in marketing research 42; in health studies 42; in political science 42–3; research design 45–6; crafting a research problem 45–6; crafting a purpose 46; crafting research questions 46; data selection 47; data collection 48–9; coding of objects 50–1; coding of participants 51; coding of settings 51; coding of color and light 51, 52; coding of typography 52–3; coding of composition 53; case example 54–5; presentation of results 56
quantification 37
quantitative content analysis 25–7, 37–8, 41–2

racism 16, 65, 80, 86
random sampling 47
recontextualization 90, 94
reddit 140
remediation 138
replicability 45
researcher participation 144–5
research question 68, 96, 98, 130, 132, 134
Rhetoric of the Image 43
roles, active and passive 41, 45
Roma 3, 5, 6, 13, 105–106

sampling 70, 98
sampling bias 48
Second Life 136–7
self-branding 13, 96, 107
self-management 74–75
self-promotion 103, 117, 131
selfie 102
semantic macro analysis 69, 98
semiotic resources 87
semiotics 61
settings 88, 94, 99, 103, 107
simulation 120
slacktivism 13
Snapchat 25, 47, 140, 152, 167
social justice 82, 119
social semiotics 85
Spotify 39
storytelling 107–108

technologization 87
text-image relationship 44; anchoring 44; relay 44
texts 28
texture 84
thematic analysis 69–70, 98, 133
TikTok 47, 162

transcript 109, 133
transparency 38, 45, 57, 175
Twitter 2–4, 11, 16, 21, 30–2, 42, 47, 54, 59, 68, 80–81, 95, 98, 137, 140

unit of analysis 33, 43, 50

validity 38, 45, 146
viewer engagement 92
violent abstraction 17
virtual reality 137; dichotomy of virtual and real 137; dichotomy of online and offline 137
visual culture 39
visual coordination 95
visual hierarchies 95
visual material, commercial use 39
visual material, proliferation of 39
Visual Pleasure and Narrative Cinema 45

Weibo 68–70, 80, 95, 98, 103, 113
World of Warcraft 136, 137

YouTube 39–40, 52, 54, 63, 95, 103, 105, 140, 141

"An indispensable guide for those who want to learn about, and practically undertake, qualitative social media research of popular platforms."
Professor Per Ledin, *Södertörn University and author of* Doing Visual Analysis, From Theory to Practice

"Bouvier and Rasmussen provide an informative, clearly written and indispensable guide for readers investigating social media data or contemplating doing so. A welcome handbook for all research methods courses that seek to remain informed and up to date."
Paul Cobley, *Professor in Language and Media, Middlesex University*

Do you want to study influencers? Opinions and comments on a set of posts? Look at collections of photos or videos on Instagram? *Qualitative Research Using Social Media* guides the reader in what different kinds of qualitative research can be applied to social media data. It introduces students, as well as those who are new to the field, to developing and carrying out concrete research projects. The book takes the reader through the stages of choosing data, formulating a research question, and choosing and applying method(s).

Written in a clear and accessible manner with current social media examples throughout, the book provides a step-by-step overview of a range of qualitative methods. These are presented in clear ways to show how to analyze many different types of social media content, including language and visual content such as memes, gifs, photographs, and film clips. Methods examined include critical discourse analysis, content analysis, multimodal analysis, ethnography, and focus groups. Most importantly, the chapters and examples show how to ask the kinds of questions that are relevant for us at this present point in our societies, where social media is highly integrated into how we live. Social media is used for political communication, social activism, as well as commercial activities and mundane everyday things, and it can transform how all these are accomplished and even what they mean.

Drawing on examples from Twitter, Instagram, YouTube, TikTok, Facebook, Snapchat, Reddit, Weibo, and others, this book will be suitable for undergraduate students studying social media research courses in media and communications, as well as other humanities such as linguistics and social science–based degrees.

Gwen Bouvier is a professor at the Institute of Corpus Linguistics and Applications, Shanghai International Studies University, China. Her main research interest is digital communication, specifically civic debate and activism on social media. Professor Bouvier's publications have drawn on critical discourse analysis, multimodality based on social semiotics, and online ethnography. She is the Associate Editor for the journal *Social Semiotics*.

Joel Rasmussen is a senior lecturer in the School of Humanities, Education and Social Sciences at Örebro University, Sweden. His research focuses on how communication processes shape responsibilities and measures regarding risk and health in organizations and society. He is interested in how public-sector institutions are refashioning identity through social media. His work is published in international journals such as *Human Relations, Discourse & Communication, Safety Science, PLoS ONE*, and others.

SOCIAL MEDIA